FAKING IT IN AMERICA

Barry Minkow and the Great ZZZZ Best Scam

JOE DOMANICK

CB
CONTEMPORARY
BOOKS
CHICAGO · NEW YORK

Library of Congress Cataloging-in-Publication Data

Domanick, Joe.
    Faking It in America : Barry Minkow and the great ZZZZ best scam
/ Joe Domanick.
        p.   cm.
    ISBN 0-8092-4497-7
    1. Swindlers and swindling—California—Case studies.
2. Business—California—Corrupt practices—Case studies.
3. Success in business—California—Case studies.   4. Minkow,
Barry.   5. Swindlers and swindling—California—Biography.
I. Title.
HV6698.C3D66   1989
364.1'63—dc20   89-35891
                                                                              CIP

Copyright © 1989 by Joe Domanick
All rights reserved
Published by Contemporary Books, Inc.
180 North Michigan Avenue, Chicago, Illinois 60601
Manufactured in the United States of America
International Standard Book Number: 0-8092-4497-7

Published simultaneously in Canada by Beaverbooks, Ltd.
195 Allstate Parkway, Valleywood Business Park
Markham, Ontario L3R 4T8 Canada

For Catherine Cappellino Domanick

Author's Note

WHEN ROGER CLAIRE, my editor at *Los Angeles* magazine, approached me to do a story on Barry Minkow and the unfolding ZZZZ Best fraud in the summer of 1987, I was less than enthusiastic, my ignorance of the stock market and finance being exceeded only by my lack of interest in both subjects.

Once working on the assignment, however, I found that the tale of how Barry Minkow, Tom Padgett, and Mark Morze managed so successfully to fool investors, bankers, Wall Street professionals, and the media was perhaps as good a story of what America has stood for in the 1980s as one could have hoped to find.

Contents

Acknowledgments

A BOOK SUCH AS THIS is only as good as the generosity of its sources, and in this regard Tom Padgett and Mark Morze were more than forthcoming, allowing me to interview them for well over a hundred hours apiece. I am grateful to them, as I am to Joel Hochberg, Maurice Rind, Chip and Lulu Arrington, Paul Palladino, Jeri Carr, Richard Burda, Carlie Kozlowski, Arthur Uhl, Jeff Wayne, Bruce Kelton, Ana and Elenora Madrinan, John Miller, Gordon Greenberg, Jim Asperger, David Kenner, Arthur Barens, John Chesson, Patrick Lee, John Orr, and Scott Dear.

Connie Bruck's *The Predators' Ball* and Joseph Nocera's *Esquire* article "The Ga-Ga Years" also were most helpful to me in understanding the culture of Wall Street and of money in America.

I would also like to thank Roger Claire, my editor at *Los Angeles* magazine, for bringing ZZZZ Best to my attention and steering me in the right direction; John Orr, Mike Justice, and Doug Bruckner for some of the book's photos; DeAnna Hodgin for her research assistance; the Federal Court House press corps for their hospitality; David Deitch for his insight; Teresa Tanka, Frances Ring, Carol Domanick, and Charlie Lerman for their encouragement and support; Bernard Shir-Cliff, my editor at Contemporary Books, for his kindness and patience; Roberta Prior for her good cheer; Sue Horton for her always-smart advice; and most especially Jack Langguth for showing me what it means to be a journalist, Clancy Sigal for teaching me how to write like one, and Judy Tanka for everything.

Cast of Characters

THE SCAMMERS

Barry J. Minkow
: Teenage founder of ZZZZ Best, a carpet-cleaning and restoration company; at twenty-one, the leader of the multimillion-dollar ZZZZ Best scam.

Mark Morze
: In charge of the "Restoration Division" of ZZZZ Best; Barry Minkow's right-hand man and master forger.

Tom Padgett
: Early mentor of Barry Minkow's; head of the bogus Interstate Appraisal Services, the source of the phony restoration jobs awarded to ZZZZ Best.

Dan Krowpman
: Tool salesman and weight-lifting buddy of Minkow's; lends money to Barry to start his business and certifies phony equipment receipts for ZZZZ Best.

Brian Morze
: Mark Morze's older brother; functions as a troubleshooter in the later stages of the scam.

Jack and Jerry Polevoi
: Twin brothers; Jack, Barry's next-door neighbor, is keeper of Barry's slush fund; both brothers perform various services for Minkow.

Mark Roddy (the Albino)
: Tom Padgett's friend and right-hand man; assists Padgett in preparing phony restoration sites.

Norm Rothberg
: A CPA hired by Tom Padgett's bogus company to lend respectability.

THE SCAMMED

Jack Catain
: An early conduit for Minkow to big investment dollars; alleged to have ties to organized crime in Chicago and New Jersey.

ix

Richard Charbit	Loan broker who introduced Minkow to Rooney, Pace.
Ada Cohen	Investor in ZZZZ Best; recruited by Kay Rosario.
Drexel Burnham Lambert	The investment banking house interested in lending Barry money.
Sheri Elowsky	Loan officer for Prudential-Bache.
Vanessa England	Union Bank loan officer.
Ernst & Whinney	The accounting firm that helped to bring ZZZZ Best public.
First Interstate Bank	Bank that lent millions of dollars to ZZZZ Best.
Larry Gray	Ernst & Whinney accountant in charge of the ZZZZ Best account; would visit Sacramento, San Diego, and Dallas "restoration sites" with Mark Morze.
Faith Griffin	The Rooney, Pace underwriter in charge of ZZZZ Best's public stock offering.
Hughes Hubbard & Reed	Minkow's law firm during the public offering.
Steve Monchamp	The First Interstate loan officer in charge of ZZZZ Best's account.
Mark Moskowitz	The Hughes Hubbard & Reed attorney working with ZZZZ Best, advising it during the public offering.
Richard Motika	The loan manager at First Interstate Bank's Beverly Hills office.
Tim Morphy	Replaces Monchamp as First Interstate's loan officer in charge of ZZZZ Best's account.
Elaine Orlando	A heavy ZZZZ Best investor and member of Kay Rosario's financial group.
Bernard Pincus	Member of Kay Rosario's investment group.
Maurice Rind	Former stockbroker with reputed mob connections; helps Minkow make ZZZZ Best a public company.

Rooney, Pace — The investment banking underwriters during ZZZZ Best's public stock offering.

Kay Rosario — Head of a group of middle-aged and elderly women investors; Barry meets her through Jack Catain.

Susan Russell — Union Bank loan officer.

Paul Schiff (a pseudonym) — Hollywood producer and financier; one of ZZZZ Best's heaviest individual investors.

Richard Schulman — A ZZZZ Best investor with a long arrest record and alleged ties to organized crime.

Robert Victor — Introduces Barry Minkow to Rind and Schulman; invests heavily in ZZZZ Best; has a long arrest record with alleged ties to Colombo crime family.

FRIENDS AND ASSOCIATES

Chip Arrington — CEO of ZZZZ Best; close friend of Barry's; owner, on paper, of Floral Fantasies.

Lulu Arrington — Chip's wife; worked for ZZZZ Best in early years and managed Floral Fantasies.

Jeri Carr — Head of her own public relations firm, which successfully promoted ZZZZ Best and Barry to the media.

Joel Hochberg — A close friend of Barry's; trains Minkow in carpet cleaning and later manages telemarketers at ZZZZ Best.

Joyce Lipman — Barry Minkow's girlfriend.

Ana Madrinan — A friend of Barry's; worked on his PR account at Jeri Carr's firm.

Elenora Madrinan — Ana's sister; high school acquaintance of Barry's; goes to work for him as a telemarketer.

Robert Turnbow — Manager at several different banks; befriended Barry.

Jeff Wayne — Nightclub comedian and friend of Barry's.

THE LAW

Jim Asperger, Gordon Greenberg	U.S. Attorneys who prosecuted Barry and other ZZZZ Best defendants.
Arthur Barens	Barry's first defense attorney; later fired by him.
David Kenner	Barry's second defense attorney.
John Orr, Buck Sadler	The FBI agents who investigated the ZZZZ Best case.
Dickran Tevrizian	The judge presiding at the ZZZZ Best trial.

Prologue

"*The day of the arraignment, Barry and I were chained to the 'Password' guy, you know, the one who collected 100 grand from the insurance company by saying his wife had died, but she hadn't?*

"*He split when he got the money and changed his name to Patrick Quinn. Then he went on 'Super Password' and won $56,000. Well, his girlfriend in Alaska sees him and snitches him out. That's not Patrick Quinn, she tells 'em. And guess who was waiting when he went to collect his money. . . .*

"*They'd come for me the night before, around 8:30. I was sittin' at the kitchen table with my cousin Patti, and we heard a knock on the door.*

"*We figured it was her boyfriend, who sleeps outside in a van. 'What's with that guy?' I said. 'He run out of beer again?'*

"*Patti gets up, looks out the window, and says, 'Tommy, they're out there in suits.'*

"*I open the door, and there's John Orr and a couple of other FBI agents, two LAPD, and a few guys from the IRS and Treasury Department. 'Jesus Christ,' I'm thinking, 'What'd they do if I killed someone?'*

"*'Thomas Padgett?' Orr asks, as if he didn't know. I nod. 'It's time,' he says and puts the bracelets on.*

"*There was a four-car procession going downtown.*

"*As we pull up to Parker Center, I see Barry going in. Around one in the morning, they stick me in a holding cell with winos and gang members. There are metal sleeping slabs but no sheets, no blankets, no nothin'. Mark Morze is already in there, and so is Chip [Arrington], and one of the Polevoi brothers, and Mark's brother, Brian. And that fuckin' Rothberg, too. But Barry, Barry was being held in a separate area.*

"*Chip was in a daze, and I remember he kept on sayin' over and over, 'What am I doin' here, what am I doin' here?'*

"*But Mark and I had a pretty good time talking about how stupid Barry's 'I didn't know anything about what was going on' defense was. And that's when we started calling it the jujube defense. You know, like a movie theater. I was outside selling the* tickets, Mark was running the projector, and Barry, Barry was just selling jujubes at the candy counter. He never got to see any of the movies. He never got to see me doin' the hawkin' outside. I mean, it was just so stupid! Everybody knows what Barry Minkow knew.

"The next morning, they marched us over to the federal courthouse. At the arraignment we had no place to sit, and they had to clear the press out of the first two rows of seats, there were so many of them. Of course, there were eleven of us.

"My lawyer gave me a copy of the indictment—bank fraud, mail fraud, securities fraud, and RICO violations. I was facing 177 years and $8 million in fines.

"Mark was looking at 182 years and $8.5 million, Barry at 350 years and a fine of $13.5 million.

"My bail was set at $200,000, but at the time it could have been $2 million. Barry's was $2 million. We were the only ones who couldn't make it. That's when we were chained to the 'Password' guy who kept singing 'Indiana Wants Me (But I Can't Go Back There)' as they led us away.

"I hadn't seen Barry since the summer when it had all come apart, and I wondered how I'd feel, but the magic was there like it'd never gone away. Barry looked good—big—he'd been workin' out, and we started laughin' and jokin' like in the old days.

"The next day at Terminal Island [the federal prison in LA Harbor], we worked out together, and we talked about how we should have stopped at the Sacramento job. And Barry, who knew how much I had loved my house on the water at Newport Beach, laughed and said, 'Well, at least you got an ocean view again.'"

Part I
The Boy Wonder

— 1 —

THE PLACE WAS A DUMP, and the kid looked like a slob. "I've made a terrible mistake coming here," thought Jeri Carr.

It was late 1984, and Carr, an attractive, raven-haired woman in her early thirties, was visiting eighteen-year-old Barry J. Minkow at the suggestion of one of her employees. The head of her own public relations firm, Carr had been told that Minkow was a dynamic young man looking for some publicity for his fledgling business.

But she'd become apprehensive as soon as she entered the building that housed Minkow's office. Squat and ugly, it was located in a low-rent, plastic, and concrete industrial area of the blue-collar Los Angeles suburb of Reseda. On the ground floor was an auto tune-up shop, above it Minkow's dreary two-room "headquarters."

The sign on the door said "ZZZZ Best Carpet and Furniture Cleaning Co.," but the carpet within was a mess—dirty, threadbare, and upturned at the corners. The furniture was shabby, a few wooden chairs and some strictly utilitarian scarred metal desks.

Carr's doubts were only increased when she gazed for the first time upon Barry Minkow, the founder, sole owner, and soon-to-be Chairman of the Board and President of ZZZZ Best Co., Inc.

His coarse black hair was, as usual, out of control—worn long and shaggy in the manner of the high school student he'd so recently been. His ugly-handsome face was dominated by a large broken nose and dark, intense eyes under bushy brows. In profile, the hook of his nose and the darting energy in his eyes gave him the look of a nervous eagle. But it wasn't Barry Minkow's face or hair that caught Jeri Carr's attention on this, their first meeting.

It was his clothes.

He was dressed in what Carr later learned was his typical business attire: cheap tank top pulled over his powerfully muscled physique and low-slung sweatpants that revealed far more of his belly than Carr cared to see.

Greeting her, Minkow gave an unconscious, habitual tug at his crotch and gestured for Carr to take a seat. "This guy," Carr remembers thinking, "had *better* be dynamic."

And he was.

In fact, almost as soon as Barry Minkow sat down and opened his mouth, Jeri Carr's misgivings began to fade. With a reasoned passion that seemed to belie his years, he told Carr that he was as aware as anyone else of his unpolished image and lack of a formal financial or business education. But those things, he said, didn't really matter. What *did* matter was drive, motivation, and capitalizing on what you know. And what he knew—truly knew—said Barry Minkow, was people and how to deal with them—that and the carpet-cleaning business. He understood both so well, in fact, that although he was only eighteen, his business was already bringing in more than a million dollars a year. And that, he assured her, was just the start.

As Jeri Carr continued to listen, Barry Minkow began, before her very eyes, to transform himself from an awkward, muscle-bound kid into an enormously charismatic and impressive young man. He told her about his expansion plans, his desire to be a role model for children, and his belief in America, "a place where we can all succeed."

"My God," thought Carr, who was herself hustling to start a business, "this guy *really* has possibilities." It wasn't just that he obviously understood PR and made it clear he was willing to pay thousands of dollars to promote himself. Nor was it really what Barry was saying. Rather, it was the way in which he was saying it—with such sincerity, such *conviction*.

Telling him to continue, she took out a notepad, turned on her tape recorder, and began asking him more about himself, focusing on the part about how, at just fifteen (Barry's PR version), he'd begun a company that was already doing a million a year in business.

Then Jeri Carr went back to her office and put out a press release about the teenage genius she'd just met, who'd started his own business in his family's garage, had an inspirational message for America's youth, and was, not incidentally, becoming a very rich young man.

Barry Minkow, with an invaluable assist from his newly hired PR rep, had taken his first big step in the extraordinary invention of himself.

"It was the height of the Reagan era," says Ana Madrinan, who worked for Carr promoting Barry, "and the timing couldn't have been more perfect."

— 2 —

THAT SAME YEAR, 1984, Bernard Tenenbaum, then Associate Director of the Snider Entrepreneurial Center at the University of Pennsylvania's prestigious Wharton School, observed a tumultuous scene: more than 750 frenzied students jostling with each other in a vain attempt to fit into a hopelessly inadequate hall booked, it appeared to Tenenbaum, for a celebrated rock or movie star. Hurriedly, another room was prepared and linked to the first by closed-circuit TV.

Nevertheless, additional shoving students spilled out into the hallways, and loudspeakers had to be erected to accommodate them. "It was," says Tenenbaum, "like they were lining up for the last tickets on the Celestial Train."

The students, however, were not jockeying for position in order to revere the latest rock idol, as had been the case for the previous two decades, but instead were there for his 1980s equivalent: Donald Trump, New York real estate mogul and superstar extraordinaire in the acquisitive Era of Ronald Reagan.

It was a time in America—surely not yet concluded—when money, as *Fortune* editor Marshall Loeb has pointed out, had become "the most discussed topic among consenting adults"—the New Sex.

Rock, movie, and sports stars, as well as politicians and social activists, were out as role models and heroes: T. Boone Pickens, Donald Trump, Ivan Boesky, Carl Icahn, and Lee Iacocca were in. *The New Republic* called this the deification of the CEO.

The media were quick to mirror this renewed popular interest in money and business. Expanded business sections began appearing in newspapers, and magazines like *Inc.*, *Money*, *Venture*, *Savvy*, *Success!*, and *Black Enterprise* flooded the newsstands. In March 1985, even *Rolling Stone* jumped on the bandwagon, breathlessly profiling "nine of the richest entrepreneurs in the country, all under 30," while the *Harvard Business Review* ran an editorial calling entrepreneurship "the LSD of the '80s."

Indeed it seemed to be.

Money magazine regularly put yuppies on its cover beneath intriguing headlines on how to double, triple, and quadruple your dollars. Writing in *Esquire*, Joseph Nocera, then working on a book about America's future, compared the *Money* covers with a *Playboy* centerfold. "That you had as much chance of getting rich by following the example of the *Money* centerfold as you did of sleeping with a Playmate scarcely seemed to matter," wrote Nocera. "People bought the magazine, took it home and drooled."

And nowhere, save, of course, Washington and Wall Street, was there more drooling than among the nation's young—and not just on college campuses or among their recent graduates, as Barry Minkow was soon to show.

For it was a time when the disparity between the haves and have-nots that we now take so much for granted was beginning to widen, and nobody—particularly young people conscious of shrinking opportunity—wanted to get caught on the wrong side of the line. The wrong side meant numbing regimentation, fast-food jobs, and futures with no prospects or expectations.

By the early eighties, it had become not just OK for America's young people to want to make a lot of money, but entirely appropriate. "If you weren't making money," says Bernard Tenenbaum, "you were a nerd."

— 3 —

BARRY MINKOW'S INCESSANT RAPPING on the door always made Joel Hochberg's hung-over head feel, as Mike Hammer used to say in the old Mickey Spillane novels, "like ten thousand little green men with sledgehammers were pounding away on it."

Even so, Hochberg would play out the ritual he'd established with his fourteen-year-old partner, crawling off his couch, grabbing his wallet, and handing Barry a couple of bucks before trying to catch a few additional minutes of sleep.

Minkow, usually shirtless now that he was working out at the West Valley Gym and wanting to show off the first faint traces of muscle on his reed-thin physique, would take the money, go to the local 7-Eleven, buy milk and doughnuts for himself and coffee for Joel Hochberg, and head back to Hochberg's room in the back of the Dunn-Rite Carpet Cleaning office.

There, Joel would sip his coffee and try to unfog his brain just long enough so that he and Barry could load up Dunn-Rite's carpet-cleaning equipment and head back to the 7-Eleven to buy Hochberg's first six-pack of the day. ("For me," Joel would say, "7-Eleven meant seven beers before eleven o'clock.") Those first beers would be the start of at least a case of Miller's that Hochberg would consume before the day's end.

An intense, open man in his thirties, Hochberg had befriended Barry in the early eighties when the teenager had first started working Saturdays and during summer vacations at Dunn-Rite—where Carole Minkow, Barry's mother, was also employed. Barry was "a bigmouthed, annoying kid nobody else seemed to want around," says Hochberg. But Minkow's wise-guy persona and almost palpable need for attention didn't bother Joel, himself a fast-talking former cabdriver from Brooklyn who liked the spotlight. Besides, he was usually so drunk during the day that the youngster's kinetic energy and unceasing curiosity were right in sync with his beer high.

Despite having a constant buzz on, Joel Hochberg was able to perform his duties well enough to hold down a telephone sales, or "telemarketing," managerial job in the evening and his morning carpet-cleaning work with Barry as well.

Under Joel's tutelage, Barry Minkow went out on jobs throughout LA's suburban San Fernando Valley, quickly learning the tricks of the trade that enable a hustling carpet cleaner to gross as much as $1,000 a week: how, for example, to talk customers into doing extra rooms, or how to have furniture or drapes cleaned that had not originally been contracted for—extras that could double or even triple a bill.

They'd work together until about one o'clock, eating some of the eight to ten tuna or egg salad sandwiches Carole Minkow faithfully prepared each morning, and doubling up with laughter as Barry displayed the female customers' panties he'd regularly take as mementos. Then they'd head back to Dunn-Rite.

As the telemarketing night shift didn't start until 4:30, they'd hang around the office while Joel got drunker and Barry answered the calls coming in for new jobs.

It was during these hours that Barry learned the supervisory aspects of the carpet-cleaning business, like how to dispatch cleaners, ensure that the jobs got done when they were supposed to, and deal effectively with dissatisfied customers.

And even more importantly, he became familiar with a key element of his later phenomenal success: insurance restoration work, which involved cleaning and restoring water-damaged carpets, drapes, and flooring, and which was paid for by an insurance company instead of directly by the customer.

Barry's training under Joel Hochberg, however, was not the first he'd received. Unable to afford a baby-sitter, Carole Minkow had been bringing her son, from the age of twelve, to work with her at a carpet-cleaning company called Same Day Carpet Care.

There, through the summers of his twelfth and thirteenth years, Barry worked at cold-turkey telephone sales.

Such solicitation is no joy in any business. But in carpet cleaning, it is a particularly tough sale.

Largely unregulated and requiring little more than the rental or purchase of basic equipment, the carpet-cleaning industry has traditionally been fiercely competitive, and characterized by shoe-string operations, questionable ethics, and widespread consumer complaints.

Much of the criticism centers around a telephone solicitation and advertising technique called "bait and switch," in which a salesperson or an advertisement quotes an absurdly low job price. Then, when the cleaners arrive, they announce that the price quoted did not include a great deal of the necessary work.

Telemarketing of this sort was Barry Minkow's first real job.

And Barry Minkow seemed instinctively to know how to talk that talk and sell that product. And over the next several years, he would absorb the two principles vital to a master salesman. The first was the halo effect: never mind the product, you're buying *me*. The second was a variation known as the chameleon principle: I am whoever you want me to be. And, like a good actor, he would soon develop that essential gift of listening and observing language and behavior and making them his own. Then, in turn, he would give back to whomever he was selling exactly what that person wanted to see or hear.

His was not the smooth charm of, say, a classic Irish con man but that of a boy. To older men he gave more than just adulation; he gave *absolute* attention, following intently what was being said, asking questions, building up their experience. To a man who once told him he flew helicopters for a living, Barry replied, "*You* get to do that?" Then, bending forward, "My God, flying those big 'copters? Now, tell me, would you be able to . . . I mean what if something went wrong?" It was more than flattery, and Barry was more than just an audience.

With older women, Barry's charm was also that of a boy—a mischievous boy full of life—full of flirtatious fun. To his peers, he was dynamic, hip, cynical, and funny—someone around whom things were constantly happening. Later, for everyone, would be added the irresistible attractions of success. He was a kid, one would hear over and over, and he was already worth millions—had already done what they'd dreamed of all their lives.

— 4 —

BY THE STANDARDS OF, say, a twelve-year-old Hollywood runaway or an impoverished kid in Watts, Barry Minkow's childhood was not a difficult one. Nevertheless, it transformed a hyperactive, insecure little boy into a young man with an unquenchable desire to succeed.

Barry's father, Robert, had moved to Los Angeles with his family from South Bend, Indiana, while Bob Minkow was still a teenager. A gentle, friendly man who looks like a cross between Henry Kissinger and Fred Flintstone, Bob Minkow gave Barry his easy salesman's affability and hawklike profile.

In his teens, Robert Minkow underwent a serious brain tumor operation that left him, according to his daughter Sheri, "a bit handicapped." He was the kind of man who always has a smile, a pat on the back, a quick handshake, and an awkwardly bad joke each time he encounters you. ("Man who fight with wife all day get no piece at night.") Robert Minkow's limited mental capabilities were to cause frequent turnovers in his later jobs as a night watchman and real estate agent.

There were, as a result, stretches of unemployment that forced him to take out second and third mortgages on his modest suburban Los Angeles home in order to pay his family's living expenses. At other times, the gas, phone, and electricity were turned off because of unpaid bills.

Carole Winkelman Minkow, Barry's mother, had been reared in a comfortable Philadelphia family (her father and grandfather had both been attorneys) before coming to California and in 1960 marrying Bob Minkow.

After the slim, dark-haired Carole had moved with her new husband to the San Fernando Valley, two daughters—Gail and Sheri—were born. Then, in 1966, she gave birth to Barry, her only son.

Shortly thereafter, Carole Minkow converted from Judaism to Christianity, and over the years joined and regularly attended meetings of Emotional Health Anonymous and Overeaters Anonymous. ("The woman was Anonymous everything," says an adviser to Barry.)

High-strung and withdrawn, Carole Minkow worked at a series of low-paying jobs in the carpet-cleaning industry and "was always," according to her daughter Sheri, "one step away from hospitalization for mental reasons."

But Barry Minkow's most vivid surface memories of his childhood seem not to have been of his mother's emotional instability but of the shame he felt at his family's sporadic poverty. "Once," Barry wrote in *Making It in America*, the self-published book he had ghostwritten for himself at nineteen, "we had our gas turned off when I was a kid, and the lights, too. We made a joke out of it, my sister and I, but we took notice of it. It wasn't just happening on TV. The TV was *off*.... [When that happens] you remember it. You ... learn from it."

Similarly, in an interview he later gave *Barron's*, Minkow spoke of his humiliation when his parents' phone was temporarily disconnected because they couldn't pay the bill. "What do you say to your friends," he asked, "whey they call and find out your service has been cut off? I mean, what do you do?"

Such experiences must have been especially searing to Barry Minkow, raised as he was in the massive bedroom suburb of LA known as the San Fernando Valley. Built on former citrus groves and cabbage fields, the Valley, like so many suburban areas ringing America's cities, had filled with young families in the decades following World War II. By the early eighties, it seemed to a casual visitor a place characterized by endless rows of tract housing interrupted only by mini-malls and the golden-arched, plastic-chicken-bucket signs that clutter its main thoroughfares—a western outpost in America's vast urban sprawl, no different from thousands of others.

But by the time Barry Minkow was coming of age, a distinct culture was developing among many Valley teenagers, perfectly defined by Moon Zappa in her song "Valley Girl." A kind of blending of Jewish-American Princess materialism with Southern California youth culture, its values seemed most influenced by the flash of the Hollywood film industry and the gaudy wealth of nearby Beverly Hills. As Barry entered high school, the Valley and its teen culture had become a place celebrated for celebrating the vacuous. A place of $1,500 prom nights. A place where in its more affluent areas twelve-year-old girls went to beauty parlors to have their faces massaged, their legs waxed, and their toenails done. A place where Guess jeans were the currency, and the shopping mall was the center of one's social life.

When Barry Minkow entered the seventh grade, much of this was hammered home to him. In an effort to harness the compulsive wild energy that could not be repressed even with large doses of Ritalin and Thorazine, Robert and Carole Minkow scraped together every penny they had and sent Barry to the expensive Ridgewood Military Academy in the well-to-do community of Woodland Hills.

"While at the military academy, I got my first introduction to money," Barry would later say. "All of the boys and girls that went there were wealthy. I was the *only* kid from Reseda to go to an elite private school in Woodland Hills. Unfortunately, my parents went broke sending me there, and at the end of the eighth grade, I returned to public school. My future success [had] become linked with wanting to be superior . . . and it took a while before other reasons for success began to emerge. Military school had motivated me, that's for sure."

— 5 —

IT WAS LATE 1981 when Barry Minkow first started talking to Tom Padgett about carpet cleaning.

The two had met and become friends about a year earlier at the West Valley Gym, drawn together by their fanatical dedication to weight lifting.

Skinny at fourteen, Barry, was going to the gym after his job at Dunn-Rite, intent on building up his scrawny body.

Tom Padgett, devotee of the god Odin, member of the White Aryan Resistance, ex-biker, ex-factory worker, Vietnam veteran, and holder of a master's degree in international relations from Boston University, was at the West Valley Gym to get into shape of a different kind. A hard-drinking lover of Corona Extra and Dos Equis, Padgett at thirty-one was fighting a losing war with his thick body's tendency to turn to fat. A man who never did anything halfway, he was now doing everything but taking steroids to get himself back into shape: applying electronic muscle stimulation, drinking huge quantities of foul-tasting protein drinks, eating twenty to thirty eggs a week, and even attempting self-hypnosis before workouts.

One day after Padgett had just finished a set of killer squats and was literally shaking from the effort, Barry Minkow, oversized shorts hanging down to his knees, walked into the power-lifting room and said to Tom and his workout partner, "Man, you guys are working like *animals*." He then stayed around, watching intently and asking questions, step by step, as Padgett and his partner completed their sets.

When he wasn't at Dunn-Rite or at school during those years, Barry invariably would be found at the gym, working out hours at a time, four days a week, and scrubbing the showers on weekends to pay for his membership. West Valley was a small gym where everybody knew everybody else, and often when Tom Padgett was working out, Barry would come over to watch.

Padgett, a large, pockmarked, friendly man who'd never married, gradually became aware that he really *liked* having Barry Minkow around and didn't mind at all the high energy and curiosity that others at the gym found so annoying.

Soon they began working out together, and Tom Padgett, who'd been living alone since moving to LA from Akron, Ohio, just a few months earlier, began to regard Barry Minkow as the little brother he'd never had but always wanted. Tom Padgett was, after all, a man who'd been around and had much to tell. And as he told it—whether weaving a war story or dispensing advice—Barry Minkow listened enraptured, hanging on every word.

But there seemed something more to Barry Minkow than just the skinny kid eager to ingratiate himself. Something that Tom Padgett, along with almost everyone who met Barry, was to find disarming: a surprising maturity existing within this typical teenager.

Once, for example, Padgett got involved in a series of amateur prize fights at a country and western bar in Pomona called the Last Chance Saloon. It was no big deal, a few rounds in the back of the bar in a ring the size of a phone booth. Padgett, having turned thirty, felt good getting in there a couple of times, mixing it up, and winning.

By his third fight, however, he'd more than met his match. The guy he was fighting was young and fast—far too fast for the aging, beer-loving Padgett, who was getting whacked senseless.

Badly battered and bruised, his face a mess, Padgett walked into the gym several days later, only to be mercilessly goofed on by the boys at the weight racks. The West Valley Gym for Padgett was like a bar, a home away from home, filled four days a week exclusively with men—normal guys who were his friends, not pretty boys at some unisex Sports Connection. And now, everybody it seemed was laughing at him.

Everybody but Barry Minkow. Instead, Barry stood up for him. "At least," he told them, "Tom had the guts to get in the ring." It was a small thing, but Padgett didn't see it that way. Barry had tried to rescue him from a humiliating moment and had shown a lot of class for a kid.

After that, they became even closer. Following workouts, they'd go out to lunch, and by the summer of 1981 they were going out to eat and see movies together.

It seemed an odd friendship, even to Padgett. "Here's this Jewish kid from the Valley with me—the image of the Irish wild man, the biker, the gun collector, the mercenary," Padgett would later say. "I'm like something out of a comic book, and here's this skinny little kid. I don't know why he was hanging out with me."

Nevertheless, over the course of a year or so, they became tight friends. In addition to their workouts together, Barry would often stop by the room Tom had rented in Woodland Hills and watch Padgett's "Twilight Zone" tapes, to which they were both addicted.

Padgett, who'd spent two tours in the army, including stints in Vietnam and Germany, considered himself an amateur philosopher, and after discussing the feasibility of Barry setting up a carpet-cleaning business, they'd often talk philosophy and politics.

They'd talk in particular about "the Jews," then and now a consuming passion in Tom Padgett's life, and about the "one-sidedness of the U.S. position in the Middle East, which," Padgett says, "nobody was talking about back in 1981."

And he'd tell Barry about the "kosher tax," which really incensed him. He explained that a *K* or a *U* on a product like ketchup or bread meant that a rabbi had been paid to bless it and how unfair it was that everybody had to pay a higher price as a result. Working-class Jews included. It was, in fact, only a small percentage of the Jews who were causing all the problems, Padgett told Barry.

Why then didn't *everybody* know about it? Well, Tom Padgett patiently explained, look who controls the media.

But Barry Minkow, Jewish or not, had carved out a special place in the affections of Tom Padgett, and when Barry told him he was thinking of starting up his own carpet-cleaning business and asked Tom for his help and advice, Padgett was only too willing to do what he could.

Tom had just gotten a good, steady job as an insurance claims adjuster for Allstate, and was now in a position to steer some work to the carpet-cleaning business Barry wanted to start. But first, he advised his young friend, finish high school, stay with Dunn-Rite part-time, and meanwhile he'd see what he could do.

In late 1982, at age 16, Barry Minkow got his first big break. Dan Krowpman, another gym acquaintance, agreed to give Barry a loan to start his own business. It wasn't much—$1,500—and he'd have to split the profits fifty-fifty with Krowpman, but Barry was ecstatic.

With the $1,500, Barry Minkow went to a local janitorial supplier and bought a shampooer, a steam cleaner, and some chemicals. Then he ordered some business cards for "ZZZZ Best Carpet and Furniture Cleaning Company, Inc.," stored the chemicals in his bedroom, turned his family's garage into an office, and had a telephone installed.

Less than five years later, Barry Minkow's share of ZZZZ Best's publicly held stock would be worth a purported $100 million.

After hiring Carole Minkow to do telemarketing at $25 a week and paying his father $150 a month in rent for the garage, Barry Minkow was officially in business. In the mornings, he would go to school; in the afternoons and on weekends, he'd clean carpets. But because most people wanted their carpets cleaned in the morning so they'd be dry by the time they got home from work, his weekday business was limited.

So deciding he needed further help, Minkow called a casual friend named Chip Arrington.

Barry had met Chip at Dunn-Rite in the early 1980s. Arrington, a twenty-one-year-old with wholesome, all-American blond good looks, was working on one of the half-dozen or so carpet-cleaning crews.

The son of a well-to-do corporate lawyer and a graduate of an expensive preparatory school, Arrington, by class and background, was not exactly a typical carpet cleaner. But he liked the independent, stress-free nature of the work and had been at it for several years when Barry called.

Chip remembered Minkow as an outgoing kid who always wanted to arm wrestle and constantly bugged the cleaning crews to take him along on jobs. He was therefore more than a little surprised when Barry told him he'd started his own business and wanted Chip to work for him. Minkow offered Chip a fifty-fifty split to do the jobs he (Minkow) couldn't do during school hours. Shortly thereafter, Arrington began working at ZZZZ Best, starting down the road that would lead to his becoming chief operating officer of ZZZZ Best, as well as right-hand man and gofer to its soon-to-be-celebrated multimillionaire teenage founder.

After hiring Chip, Barry Minkow called on his old friend Tom Padgett at his new job as a property appraiser for Allstate. "Tom," Barry said, "you handle plenty of property claims, and I gotta have some work. Can you steer some my way?"

As it happened, Tom Padgett was indeed in a position to give Barry some business.

If an Allstate customer were to call in, for example, with a large hole in her rug, and had no one in mind to repair it, a claims adjuster like Padgett could send someone of his or her own choosing to do the work.

Since his responsibility to Allstate was to keep prices down, an ethical adjuster would send someone known to be good and inexpensive, and expect nothing more in return than an appreciative phone call. Others might expect lunch or a kickback, typically 10 percent.

Tom Padgett was a 10 percent kickback guy.

He and Barry agreed on the kickback, but the money was not Padgett's main concern. His main concern, in addition to helping Barry, was bad work. He could not *deal* with bad work. Bad work meant callbacks, and callbacks are the bane of a claims adjuster. People are not normally happy when they call to report that their car has been in an accident, their home has been wind- or flood-damaged, or their carpet and furniture destroyed in a fire. They are stressed out and not on their best behavior. A callback was only extra aggravation that Tom Padgett *did not* need. Did Barry understand that? "Hey, babe, no problem," Barry told him.

The first claim Padgett sent Barry out on was a patch job on a rug for an old lady, who immediately called back to complain.

When Barry returned, he gave Padgett a slip of yellow paper on which he'd written his estimate of what the job had cost. "Jesus Christ," thought Padgett, "here he is dealing with the second largest insurance company in the nation, and he turns in his estimate on a fucking piece of scrap paper!"

He told Barry to forget about getting paid, that he'd have to send a more experienced contractor out to redo the job. But then Barry gave him the patented Barry Minkow look—that sheepish beagle-eyed look that always got to Padgett—and he quickly relented. He gave Barry some money for business stationery and promised to send him out on future jobs.

Padgett did assign more jobs to Barry, but in early 1983, he was transferred out of homeowner claims to drive-in car appraisals. Barry, however, would still stop by and watch Tom Padgett deal with the customers driving up in their dented and smashed autos. Tom would introduce Barry as his "little brother," and the customers would think it was great, two brothers so close that one would come and spend time with the other that way.

Barry wasn't just socializing, however. He was learning from Tom Padgett the ways of the world of insurance, as he had studied with Joel Hochberg the business of cleaning carpets. And there was much to master. Padgett wasn't just estimating damage; he was also steering work to auto repair shops, in effect "selling" the shops at which he wanted his customers to have their cars repaired, and receiving a kickback in return. As he did so, he lectured Barry about insurance and sales and reintroduced him to the halo effect, using President Reagan as an example. "Look at Reagan," he'd say, "look at all the shit he gets away with. Why? Because people like him so much that they don't look at the particulars. They buy his whole package, think he's on their side. He's like an angel. People think he can't do anything wrong."

"Reagan," explained Tom Padgett to Barry Minkow, "has the halo effect."

— 6 —

IT WAS HEADY STUFF, and Barry Minkow loved every minute of it, riding around the Valley with Danny Krowpman in his eighteen-foot tool truck, watching him sell wrenches, screwdrivers, and other hand tools to auto mechanics.

Barreling down traffic-choked Ventura Boulevard, feet propped up on the dash, right arm hanging out the window, Barry Minkow felt good, alive, in sync with the world. He was with his idol. He was with Danny Krowpman.

It wasn't his two trucks and certainly not the tools he was selling that caused Barry to regard Danny as his hero, as "everything." Even at sixteen, Barry knew that in the best of years, selling tools was just a living.

But Dan Krowpman "was money." He was *money*. Hundred-dollar bills—ten or fifteen at a time—were always in Danny Krowpman's pocket. And they weren't there just for flash. As Barry saw, they were there to float loans, to cash checks at 5 percent, to make book on Sunday's game, or to make change if you wanted to buy the tools, porno tapes, or fireworks Danny was selling off his truck.

For Danny always had a scam. Not that he thought of himself as a criminal. He simply operated in the twilight zone where so many American men spend a little time. An area of bets, an occasional hooker, maybe a joint once in a while, or a little coke. A place that mocks the straightlaced "good guys, bad guys" puritanism that's become so prevalent in the late eighties. Why, as Danny himself used to say, he was "deviating just a little from that straight line down the middle."

So it was only natural that Barry had gone to him when he needed a loan to start his business. By sixteen, he'd come to think of the tall, powerfully built Krowpman as "the father he'd never had," a man he could talk to as he never could Bob Minkow. Besides, where else was he to turn? Banks were not exactly eager to lend money to teenagers with no collateral or track record of any kind.

And it had been equally natural for Krowpman to loan Barry the $1,500 start-up money. Like Joel Hochberg and Tom Padgett,

Danny had a great deal of affection for Barry and wanted to help the kid out. Minkow was smart, willing to take advice, and eager to hustle for a buck. The loan, therefore, appeared a safe one.

Danny hadn't expected Barry to become a headache—one of his "deadbeats" who on Monday nights—"*deadbeat* night"—Dan Krowpman would have to call and cajole for his money.

But he did.

First, there was the loss of Minkow's steam-cleaning equipment just two months after he'd loaned the kid the money for the machines. They'd been stolen, Barry claimed, by a couple of guys who'd just started working for him, and as a result he was claiming to be "washed up." Naturally, he was uninsured and had no way of paying Danny back.

But when Minkow asked for an additional loan to start over, Danny came through with it, perhaps because he saw it as the best way to recoup his investments, perhaps because of his mentor-buddy relationship with Barry—perhaps because of both.

With the money, Barry decided to move out of his parents' garage and into the two tiny rooms over the auto repair shops in Reseda where he would later meet Jeri Carr.

"I was sixteen, and I had an ego, and I wanted to have an office to be important," Barry would later say. But there was another factor as well. His mother's ring—her *wedding* ring—had been taken during the theft of Barry's equipment, and his parents were pressuring him to move his business out of their house.

It was never Barry Minkow's style to think things through and have a cost analysis done before opening a new location or to keep careful profit-and-loss statements so he'd know where he was at any given moment.

His method of determining ZZZZ Best's payroll, for example, was to sit on his living room floor with Chip Arrington on a Sunday night, time cards in hand, and holler out the number of hours an employee had worked. Then, Chip, using a calculator, would shout back the amount the employee was to be paid. Barry Minkow had little time for details and no use for facts. He was intent on expanding, no matter what the reality. And the reality was he simply could not afford to.

It wasn't as if ZZZZ Best was failing to make money cleaning carpets. Barry had quite correctly understood from the start the importance of telemarketing in obtaining jobs, and by devoting valuable resources to that technique he was getting ZZZZ Best its share of work.

Once inside a customer's home, he and his crews were adept at taking a four-room, $39 job and boosting the price to $100 or $120 with extras. But how much money can you *gross* with just one small-time outlet? Maybe $3,000 or $4,000 a week.

Barry Minkow wanted *big* money, and not in five or ten years. So having just turned seventeen and already in debt, he decided to open a second location. And to steal his grandmother's pearls.

The pearls were worth several thousand dollars, her solid-gold bracelet somewhat less. No one seems certain how much. But everybody agrees that Barry was grossly underpaid when he sold the jewelry at the Gold Exchange after having taken it from his grandmother's house. It was later said, in fact, that he'd gotten only $35 for everything, although Barry would indignantly insist it had been "a lot more."

But whatever the amount, it wasn't even close to what Barry Minkow needed to dig himself out of the financial hole in which he found himself after just six months in business.

Opening that second office in Thousand Oaks had been a major mistake. Barry was now bouncing checks all over town and was forced to move from bank to bank as his accounts kept closing. His sloppy and irresponsible management style along with his newly acquired big spending habits had all played their parts in the failure of the Thousand Oaks office, and his mounting debt.

Then in June his father discovered Barry's theft of his grandmother's jewelry and began blaming him for the earlier theft of Carole Minkow's wedding ring as well. Worse, he was now demanding that his son take a lie detector test *and* see a psychologist.

Barry, understandably, was not keen to do either. But he did agree to see the psychologist and eventually admitted stealing his grandmother's jewelry.

"I needed the money for the business," he said. This was particularly distressing to the Minkow family, since his grandmother had already lent him $2,000 to open the Thousand Oaks location.

Still, things *were* coming down on Barry Minkow. In addition to the $2,000 he'd borrowed from his grandmother, he'd also borrowed another $1,000 from Dan Krowpman. Plus, he'd taken out a $3,500 leasing agreement underwritten by Krowpman to buy equipment and chemicals for his new office, run up a Diner's Club bill of over $5,500 at local restaurants, and was falling further behind in his loan payments to Danny. By August Barry was asking Krowpman for still *another* $1,000 loan (which he got) simply to pay his employees. "I couldn't meet the payroll," Barry Minkow would later say. "I was dead in the water."

So, out of options, Barry decided to pull off his first insurance scam, the one he hoped would bail him out of debt. He would falsely claim to his insurance company (for Barry was now insured) that his cleaning equipment had been stolen.

As a name for the nonexistent, stolen machines, Barry chose the Cornwell Triple-Vac Dual-Pump Water-Heated Steam Cleaner. It was perfect. It sounded, Barry thought, so "expensive," so "extravagant," well worth the $1,000 loss per machine Barry was claiming. And, of course, there was no way an insurance adjuster could check out the cost. Where, Barry reasoned, was the insurer going to find a machine that didn't exist?

So one August evening in 1983, after ZZZZ Best's offices had been closed and everybody had gone home, Barry returned, kicked a big hole in the door, and left. The next morning, he came to work, glanced at the door, and said, "Oh, look, my office is broken into," called his insurance adjuster, and filed a police report complete with made-up serial numbers of the nonexistent machines.

Then he presented a sworn statement to State Farm claiming that the machines had been stolen, along with invoices from Cornwell Quality Tools and Equipment (the company that supplied Dan Krowpman's tools) that proved ZZZZ Best had indeed purchased the equipment.

The break-in netted between $10,000 and $16,000; Barry would later have trouble remembering exactly how much. In the months to come, he would repeat the scam at least three more times at different ZZZZ Best locations, receiving about $8,000, $6,000, and $5,000.

He would simply submit the paperwork and give the insurer what he said was Krowpman's phone number. When Danny (or Barry pretending to be Danny) received the insurer's call, he'd verify having sold the equipment to ZZZZ Best, and "bam, bam," says Barry, "that was it."

In late September 1983—just a month or so after the faked break-in of his office—Barry Minkow stopped by Tom Padgett's apartment for a visit. It had been a while since they'd seen each

other, and as they spoke, Padgett was struck by how much Barry
had changed from the boy he'd known three years earlier.

Aided by anabolic steroids and grueling four-day-a-week, two-
hour morning workouts, Minkow had grown from a skinny kid into
a powerfully muscled young man who—as he approached eighteen—was entering his senior year in high school and running, it
appeared, a very successful business as well. Sitting together that
day, bullshitting about the guys at the gym and ZZZZ Best, it
became clear to Padgett for the first time that he was speaking
with an equal.

Finally, Barry got around to the reason for his visit. He was
caught short and needed a loan to tide him over—some cash to
replace equipment that had been stolen and to cover a few problems
at his new Thousand Oaks location. Four or five thousand dollars
would do it. His parents didn't have it, and Tom was really the only
one he could turn to.

So Tom Padgett, a man who valued his friendships, went with
Barry to Security Pacific Bank in Woodland Hills and secured a
savings book loan in his name for $4,500. The security for the loan,
it was agreed, would be Padgett's savings—about $5,000. Barry
would make the monthly $400 payments.

When Minkow missed the first payment, Padgett wasn't even
pissed. After all, Barry was a kid. It was understandable. And
when he called, Barry was so contrite. "I forgot. I feel like such an
asshole. It was just an oversight." He had twenty excuses, but the
bottom line was that it would never happen again.

The next month it did.

He missed not only the second payment but the third one as
well.

And not only that, but Security Pacific was calling Padgett at
Allstate, asking him why *he'd* missed the payments.

Now Padgett *was* pissed.

He called Minkow, who immediately started to apologize, but
Padgett cut him off. "Barry, don't give me that same song and
dance. Just tell me what the fuck is going on. I don't need this shit
coming into the office and getting phone calls. Don't"—Padgett was
shouting now—"*do* me this way."

Barry said he needed to see him, and they agreed to meet at
the gym.

When they got together, Barry explained the problem: he
simply didn't have enough business to meet his payroll and ex-

penses while expanding at the same time. "Tom," Barry asked, "can you help me out? Maybe talk to some of your friends in property claims? I won't disappoint you."

Padgett said he would try, and he laid down the rules.

"Do everything straight," he told Barry. "I'll tell you who plays [the kickback game] and who doesn't. Don't offer 10 percent until you really feel someone out. Most of the adjusters here are straight anyway, so the most important thing is to just do a good job. No callbacks. If you do all that, you'll get stacks of work at Allstate and can branch out to State Farm and other companies."

So Barry gave out his ZZZZ Best card to Tom Padgett's friends at Allstate, but all they sent was about $1,000 worth of small jobs to ZZZZ Best.

— 7 —

AT ABOUT THE SAME TIME that Barry Minkow was struggling to keep his business solvent and Dan Krowpman and Tom Padgett at bay, a young woman named Elenora Madrinan was entering Grover Cleveland High School in Reseda.

At fifteen, Elenora was the second daughter of a hardworking Mexican-American family. Her pale skin, light sandy hair, and freckles belied her Latin heritage, as her wide-eyed, unaffected naïveté reminded one of Debbie Reynolds in those MGM musicals back in the fifties. Talking with her, it was always a bit surprising that Bobby Van didn't suddenly appear and, in tandem with Elenora, break out in a chorus of "The Aba Daba Honeymoon."

One day in early 1984, Elenora Madrinan was sitting in one of her tenth-grade classes, chatting with some girlfriends and waiting for the class to start, when in walked Barry Minkow. It was the first time she'd ever seen him, and she and her girlfriends immediately broke into a fit of the giggles.

He was dressed in a sky-blue polyester suit and was carrying a briefcase. Not exactly typical attire for a Valley high school where kids with shopping mall mind-sets dressed either studiously casual, or latest-fad hip, but *never* in pale blue polyester.

But it wasn't just Barry's suit or even his hair, which as usual was in wild disarray, that Elenora and her girlfriends found so hysterical. It was the *combination* of the suit and hair, along with Barry Minkow's walk. Elenora had never seen anyone sway quite like Barry when he moved. It wasn't anything like the graceful pimp roll of the black guys at school. It was rather just the opposite: awkward and lumbering. For Barry had become so huge and muscle-bound that when he walked across the front of the room to talk to her teacher, he reminded Elenora of an ape in a suit.

"Who," Elenora remembers asking her girlfriends, "does *this* guy think he is?"

Later she found out. Barry Minkow was a senior and owned his own company. She wasn't really interested in knowing much more. He was too weird. And frankly, Elenora, who'd always been shy and quiet, was intimidated by him.

Not only did he appear physically huge to the diminutive Elenora, he was figuratively becoming a big man on campus as well, soon to be voted both Most Likely to Succeed and Class Clown in this his senior year—despite his barely passing grades.

And he *was* a clown in Elenora's estimation—a loud, obnoxious one, too, with the kind of quick put-down wit that could make you cringe in embarrassment.

But nevertheless, a lot of people at Grover Cleveland High seemed to like Barry Minkow.

Not nearly as many, of course, as *idolized* Bret Saberhagen, later to be the star pitcher for the Kansas City Royals. Saberhagen was also the star of stars at Grover Cleveland when Barry Minkow went there, and pitched a no-hitter in Dodger Stadium his senior year, making Barry feel like a nobody. Although Saberhagen had never done anything to him personally, Barry never forgot, and as he grew rich and his horizons seemed limitless, he'd frequently mention to Joel Hochberg and others his plans for revenge: one day he would buy the California Angels from the aging Gene Autry, trade for Saberhagen, and then send him to the minors. "And he was *serious*," says Hochberg. "I'm telling you, he was serious. I never met anybody with a bigger ego."

In any case, things probably would have remained much the same between Barry and Elenora—he at the center of his circle of friends, and the shy Elenora on the fringes. Except that Elenora needed a job.

Despite her youth, she was already working at a stationery store. But she hated its monotonous, dead-end predictability and was looking for something more adventurous when a girlfriend told her that Barry might be hiring telemarketers. Elenora said it sounded interesting.

Several days later, she was hanging around during nutrition, when the man himself, seated at a nearby table, spun around and without any words of introduction, spoke to her for the first time: "So I hear you want a job at my company. Why don't you come in today after school, and we'll talk about it?"

That afternoon, Elenora went to Barry's office in Reseda and was surprised to find it was a "dumpy little place." Barry told her to sit down, and she was conscious that, despite his obnoxious reputation, he was going out of his way to make her feel comfortable. He introduced her to two telemarketers: his mother and an old friend of Mrs. Minkow's, Vera Hojecki.

He then explained a bit about how to go about calling people cold on the phone, made a few calls himself by way of demonstration, and told her to try it. She did and astounded him by booking her first call. "Luck, pure luck," said Barry. "Try it again." The next person wasn't interested, but on her third call, she was once again successful. "OK," Barry said, "you're hired." He offered her minimum wage, as he did all new telemarketers, and Elenora Madrinan started work that very day.

Initially, she took the job as a goof—something to get her away from the stationery store and keep her in spending money. Barry's company was known around campus as a joke, and that's the way Elenora initially took it.

Over the next several months, however, Elenora began to develop an unexpected affection and respect for Barry Minkow.

Like Jeri Carr and so many others meeting Barry for the first time (and if he was not on his salesman good behavior) Elenora was at first put off by the boy in Barry—the gross, pizza-every-day-for-lunch, crotch-grabbing, egotistical clown side of him, the loud-mouth whose idea of humor was to goose somebody or to badger his young female employees with half-serious come-ons like "Don't you wanna do me?" and taunts like "When are ya gonna grow some tits?"

Still, on many occasions, just one on one, the fast-talking, high-strung, wiseass put-down artist evaporated, and in his place would materialize a sweet, decent guy who would listen to you with *absolute* attention, and—once he liked you—would do his best to be the most loyal friend you ever had.

In time, for Elenora, his warmth, charm, and sheer joy of life far outweighed his crudeness.

Although there was no romantic or sexual relationship between them, there was an intangible quality about Barry that went beyond mere charisma and that was so strong that Elenora found herself inexplicably drawn to him. She just had never, ever come across anyone like him. Over the next several years, like many of his employees, she grew to love him, both as an employer and a friend.

And while not everyone who worked for Barry was as enthralled as Elenora, Minkow's soon-to-be highly publicized skill at motivating people was far more than just a sales pitch or PR ploy—it was very real indeed, whether he was dealing with bankers and investors or with people who came, like himself, from marginal economic or social backgrounds.

Principally, the kinds of people Barry would hire were, like Elenora, young and possessed of few prospects. But most had enough awareness to sense that, unless they got a break at a time when upward mobility for working-class kids was becoming far more difficult, they would be left out in a society where status—after a brief twenty-year hiatus—was once again based almost exclusively on material success.

The nice home, the new car, the good clothes, the vacation in Hawaii or at the Club Med would be closed to them in a 1980s economy that was offering young Harvard MBAs spectacular wealth and people like themselves little more than low-paying, dead-end, service-industry jobs.

Barry Minkow seemed to have grasped this instinctively, and learned to use it to his advantage.

"I was one of the 'working broke' when I started with Barry," Chip Arrington was later to say, "and he paid me far more money than I'd ever made before. [Then later] when I'd complain about busting my ass or object to something he wanted me to do, he'd use the old Reagan line on me, you know: 'Are you better off today than you were a year ago?' And the truth is, I was. *Much* better off. That's one way Barry'd get his power over people: by putting them in a better situation and then constantly reminding them of it."

Barry also knew the benefits of always promising more. At ZZZZ Best, the prospect of high-paying, status-filled positions in the company—and of promotion from within—was the major tool

Barry Minkow used to motivate his employees. As his business and
its revenues appeared to grow, in just a few years, to startling
proportions, the message repeated over and over was that *his*
dream could be *your* dream, that as ZZZZ Best grew and pros-
pered, so too could you.

Three years after Elenora was hired, for example, she was
promised the job of producing ZZZZ Best marketing and training
videotapes as the company was about to go national and became a
multimillion-dollar enterprise; Don Sanelli, who did ZZZZ Best's
advertising, was going to head one of the top ten advertising
accounts in the nation, meeting with top directors and producers,
dining at the Four Seasons. Elenora's sister, Ana, was going to
leave Jeri Carr's PR agency and work for ZZZZ Best full-time as its
in-house publicist; and Chip Arrington, by late 1985 already the
CEO of ZZZZ Best instead of the bone-wearying carpet cleaner
he'd been, was going to ride the seemingly limitless crest of success
right beside the Boy Wonder.

"I was in my late thirties," says Joel Hochberg, who, newly
sober, was hired by Barry in November 1985, "and Barry showed
me a suit and tie and a future where I wasn't gonna be a carpet
cleaner, car salesman, or bum all my life. I was going to the top
because 'the sky was the limit,' and 'tough times pass, but tough
people last.' I really believed him when he said all that. I'm forty
years old, and he was the best bullshit artist I ever met from
Brooklyn to California."

In fact, almost everybody who worked for ZZZZ Best became,
in time, infused with Barry's optimism and began, like him, to
dream big dreams of their own. "ZZZZ Best was the place," Ana
Madrinan later said, "where we were going to spend the rest of our
lives. This was where we were going to be twenty or thirty years
from now. We all loved and believed in Barry."

Soon after, when he became the darling of the local media,
stories would abound about Barry, the "nineteen-year-old millionaire who insists that his employees call him *Mr.* Minkow"; about
Barry, the hard-nosed taskmaster who would literally chew pencils
to pieces in hyperkinetic frustration; about Barry, who said he'd
fire his parents (both of whom became his employees) if they didn't
meet his exacting standards. But few who worked for ZZZZ Best
were concerned by any of that. What they wanted was a share of the
pie that Barry was offering. And if he was crude and chewed
pencils and all the rest, he was also at the office twelve or fourteen

hours a day, every day, making it happen for everybody.

In those early months of 1984, nothing infuriated Barry Minkow more than Chip Arrington's go-slow counsel. "Arrington," he would say, "you are one conservative motherfucker. You'll never understand that if you don't go for it, you don't get it. Your attitude, the kind of shit you're saying, will get us exactly one place—nowhere."

Specifically, it was Chip's protestations that it was financially too risky to open a third location in Anaheim—a city located more than fifty miles south of the San Fernando Valley—that had brought on Barry's tirade. But Barry insisted on going ahead anyway, in spite of the recent fiasco at Thousand Oaks.

Chip's analysis proved exactly right. The Anaheim office *was* a financial disaster. Barry seemed to think, said Arrington later, that if "he just did enough volume [in his business] . . . he would overcome anything. It was an obsession with him."

But then again, Chip had no way of knowing about the problems Barry Minkow was struggling to overcome.

In September, using the immediate credit that ZZZZ Best had recently been granted at West Valley Bank, Barry had quickly rung up almost $20,000 in charges. When payment was not forthcoming, the bank had demanded its money and threatened to notify the FBI.

Barry had taken care of *that* problem by arranging to pay it back at the rate of $300 per week, signing a note for $20,000 in the process. But now there were also the losses resulting from the Anaheim opening to contend with, losses that even Barry described as "awful, terrible."

And, of course, he still had to make at least token payments to Tom Padgett and Dan Krowpman, and deal with the overcharges due on his Diner's Club bill and various lawsuits and judgments stemming from his Thousand Oaks mismanagement. At the age of 18, Barry Minkow was fast finding himself in a classic Ponzi trap, having to constantly borrow from new lending sources in order to make payments on previous loans, increasing the number of people he owed money to—without any increase in his income.

In his effort to stay afloat, Barry Minkow began casting about for bank loans. Loan officers, however, didn't want to talk to him without first looking at his financial statements and tax returns.

The fact that he'd never prepared or filed either posed a problem. But that problem was quickly solved. Barry found a woman who did accounting work and was willing, for a price, to prepare fraudulent statements and returns.

Minkow had them done for 1982 and 1983, even though he hadn't even started in business until October 1982. Over the next year or so, he would have about ten different versions of the same paperwork created, each reflecting different amounts of income earned for the same year.

But despite Barry's creative paperwork, banks were refusing to grant him a loan. He was just eighteen; he was in a service industry; he had little collateral; his was a small business, and small businesses in general have high failure rates; and his unpaid Diner's Club bill and other bills were now showing up on his TRW credit rating.

So, following a warning from West Valley Bank because he'd missed a couple of his $300 weekly payments, Barry turned his attention to private investors and placed an ad in the *Los Angeles Times*. A man named Wallace Berrie responded, and Barry charmed him into a $30,000 loan.

Along with his bogus tax returns, Barry showed Wallace Berrie a breakdown of where the money was going, mainly to open new offices and buy new equipment. As with the insurance "thefts", he simply made up the names of some expensive-sounding equipment that he *had* to have, including a nonexistent "drapery cleaning machine," and Berrie bought the package. But the cost was steep: over $1,200 a week in payments, $500 of which was interest partly hidden as a consultant fee.

However, Barry Minkow, even for a teenager, was a guy who lived for the moment. Tomorrow could always be dealt with tomorrow. There was just one snag, however. The loan wasn't due to fund until late July, four *long* months away.

In the meantime, Barry still had to confront reality. So in late March, while at Rick's Check Cashing—where he frequently did business and which was located right by his parents' house—he managed to steal over $10,000 worth of blank money orders and use them to pay some of his more pressing bills. Among those he filled out and used were a whole series to Pacific Bell that saved him from the calamity of having his phones turned off—a terrible fate to befall any business, but a particularly disastrous occurrence for a carpet-cleaning company, which relies so heavily on telemarketing.

The stolen money orders enabled Barry to hold on until the Wallace Berrie loan came through. They were the first of what Barry and his partners would later come to call "mini-cures"— immediate solutions to pressing problems.

In retrospect, it seems entirely logical that Robert Turnbow, the vice president and manager of the West Valley Bank, would become Barry Minkow's next mini-cure.

Barry, after all, prided himself on how well he had the man pimped. "Turnbow?" he would say, "Turnbow? I *own* the guy. He's in my pocket."

A hesitant, inoffensive man with more the blow-dried look of a K mart manager than the appearance of the banker he'd been for the past twenty years, Robert Turnbow had been much taken with Barry Minkow—an "eager, energetic young man who was going to make something of himself"—when Minkow opened his bank account at West Valley in early 1983.

Because Barry was just turning seventeen, Bob Turnbow took to meeting with him regularly and granting fatherly financial and personal advice.

Turnbow had been the man largely responsible for ZZZZ Best being granted instant credit at West Valley, so naturally he was not happy when Barry had bounced all those checks.

But in early August, Robert Turnbow's faith in Barry Minkow was fully restored. Using the $30,000 Wallace Berrie loan, Barry completely paid off his $20,000 note to West Valley Bank.

Several weeks later, Barry asked for and was granted mini-cure number two: a merchant credit card account. With the credit card account, Barry planned on giving ZZZZ Best customers the option of paying his company with their Visa or MasterCard, an obvious advantage for a small business.

More importantly to the cash-poor young businessman, however, was the float or lag time he'd also get on the new credit card billings, time when he'd have the use of his customers' money.

What Barry intended to do was relatively easy, so easy, in fact, that credit card fraud has become one of the most abused forms of theft in America. In 1985, for example, about $200 million worth of credit card frauds were committed. In most cases, a credit card payment is made for a service performed, and instead of running off one bill, the vendor runs off half a dozen blanks and later adds various amounts and forges the customer's signature. Or some zeros are added after the customer has signed.

Barry decided to use the overbilling technique. Taking a customer's credit card bill after a carpet cleaner had brought it in, he'd forge the customer's name and credit card number on another draft and then bill the customer for hundreds of dollars (usually between $500 and $800) for cleaning services never performed.

Then he'd deposit the phony bills along with the real ones at West Valley Bank and receive instant credit on all of them.

The bank would send out the billings to the various credit card companies, which would send the charges to their customers on monthly statements. The lag time between when a cardholder discovered the overbilling and complained to Barry or the credit card company, and the time when the cardholder would eventually have to be reimbursed, could be anywhere from forty-five days to six months. In the interval, Barry would have the use of the bank's or customer's money as kind of a short-term loan or "float."

Luck and circumstances, however, were to provide Barry with far more of a float than he had ever anticipated. In February 1985, West Valley Bank went bankrupt. The timing, for Barry Minkow, was perfect. In those four months, West Valley had paid out about $70,000 in instant credit to ZZZZ Best for phony credit card charges without getting reimbursed—the victimized credit card holders being understandably unwilling to pay the overcharges.

Had the bank not gone out of business, Barry would have been in deep trouble, but he got a free ride. The credit card companies let the false charges drop; they, after all, weren't taking the loss. And most of the customers, after refusing to pay, were issued new cards. It was the *bank* that took the loss, with the overburdened, understaffed, and slow-moving Federal Deposit Insurance Corporation responsible for the collection.

With the breathing space and, of course, the money, Barry was able to relax just a bit and do a little catching up. He paid off the first of three tax liens and put $6,000 on a new $21,000 Datsun 300 ZX sports car (creating, in the process, false pay stubs that showed he was making $1,100 a week so he could qualify for the $480 monthly payments on that 300 ZX). Then, he placed a $5,000 down payment on a $100,000 condo he was purchasing.

It had worked out for Barry Minkow, just as he knew it would. Maybe not quite the way he'd anticipated, but it had worked out nonetheless, underlining the philosophy by which he lived his life: say anything, do anything, just get the money first, and worry about it later. He even had a parable he'd tell the faint of heart when he wanted to illustrate the point: the Jewish doctor story.

One day, went the story, a king got angry at his Jewish doctor: "You're not doing a good enough job taking care of me; I'm going to order your death."

"Please, your majesty," said the Jewish doctor, "there must be something I can do to change your mind."

Thinking a moment, the King said dismissively, "Yes, you can teach my dog to speak Spanish."

"Thank you, your majesty," the Jewish doctor replied. "How long do I have?"

"Thirty days," said the king.

The doctor told a friend how lucky he was. "Are you nuts?" the friend asked. "Dogs can't talk, and *you* can't even speak Spanish."

"True," answered the Jewish doctor, "but a lot can happen in thirty days. The dog could die, the king could die. Who knows?"

It was a story Barry Minkow would have occasion to tell many times over the next several years.

When Barry Minkow hired Jeri Carr to do his PR at $1,500 a month, she had no idea just how good he would be. The idea was simply to get ZZZZ Best some free press so that when people wanted to get their carpets cleaned or were solicited over the phone, they (and bankers) would be familiar with the company's name.

Initially, Carr managed to get Barry, who was incredibly nervous, on a few talk shows on small local radio stations. The first interview, done when Barry was eighteen, took place at tiny KMAX in Pasadena. In spite of Barry's nervousness, he did quite well, impressing the interviewer with his "big dreams" rap and his "message to youth."

Afterward, responding to the barrage of press releases the hustling Carr Agency was sending all over town, Cleve Hermann, a well-known features reporter for KFWB, a popular all-news radio station, agreed to interview Barry for his show, "On Location."

Barry was ecstatic. Hermann was coming out to interview him at *his* office, and although the piece was only two minutes long, the interview would air on the hour, twenty-four hours a day for two days!

Moreover, Barry *loved* Cleve Hermann. When Hermann walked into ZZZZ Best's offices, Barry appeared momentarily overwhelmed, and after the reporter left, he could barely control himself. "Was I good?" he kept asking Carr over and over. "Was I really good? Did I say anything stupid? Did I say the wrong thing?

Man, Cleve Hermann," he repeated, "Cleve Hermann! I can't believe Cleve Hermann really interviewed me!"

But after just a few more tries, Barry Minkow became a pro—a complete press package with perfect pitch and superb media instincts who no longer needed tutoring in how to promote himself.

After a while, all Carr needed to do was line up the press interviews. By the following year, the Carr Agency began to produce spectacular results as Barry began appearing on virtually every local—and some national—TV news magazine, talk show, news program, and newspaper and magazine.

For the present, however, the interviews and a slick press kit were doing their jobs: making Barry a well-known personality, giving ZZZZ Best priceless publicity, and providing indispensable credibility to a company that would soon be seeking investors.

— 8 —

IT WAS RIGHT ABOUT THAT TIME—late 1984 or early 1985—that Barry fell in love with the "cat's head" joke.

He'd first heard it at the LA Cabaret, a comedy club located in a faceless Valley mall that had become his habitual haunt.

Barry just couldn't hear that cat's head joke enough, and each time he showed up at the Cabaret, he'd request it.

After having become acquainted with the man who was telling it, a cynical Vegas-lounge, Jersey Shore–style comic named Jeff Wayne, Barry would burst into the Green Room, wave a $50 bill, and scream, "I'll give you fifty bucks if you tell that cat's head joke!"

Wayne, a squat, venom-filled man in his early thirties, would have told it without the tip; after all, it was part of his shtick, and with Barry—who was a great laugher—in the audience, it always went over well.

But Wayne always took the $50 anyway. What the fuck, the kid was offering it.

And Barry loved that. That *attitude*. That cynical, "fuck you" attitude of Wayne's so personified in the cat's head joke was exactly Barry's sense of humor. As a result, Barry was crazy about not only the joke but Wayne as well.

It was almost as if dwelling within the eternally optimistic

Ronald Reagan–Southern California–used-car-salesman side of Barry Minkow was a darker side as well—a Richard Nixon–Bronx-street kid for whom cynicism was both a world view and a badge of honor.

So when Barry would make his twice-weekly visits to the Cabaret, sometimes with Joyce Lipman, his willowy, blond girlfriend, but more often with a party of young sycophants, he'd head directly to the Green Room to see Wayne, who was also the club's master of ceremonies and house comic.

"That joke you told last time was great!" he'd shout. "You're great. What are you doing here? You should be on television."

Barry Minkow was more than just a fan of Jeff Wayne's. In Barry's eyes, Wayne was a God of Comedy, a guy who could do with a crowd exactly what the attention-hungry Minkow craved: be obnoxious, be funny, *and* be liked!

Take the cat's head joke as an example. Wayne would slowly build his impatient, perpetually disgusted, talking-out-of-the-side-of-his-mouth persona and then slide into it: "Now, I'm a nice guy, right?" (Nervous laughter from the mostly youngish Valley crowd—too tired, too high, or too satisfied to make the fifty-minute trek into the major-league Comedy Store or the Improv in West Hollywood.)

"But nothing goes right, you know what I mean? My kids want a cat. You'd think buying a cat would be easy.

"But no.

"I buy a cat and bring it home.

"We open the box, and what pops out?

"The most vicious cat you've ever seen. A horrible beast who runs immediately into a closet. And whose closet do you suppose it runs into? My kids'? No. My wife's? No. You got it. *My* closet.

"So for three days I try to get that cat out with a plate of milk.

"'Here, kitty. Here, kitty, kitty, kitty.'

"But nothing.

"So I call Pet Pride, a humane society for animals.

"'Hello, Pet Pride?' I say. 'I've got this mean, vicious, killer cat in my closet for three days, and I can't get it out. What do you suggest?'

"'Sir,' she tells me [here Wayne holds his nose and imitates a high-pitched female voice], 'Sir, you're not looking at it from the cat's point of view. A cat needs three weeks to adapt to a new environment, not three days. Please call back then.'

"And she hangs up.

"So fifteen minutes later I call her back. In the background there's a revving sound.

"'Hear that revving sound?' I say.

"'Yes, sir.'

"'Well, I've just provided the cat with a nice, new environment. That's the cat's head in the fuckin' blender. How's that for a change of environment? Sorry I can't get your fuckin' head in there, too.'"

The joke never failed to elicit gales of laughter from the Cabaret crowd, but none louder than from Barry.

He liked Wayne so much that he asked him how to fulfill a longstanding dream to be a professional comedian. Wayne, who'd worked small towns and small clubs for a decade, told him to work out a five-minute routine and start performing anywhere he could. Barry, who, says Wayne, had "brass balls" and was not a bad public speaker, had *no time* for that. As with everything else, he wanted to start at the top.

His humor, however, seemed too crude, even to someone like Wayne. And there was also a smugness about Barry when he told a joke—a hint of demand, an expectation that you *would* laugh—that blunted his charm for a lot of people.

One evening after a particularly successful set by Wayne, Barry came back to the Cabaret's Green Room.

"Jeff," he said in that rapid-fire way he had of talking, "What the fuck you doin' in this place? You're too talented; you need to get out of here. Who's your PR? That's what you need, PR! You're a big talent; you oughtta be on TV."

Wayne told him he didn't have any PR.

"What, no PR? Are you shitting me?" said Barry. "Come to my office. We're gonna get you some."

So three days later, Wayne went to Barry's Reseda office. The employees seemed very respectful, and the walls in Barry's office were already becoming lined with the citations and awards he so loved.

"Come in. Sit down," Barry said, closing the door. "Jeri will be here in a minute."

He then sat down and went into his "I've got big plans for you" rap. But as he did so, he started fondling himself, stroking his crotch in an absent-minded but embarrassing way. "What the fuck's going on here?" thought Wayne.

He had noticed Barry's habit of playing with himself before, but hadn't really thought much about it: "I mean, the guy wasn't walking around wearing lavender or lisping."

Later Wayne was to recognize Barry's behavior for what it probably was—a kid's unconscious habit, yet to be broken. But now it was making Wayne very uncomfortable. The tension was broken by the arrival of Jeri Carr.

Barry introduced Carr to Wayne, told her about him, and asked how much it would take to promote Wayne.

"About $15,000," replied Carr.

"Fifteen thousand!" said Barry. "I'm not gonna pay that; you're already getting too much from me." Turning to Wayne, Barry asked, "How much can you pay?"

"I can't pay anything," said Wayne. "I've got a wife and kids."

Minkow then started arguing with Carr about the price, much to the embarrassment of both Carr and Wayne.

"We'll talk about it later," Carr said, and the meeting broke up.

When Carr left, Wayne said, "Barry, why are you doing this?"

"Hey, man," said Barry, "I just want to help you out."

A week later, Minkow dropped by the club and told Wayne the PR would have to be put on hold. About a month afterward, Minkow offered to finance a one-hour comedy special that Wayne was trying to produce for cable television. But as with so many of Barry's promises, nothing ever came of that either.

He did, however, pay Wayne to write jokes for his motivational speaking engagements and later to emcee, at $1,000 a clip, the roasts and award ceremonies that were so much a part of Barry's "one big family" managerial style.

Wayne was grateful for the work, and not at all angry that Barry had failed to come through on his promises. Those things happen, especially in show business.

Barry was a serious guy. Why, after all, would he go through all that trouble if he weren't serious?

While Barry Minkow appeared to be growing prosperous, Tom Padgett was struggling just to get by. His problem was once again Barry Minkow. One night while attending a party at Tom's, Barry had stolen some Allstate drafts used to pay customers for damage, from Tom's car. Then Minkow had tried to cash them. In the ensuing flap, Barry managed to talk Allstate out of pressing charges, but Tom was fired. Desperate, Padgett took a job at a pistol range as an instructor. His duties included sweeping up. The job paid four dollars an hour.

Then after months of further job hunting, Padgett got a break. He was not overly delighted, since the job didn't pay the kind of money he felt entitled to, but it was a break nonetheless.

He was hired as an auto appraiser at Travelers [insurance] Corp. for $1,600 a month. "Sixteen hundred dollars. For one month," he would later say with a smirk. "Wasn't that generous of them?"

Still, there were compensations. He had to appraise only about four cars a day, so with thoughtful scheduling, he could do them all in a morning or afternoon and have the rest of the day free to do what he wished.

He always kept Friday afternoon free to visit Barry and pick up his $50 or $100 or $150 loan payment—whatever Minkow could spare that particular week.

Over the months of Friday collections, he began to notice that Barry *really* seemed to be doing well. Not only was his business still growing, but his staff also appeared to be expanding. Moreover, Barry was talking about taking ZZZZ Best public and buying himself a new two-bedroom condo. In fact, by the end of 1984, Barry Minkow was claiming in interviews that he had—at just eighteen—done more than $1 million worth of business that year.

Goddamn, Tom Padgett remembers thinking after reading one of Carr's handouts, the guy's grossing a million a year. And all on $39 four-room specials.

One evening in the spring of 1985, Barry Minkow asked Tom Padgett over to show off a few of his recent acquisitions. One was his sparkling Datsun 300 ZX sports car, the other his new condo.

Impressed by the car and condo and not knowing about the credit card fraud that was helping to pay for them, Tom Padgett couldn't contain himself. "Jesus, Barry," he said as they sat relaxing in Minkow's living room, "things are really going good for you. I never knew there was so much money in cleaning carpets."

"Well, I'm not making all this just from carpets," replied Barry.

He'd had a stroke of luck, he said, and met a man named "Jim." "Jim" was the owner of a small independent insurance appraisal company who was giving Barry a lot of restoration jobs on fire- and water-damaged property. A *lot* of jobs. And not only were they numerous, they were also big—some for as much as $200,000.

"Man," thought Tom, "this guy's business is *going*."

He'd made a deal with "Jim," Barry continued, an elaborate kickback scheme. "Jim" would vastly overestimate the damage to a building. Then ZZZZ Best would repair it cheaply, and "Jim" and ZZZZ Best would split the excess profits.

It was a great deal, Barry said, but they were also having a problem. ZZZZ Best was trying to arrange loans from several banks for up-front money to pay for labor and materials to the jobs. But neither he nor "Jim" wanted the banks calling "Jim's" insurance companies to verify the job. It might make the insurance companies suspicious and cause them to ask why ZZZZ Best was getting all "Jim's" work and why "Jim" wasn't spreading it out and getting competitive bids from other cleaning and restoration companies.

So Barry had a favor he wanted to ask. Now that Tom was working as an appraiser at Travelers, could he verify some of his jobs to a few banks, a few of his investors?

Tom Padgett later claimed he was appalled at the suggestion. "Jesus Christ," he told Barry, "I'm just an auto appraiser, a bump-and-dent guy. If this got back to Travelers, I'd be history."

However, after an offer of $100 a week if he'd help out—Tom Padgett quickly agreed to the deal. "OK, what do I have to do?" he asked Barry.

"Step one," Minkow replied, "get me some Travelers stationery. Step two, be prepared to verify any calls you get about ZZZZ Best jobs."

Such was the story, filled with disingenuous naïveté, that Tom Padgett would later tell. A more likely scenario, however, is that Barry Minkow dreamed up the restoration scam, told Tom about "Jim," who probably never existed at all, and that Padgett realized it and simply didn't care. As one of Barry's investment partners would later say, Padgett would have had to have been "a fuckin' retard to believe *that* story."

In any case, what is *not* in doubt is that Tom Padgett did indeed steal fifteen or twenty sheets of stationery on which was printed both the letterhead of Travelers Corp. and the name of Tom Padgett's boss. Shortly thereafter, he began to verify restoration jobs that did not exist.

With the Travelers stationery and Tom Padgett answering the phone, Barry Minkow had created his masterwork: a scheme as ingeniously simple as it was outrageously audacious.

On the stolen stationery, Barry typed several letters addressed to himself that said something like, "Dear Mr. Minkow, The following is a list of restoration jobs we want you to do for us, along with your approved bid. Please let us know when you'll be ready to start." Then either Tom would sign the letter, or Barry would forge Padgett's signature or that of his supervisor, Dave Tengberg.

All Barry now needed was potential investors he could take the letters to and say, "Look, I have these guaranteed restoration jobs that have tremendous profit margins, but I need capital for materials and equipment in order to do them. I've come to you because I'm just a kid, and it's difficult to get a loan from a bank, even though the profits will be enormous. I'll give you an amazing return on your investment, and it's risk-free. If you have any doubts, just call Tom Padgett at Travelers; they're paying for the jobs."

Although Barry mentioned the Travelers jobs to Wallace Berrie when he got two more loans from him totaling $30,000 in early 1985, Robert Turnbow was to have the unhappy distinction of being the first to be officially scammed in the insurance restoration scheme that eventually raised Barry Minkow to heights that not even he could have imagined.

Barry had gone to see Bob Turnbow after the West Valley Bank folded and Turnbow became manager of another small bank called Valley State.

By mid-March—when Barry applied for a loan from Turnbow to finance insurance restoration work that in fact did not exist—he had already rung up $15,000 worth of fraudulent credit card charges at his and Turnbow's new bank.

Fortunately for Minkow, Robert Turnbow did not become aware of these charges until more than a month after the restoration loan had funded.

Barry had worked his way into Turnbow's good graces by paying off his $20,000 loan and showing up at Turnbow's new bank with *an additional* $20,000—the proceeds of a loan he'd just received from yet another Valley Gym friend—which he deposited in Valley State. He would use part of the money he'd get from Turnbow, of course, to repay *that* loan, floating money, borrowing money, paying it back, and borrowing again, trying always to stay one day ahead in a spiral that was never to end while ZZZZ Best existed.

Applying for the restoration loan, Barry told Bob Turnbow that he had a $60,000 insurance contract to repair a fire- and water-damaged building and needed a $15,000 loan to pay for up-front labor and material, as the insurance company wouldn't pay *him* until the job was completed.

Along with a billing showing the square footage of the building to be restored, Barry brought with him a personal financial statement showing assets of over $320,000. The billing, like the job and the financial statement, was bogus. So was the downtown LA address he gave as the job site.

Over the course of their meetings, Barry told Turnbow he had an "in," a contact he'd developed in the insurance industry named Tom Padgett, and mentioned in passing a job he had in a little Central California town called Arroyo Grande. Oh, he wasn't trying to get a loan from Valley State to handle *that* job, he wanted Turnbow to understand. He knew Valley State was far too small to finance a contract of that size. No, he'd have to go to his other banks—Union and First Interstate, where he had his major accounts—for the Arroyo Grande funding. It was, after all, for $3 million.

As Barry appeared to be doing so well, Robert Turnbow was rather surprised later to receive a call from the operations officer at the old West Valley Bank, which had since been resurrected as a branch of First Interstate. She asked if Barry Minkow had opened an account at Valley State, and when Turnbow confirmed that he had, told him to be careful, that a lot of credit card charges had been coming back from ZZZZ Best and were being referred to the FDIC.

Almost simultaneously, Bob Turnbow got a second call, this one from an administrator at his own bank. Close Barry Minkow's account immediately, he was told without explanation. Shortly afterward he found out about Barry's new credit card overcharges.

When Turnbow got in touch with Minkow, Barry told him that, yes, he knew about the problem, and it was driving him nuts, some goddamned employee running up all these charges and leaving him holding the bag. Not only was it embarrassing, but it was *really* hurting business.

In the following days, after borrowing $5,000 from Dan Krowpman, Barry met with Robert Turnbow and, as he'd done previously, worked out a weekly payment schedule to make good on the overcharges.

Once again, Danny Krowpman, who Barry would later say was

constantly threatening him for his money, and Robert Turnbow, who resided in Barry's pocket, had come through with a mini-cure.

March 1985 was also the month that Barry decided to furnish his new condo. He would later deny spending $11,000 on the job, claiming it was in fact only $5,000 or $6,000 because he'd got the furniture wholesale through his aunt. In fact, the purchase of the furniture, like that of the condo, was, said Barry, "a money-making deal." That's why he'd bought it, because it was "a great invest-ment."

The following month, Wallace Berrie sued Barry and sought a writ of attachment against all of ZZZZ Best's equipment because Minkow had defaulted on his loan. Moreover, between $6,000 and $7,000 worth of ZZZZ Best's payroll checks had just bounced at a check-cashing service that many of his employees used. "I was in the hole . . . for the checks," said Barry. "Everything was terrible."

— 9 —

IN JUNE 1985 Barry got a call from his uncle. There was a problem with a carpet ZZZZ Best had installed in a townhouse in Tarzana, and he wanted Barry to look into it.

Since his uncle's development corporation was involved in the project and was giving ZZZZ Best all its carpet work, Barry told him he'd take care of it personally. "Good," said his uncle, "get over there as soon as you can. The guy's name is Jack Catain."

Like everyone else, Barry badly misjudged Jack Catain's age when he first saw him. Gray-haired and heavy, Catain looked to be at least in his midsixties but was in fact a decade younger.

He was dressed that day in the outfit he habitually wore: slacks, an open-collar shirt, and a windbreaker that said "Members Only" on it, although it was never clear to anybody who knew him exactly what he was a member of.

Sallow and overweight, Jack Catain was then playing out his final scene, having recently had surgery on his hip and a heart bypass operation. For the rest of his life, he would be forced to use a cane or walker just to get around.

Lighting one of the dozens of cigarettes he chain-smoked daily despite his heart condition, Catain told Barry to take a seat and, after talking briefly about his carpet, asked him if he wasn't the kid he'd just read about in the *Los Angeles Herald-Examiner*.

Barry replied that he was indeed. Jeri Carr's press releases and resultant media stories were starting to pay off, and increasingly Barry was becoming recognized around the Valley as the amazing Boy Wonder of carpet cleaning. In fact, through Carr's PR, Barry had recently been awarded a scrolled commendation from Los Angeles Mayor Tom Bradley.

Barry and Catain began talking about ZZZZ Best's success, and gradually the conversation turned to cash flow and other financial questions.

Because of his age and ZZZZ Best being a service industry, it was very hard to raise any capital, Barry told Catain, adding that it was a shame, because there were really two sides to his business: the everyday carpet-, furniture-, and drape-cleaning side and the restoration business. It was the restoration end that was growing out of control, producing big profits but requiring lots of capital. The reason he could produce those large profits, he continued, was that a friend of his who was an insurance appraiser was steering a lot of lucrative jobs his way, while another—in discount carpeting— was selling him irregular and discounted carpeting at rock-bottom prices.

Catain seemed more than interested and over the next half hour or so asked a good many probing questions.

The next day Barry called Tom Padgett and told him about the meeting and another he'd had that night with Catain and one of his financial advisers. "Look, he wants to stop by my office tomorrow, and I think it'd be really good if you were there. He's *definitely* interested."

Padgett agreed to be present, in the process escalating his involvement from that of a passive confirmer of jobs over the telephone to a far more active role. After rehearsing what they intended to say the following day, Barry reminded Padgett to wear a suit and hung up.

The next morning, Tom arrived at Barry's office before Catain, and once again they practiced the little skit they'd planned earlier on the phone—Padgett playing the insurance appraiser responsible for awarding Barry a growing number of highly profitable restoration jobs, and Barry the hustling young businessman.

A few minutes later, the phone on Barry's desk rang. "Mr.

Minkow," said Barry's secretary, "Mr. Catain to see you."

Barry told her to send him in, and dressed uncharacteristically in a suit and looking to Padgett "like somebody's grandfather," Catain walked in.

After some brief introductions, the three men talked in a general way about insurance restoration before Tom, switching gears as planned, turned to Barry, picked up several sheets of paper from Minkow's desk—on which were printed the letterhead of Travelers Corporation—and began reading from a list of restoration jobs and giving Barry instructions. "All right, Barry," he said, "at the Westminster job, you've gotta get the plumbers moving, the electricians are still fuckin' off in Torrance, and the drywalls are slow at all the sites. How many times I gotta tell you not to overload yourself?"

Then he turned back to Catain. "Sorry," he said, "we've got to get this straightened out."

"Don't let me interrupt nothin'," replied Catain in his gruff Chicago accent.

Then, after making a little more small talk, Padgett excused himself and rose to leave.

"Keep on top of this kid," Jack Catain said to Padgett as Tom walked out. Barry just sat there at his desk with a sheepish grin on his face.

Barry Minkow's master scam—in which he would continuously borrow money to perform restoration jobs that did not exist in order to live high and pay back previous loans—was already working on a small, sporadic scale. With the involvement of Jack Catain, however, it would escalate to an entirely different level.

When Barry Minkow met Jack Catain, the only outlaw group to which Catain could have belonged was the "Over-the-Hill Gang." His body had about given out on him, and with the exception of one or two low-rent local thugs, the muscle he might have been able to call on in the past had all deserted him. The type of people with whom Jack Catain had associated most of his life were not known, in spite of the movie image, for their loyalty.

A street guy associated with the Jack Crone mob in Chicago, Catain had headed west as a young man on the make in the 1950s, building, after much hard work, a modest reputation among successful career criminals and street hoods alike. He always knew tough guys on whom to call, if needed, and early in his career was not loath to have someone rough up people who made him unhappy.

But he was far from being just a thug with a musclehead. In fact, Jack Catain always picked the best kinds of crimes; the white-collar ones where you can make a lot of money and not do much time if you're caught, the kinds of crimes—different in nature but not intent—that are rampant, say, in the defense industry. But Catain was never well placed enough to be involved in overpricing or government kickbacks. Instead, he was a low-level paper man involved in counterfeiting, money laundering, loan sharking, and bust-outs (opening a business, skimming the assets, and then declaring bankruptcy).

Jack Catain was said to have done *very* well at it, as he had with his straight business, Rusco Industries, which, to the amusement of Bruce Kelton, the U.S. attorney who prosecuted Catain, had manufactured the plastic security cards used to open the gates guarding access to the parking lots of federal buildings. "I always thought that was hysterical," said Kelton. "Jack Catain involved in security for the federal government."

Around 1980, the FBI investigated charges that Rusco Industries—which primarily made aluminum building products and was listed on the American Stock Exchange—was being used as a front for laundering organized-crime money, but nothing was ever proved.

At about that time, however, as part of a settlement of a Securities and Exchange Commission suit charging Catain with undisclosed insider transactions, he was forced to resign as Rusco's chairman and chief executive.

There were also allegations, never proved, that Catain was linked to the case in which Dominic Frontiere—the Oscar-winning Hollywood composer and husband of Georgia Frontiere, the owner of the Los Angeles Rams—was convicted of scalping Super Bowl tickets. Frontiere was later to claim that Catain had extorted money from him during the case, but nothing ever came of that charge either.

As a matter of fact, Catain, who had connections with the mob throughout his life but was not a "made" Mafia member, was remarkably successful in avoiding prosecution. That is, until early 1982, when he got involved with some people far less sophisticated than himself.

A guy named Stuart Noble had printed up several million dollars in counterfeit money—crude, poor-quality stuff—that he planned to have distributed in Chicago and LA. Among his major Los Angeles distributors was his cousin, Jack Catain.

Catain, through an intermediary, gave a couple of hundred thousand dollars' worth of the bills to some young guys from Chicago and told them to sell the counterfeit money to a specific buyer in Las Vegas.

When they arrived in Vegas, however, the young men, who apparently were not among the best and the brightest, had trouble locating the buyer and tried instead to pass some of the $100 bills in a casino, where they were immediately spotted and arrested.

"It shows how stupid these guys were," Kelton said later in disgust. "*Of course*, if you try to pass off a $100 counterfeit bill in Vegas, you're gonna get nailed. They got guys there that do nothing but look for that kind of stuff. It's the last place in the world you'd want to try to pass something."

Confronted by the Secret Service, the young men rolled over on the intermediary, who, in turn, gave up Jack Catain. In return for their cooperation, all three were promised probation—"a pretty good deal," says Kelton, especially considering that $1.5 million was found in the garage of one of them.

The Secret Service then had the intermediary—a friend and associate of Catain's named Ray Cohen—call Catain and tell him they'd found a new buyer in Vegas who they wanted him to meet. The buyer, in fact, was an undercover Secret Service agent.

Catain and Cohen, who was wired, met with the undercover agent in Los Vegas and, after displaying some samples, negotiated the sale of well over $1 million of the money.

After several other tape-recorded meetings and a search of Catain's office, in which more counterfeit bills were found in his desk, Jack Catain was arrested.

He'd finally been nailed. And good. The case was airtight. The government had him on tape negotiating with an undercover Secret Service agent to sell the money. They had the counterfeit samples found in the desk, and they had the witnesses against him. They had it all, and they felt really good about the case.

Then one day Kelton received a call from Jack Catain's lawyer.

He was going to file a motion to have the trial postponed for six months, he said. Jack Catain had had a heart attack and was too ill to stand trial.

At the hearing on the motion, Catain's doctor said he couldn't go to trial, the stress would kill him. The government's doctor countered that the stress of a trial could kill *anyone*, and while Catain did have a serious heart condition, arrangements could be made to ensure he'd survive the ordeal. Kelton was annoyed. He felt Catain's doctor was lying and Catain himself exaggerating the severity of his symptoms.

But the judge, who had a heart condition himself, sided with Catain and postponed the trial. On several occasions, as the case was rescheduled to go to trial, Catain checked himself into the hospital and his lawyer asked for another delay.

Meanwhile, Kelton had the Los Angeles police and the Secret Service shadowing Catain for six or eight hours at a stretch, a couple of weeks at a time, trying to find evidence that he was playing golf or exerting himself in other ways.

But if he was, he was too clever to get caught. Finally, after about a year, the judge dismissed the case "in the interest of justice." The case is a felony, said the judge—William Gray—but it's not that serious a charge. The man has a heart condition. "Your doctor," he said to Kelton during the final hearing, "says he [Catain] will survive the trial; his doctor says he won't. I'm just not going to take the chance. I don't want anybody dying in my courtroom."

Jack Catain was once again a free man, although only momentarily.

Shortly thereafter, a *second* batch of money was distributed; Catain was linked to it and was indicted again. This time the indictment stuck, and in November 1986, Jack Catain was finally convicted on a counterfeiting charge.

It was right in the middle of this time—when Jack Catain was having terrible money, cop, and court problems—that he met young Barry Minkow. Like many others to follow, he was immediately impressed. For one, Barry's presentation had grown increasingly smooth. ("I own 100 percent of the fastest-growing carpet-cleaning business in California. We're in the process of opening our San Diego location—our fourth in two years. A $1.5 million restoration job in San Diego is just waiting for the capital.")

Also, under the guidance of Jeri Carr, Barry had began passing out impressive-looking autographed copies of his book, *Making It in America*, an ode to himself, the virtues of positive thinking, and the glories of the free-enterprise system. Further, an extraordinarily slick, glossy press kit had been created by Carr and her staff and was being enthusiastically distributed to all who might conceivably have a desire for one.

But in addition to all that, Jack Catain—like Joel Hochberg and
Danny Krowpman and Bob Turnbow and Tom Padgett—genuinely
liked Barry Minkow. "The kid's sharp," he told John Miller, a loan
broker with whom he shared an office. "I've never seen a kid so
smart."

And in just a short time, Jack Catain and Barry Minkow
seemed to develop a father-son relationship, with Jack unstintingly
giving advice and expressing concern on a wide variety of subjects,
including Barry's newly developed bleeding ulcer, the result, no
doubt, of the unrelenting stress he was under combined with the
steroids he was taking regularly.

On several occasions, Jack Catain actually mentioned to John
Miller that he wished Barry was really his son. Catain, in fact, had
two sons of his own. One had tragically died at thirteen of leuke-
mia. (Catain, when he was wealthy, had donated generously to the
City of Hope in his honor.) The other son was about twenty-eight,
but Jack, it was rumored, had little use for him, fearing he might
be involved with drugs, which Catain hated. He also had a daughter, but it was his dead son to whom he'd been closest, and perhaps
it was the boyish, youthful spirit of Barry that so reminded Catain
of his son, to which he was partly responding.

There *was* that paternal, good-hearted side to Jack Catain that
would listen to a sad-ass story and do what he could to help. He'd
always make sure to make a buck, though. And Barry—if his story
and press clips were to be believed—looked like a great way to
make some quick money at a time when Jack Catain's attorney's
fees and other expenses were far exceeding his income.

As for Barry, Jack Catain was a guy who appeared to have a lot
of money to invest and seemed willing to do so, much like Wallace
Berrie or his friend from the gym, Hal Berman, who'd loaned him
that $20,000 he'd briefly deposited in Bob Turnbow's bank.

Moreover, for Barry, Jack Catain well fit the part of the proper
father for whom he never stopped looking. If Danny had the
muscled physique—and with it the power—Jack Catain had the
connections that meant power. By this time, unfortunately for Jack,
those connections existed mainly in his head. But when he was
drinking, he'd still talk a big story. "Catain was such a bullshitter,"
says John Miller, "that when he died, the only reason I went to his
funeral was to make sure he was in the box. [Catain died of a heart
attack in February 1987.] But Barry ate all that organized-crime
stuff up."

Miller had first met Catain at Rancho Bank in San Dimas when Catain was looking for a loan to buy his new townhouse and Miller was working as a mortgage broker. Initially, he had liked Catain, but by the time Jack introduced him to Barry about three months later, Miller had become more than slightly disillusioned. Over the first several months of their friendship, Jack had lent him about $9,000, and Miller was most unhappy when Catain told him he was expecting $20,000 back. After Miller had paid Catain $15,000 and let him know that he (Miller) thought that was more than adequate, Jack, in return, let *him* know, "in a very nice, nonbelligerent" way that he certainly hoped he would not "have to send Carmen [DeNunzio, a small-time local muscleman] around."

Miller, needless to say, "didn't appreciate that shit," nor did he like it when Jack started to show up regularly at his office and, without asking, more or less expropriate a desk and phone. When Miller finally pointed out that someone was using that desk, Jack's reply was classic: "Oh, yes," he said, "and did that person just loan you nine grand?"

What could Miller say? The desk became Jack's, and Miller's office a front to work the phones and to draw up and have notarized the big-money loans that Jack Catain was to get to finance Barry Minkow and ZZZZ Best's mythical insurance restoration work.

When Jack Catain and John Miller saw Barry Minkow's bogus financial statements, it was all they could do to stop themselves from going into a Sammy Davis–style "please don't break me up" routine. "Are you shitting me?" said Miller. "If I were to show this to someone in a bank, they'd have just one question for me: 'What've you been smoking?' I can't do anything with *these*."

Miller had received a call from Catain earlier in the day, asking him to meet that evening with "this kid from ZZZZ Best, the one with the newspaper articles and all," and see if he could package a loan for him at a bank.

But with little to lose, Jack had decided to go ahead in any case and try to get Barry $75,000 in loans for a restoration project Padgett was supposedly going to award ZZZZ Best. In reality, Barry needed the money for partial payment on his rapidly mounting debts and to cover the start-up expenses on a fourth ZZZZ Best location he had already committed to in San Diego.

Miller told Barry he'd go ahead and try to secure the loans, but he'd need $2,500 up front as an accounting and packaging fee.

Twenty-five hundred dollars was about all the money Barry had, but having no options, he went ahead and gave it to Miller.

Over the next several weeks, Barry met with Miller and Catain perhaps a dozen times, discussing ZZZZ Best and trying to put together a loan package. Sometimes Barry would sit in on the meetings, which took place in Miller's office. On other occasions, he'd be told to wait outside, where he'd sit for hours, bullshitting with the secretary or running down to the cafeteria for cigarettes, coffee, or pizza.

In spite of the many meetings, Miller failed to produce any bank loans. Let him get some money in an account, keep a good balance, and we'll see, the bankers were telling Miller. He and Catain had had another set of more professional looking but still phony tax returns and financial statements prepared by someone in Miller's office, but Miller, who valued his banking relationships, decided not to use them.

Instead, he showed the bankers Barry's press clips, PR package, and Barry himself, telling them they might well get some good publicity, if they made him a loan, of the "Bank Helps Out Young Entrepreneur" variety.

But the best Miller could come up with was a bank account for ZZZZ Best at Rancho Bank and the possibility of a loan when the loan committee met in three weeks. Keep your account current for thirty to sixty days, the manager had told Barry, and we should be able to do something for you.

But no, that *very day*, Barry wrote a check for more than he'd put in the account.

A couple of days later, the manager called Miller. "What are you doing to me?" asked the manager. "I opened the account against my better judgment, and the kid's kiting checks already."

When Miller confronted Barry, his response was, in Miller's words, "OK, so I bullshitted them."

John Miller didn't like that. But it was typical, thought Miller of Barry Minkow. He'd always come to you with that naive, puppy dog face, using his age as an advantage. He was naive all right, as naive as a fox, and John Miller told him so.

The kid had a great mind for spotting people's weaknesses and manipulating them. Miller told him that, too. And he told him that he and Jack Catain were like "two peas in a pod," and that the only difference was thirty years. "Are you sure," John Miller asked, "you don't have the same mother?"

Barry just snickered.

The 280 pounds on Carmen DeNunzio's 6'1" frame consisted of a little muscle and a lot of fat. About thirty, DeNunzio always seemed to John Miller a guy straight off the back lot of "The Untouchables," for whom five hundred dollars was "a nickel," a thousand "a dime," and the money Barry Minkow was soon to owe him "the vig."

DeNunzio was Jack Catain's power—among the last of the muscle Catain could call on to enforce a deal in his waning years.

Carmen was involved for the most part in small-time activities like numbers running and poker games. But people feared Carmen DeNunzio because he was stupid. "He would not hesitate to smash your ass in front of twenty people if you pissed him off," says one observer.

It was to DeNunzio that Catain turned after John Miller proved unsuccessful in obtaining legitimate financing for Barry.

By now, Barry, who'd been counting on the loans, was once again bouncing checks and being squeezed by those he owed. He desperately needed $35,000 to cover himself.

So "a meet," as Barry called it, was set up by Catain with Carmen DeNunzio.

DeNunzio, as small-time as he is, was about the closest thing to a traditional Mafia type that LA had to offer, being an "alleged associate" of Peter Milano, said to be the local capo of organized crime.

Nowhere near as entrenched as it is on the East Coast and in Chicago, organized crime has had it tough in LA, where it has no ties to the local government establishment, and where the drug traffic is mostly controlled by Mexican and South American organizations.

Despite Jimmy ("the Weasel") Fratianno's boast that there are "100 guys in our family in LA," most law enforcement officials put the number much lower, referring to West Coast mobsters as the "Mickey Mouse Mafia"—a loose group of freelancers looking for legitimate businesses to penetrate.

When DeNunzio showed up at the meeting in John Miller's office, he was carrying a brown paper bag. In it was $25,000. (Jack had come up with an additional $10,000 from other sources.)

Carmen told Barry he'd be happy to lend it to him for as long as he needed it. But it would cost him "five points in juice," or $1,250 per week interest. Five percent a week was steep, even for a new shylock loan, but Carmen was only taking four points, with Jack getting a point for serving as an intermediary.

In fact, Carmen wasn't really lending the money to Barry, but to *Jack*, since Catain in effect was guaranteeing its return. DeNunzio, like Miller, had a bad feeling about Barry and was dealing with him, despite the not inconsiderable juice, only as a favor to Jack. Barry, thought DeNunzio, had no fear. And that made DeNunzio fear Barry, who he thought would go to the cops in a minute if there was trouble.

In the months to come, Jack Catain became a loan broker for Barry Minkow. Though generally unsuccessful with banks, the pair did much better bringing in Jack's friends and acquaintances as investors in ZZZZ Best's restoration projects.

Barry told Jack about the big jobs he could get from Tom Padgett, like the one in Gardena, which required $52,000 in upfront money for material and labor but would reap a profit of $58,000, or the $180,000 job in Westminster that would cost $95,000 to finance. Barry was offering to split the profits fifty-fifty with investors in return for the financing.

And Jack told Barry that that was big money but he thought he could come up with it. But Barry should understand it wasn't charity week.

In return for getting investors to put up relatively big money, Jack wanted a 49 percent partnership in what would be called the "Barry Minkow Insurance Company" and a consultant fee of $3,000 a month. He would throw in a 50 percent interest in his own company, L.A. Mid Cosmetics, which Barry described later as "a bullshit product that Catain and his wife have unsuccessfully been promoting for years."

But Barry *needed* Jack Catain, so he signed. On its face, the agreement was ruinous—a true disaster. In addition to paying Jack $3,000 a month, Barry had to pay back the investors' loans at interest rates of anywhere from 3 to 5 percent per *week*. Also, he had to give Jack Catain, who invested nothing, half of the remaining profits from ZZZZ Best's restoration work, none of which, of course, existed.

— 10 —

ADA COHEN AND ELAINE ORLANDO were very fond of Kay Rosario. Cohen, an elegant, middle-aged Yugoslavian émigré, and Orlando, the former wife of the singer Tony Orlando, had been close friends with Rosario for well over a decade when Kay first mentioned Barry Minkow to them.

Rosario, a rotund woman in her fifties, was the wife of the pop music conductor Bobby Rosario, who'd worked with, among others, Tony Orlando and Bobby Darin. She was also a long-time friend of Jack Catain and his wife, through whom she had met Barry.

In the course of conversations with Cohen, who was visiting from her home in Las Vegas, and Orlando, who lived in nearby Beverly Hills, Kay told her friends how she'd recently met this brilliant young man named Barry Minkow and about what a delightful, ambitious fellow he was, mentioning as well his great success with ZZZZ Best.

Because he was so young, however, he was having trouble getting bank loans to finance some insurance restoration jobs he was being given. She'd been very impressed with Barry, she told them, not just because of his "ambition and competence" but because he was such a "loving person." And *that* was very important to her, Kay said, to be able to do business with a person who was a friend and not just a business partner.

And speaking of business, Barry's was really starting to take off, Kay told her friends, and she thought "it would be wonderful to get in at the beginning of a company that will grow tremendously."

In fact, she was about to invest a good deal of her own money in ZZZZ Best's restoration projects and was in the process of putting together a group of investors to do the same. Were they interested?

Ada Cohen—who owned a half-interest in a small Las Vegas motel called the Downtowner—said that if Kay thought it such a good investment, she definitely was interested. Her motel business was not doing well and she trusted Kay's judgment.

So, without ever having met Minkow, she sold some gold she had in savings and invested $40,000 in ZZZZ Best restoration work. No papers were signed or receipts given; Kay's *word* was good enough. Nor was it exactly clear just when and how much she would get back. Kay was to take care of that.

Elaine Orlando, a woman of considerably more wealth than Ada Cohen, also placed great trust in Kay and invested $25,000, receiving a single-page "personal guarantee" dated July 1985 and made out to her. It read:

> Dear Mrs. Orlando,
> Please be advised that Mr. Jack Catain and Barry Minkow is [sic] personally guaranteeing a $25,000 loan to the ZZZZ Best Carpet Cleaning Company.

It was signed by Catain and Barry.

Elaine Orlando, like Ada Cohan, was later to be rather vague about how and when the money would be returned and what interest rate she was expecting. Perhaps she feared that the exorbitant interest she and others were to get might have violated California usury laws; perhaps she was truly unconcerned about it because of her faith in Kay. "I knew," said Orlando, "that [because of their friendship] whatever [was due] to come back to me would come back to me. I thought it was a way to invest in something that could possibly be beneficial to me down the line."

Within approximately two months, Kay Rosario and her contacts had invested $240,000 in Barry Minkow's restoration projects.

The money Kay raised was primarily from middle-aged or older women of some means but not great wealth, who were looking for a far higher return on their investment dollar than they could get with, say, a CD. Kay's word was all that was needed to secure the loans.

Kay, in return, was relying on Barry's confident rap and ingratiating, dynamic personality; the personal guarantee of Jack Catain; and documents written by Barry on Travelers letterhead outlining the terms of various restoration jobs, listing a payment schedule, and signed at the bottom with Tom Padgett's forged signature.

The short, usually one-page documents weren't much, but they seemed enough for Kay and established a pattern of minimal paperwork that would be repeated throughout the volatile life of Barry's scam.

Of course, the extraordinary profits Barry was promising may also have been an inducement—$5,000 to $7,000 a week to Kay's investment group in interest alone, the principal remaining largely untouched.

But that was OK with Barry. That $240,000 principal was paying the interest or principal on earlier loans, paying Rosario's weekly juice, and permitting Barry to live an even more extravagant lifestyle that seemed to attract future investors and feed an ego that would soon become insatiable.

When Ada Cohen and Elaine Orlando finally met Barry later in the year, they couldn't have been happier. He was everything Kay had said and more.

Four or five friends of Kay's as well as fellow investors in ZZZZ Best's restoration projects had gathered that day to shake the hand of the man responsible for returning so much interest on their investments and of whom they'd heard so much.

The meeting was held at Barry's newly purchased, still sparsely furnished home in a gated community in upscale Woodland Hills, but the house was not what impressed them the most.

It was the man himself.

He was very affectionate. That was the first thing that struck Ada Cohen, who had a son the same age as Barry. And that affection "invited very much a motherly feeling" in her. I want this man to meet my son, she thought. Perhaps his affection, his joie de vivre, his energy will rub off.

Kay had been right to trust Barry, Ada felt. *She* trusted him already, not just 100 percent, but 150 percent if there were such a thing. "He was so loving, so eager, so understanding." Ada "just adored him."

Elaine Orlando's response was a bit more restrained, but she too was impressed with how "up," how "cheerful," how "gregarious" Barry was. Barry told her the story of the fifteen-year-old starting his business in his parents' garage, and about how he was too young to get bank financing, and about how restoration had become the priority end of his business and how he needed to raise money for materials like flooring and carpeting before he could begin each project. He even showed her some cashier's checks made out to ZZZZ Best with "Travelers Corporation" typed on top, in case Elaine Orlando had any doubts.

But she had none.

Instead, what Elaine Orlando took away from the meeting that day was a "very positive feeling." She felt very confident that "this young man was going places because of the confidence that he had in himself and the belief in his company. It was all very positive and very up. . . . He just seemed to know what was going on."

Shortly after Kay Rosario's investment dollars started flooding in, Jack Catain became suspicious and, much to Minkow's annoyance, started putting questions about the restoration jobs to ZZZZ Best's employees, all of whom were engaged in the legitimate carpet-cleaning end of the business and knew nothing about the restoration projects.

Catain, who had moved into one of the small, spare offices adjacent to Barry's at ZZZZ Best's Reseda headquarters as an additional partnership perk, had also started probing into the company files and could not have been pleased with what he found, . which was almost nothing. For Barry, in his customary modus operandi, was winging it, making up his story as he went along. Rarely were any documents prepared until they were demanded of him.

By early September, Catain's edginess was beginning to show. One day, as Chip Arrington was walking down the hall, Catain, who'd been coming to ZZZZ Best almost daily but doing very little, called him into his office, and began asking Chip about the insurance restoration jobs. He wanted to know in particular if Arrington thought Barry was investing all the money he'd been loaned for the restoration projects, or if Barry might be keeping some of it in a safe-deposit box. Chip replied truthfully that he really didn't know, and the conversation ended.

The following Tuesday night—bowling night—Barry approached Arrington at the lanes, as truly angry as Chip had ever seen him. Why, he shouted, was Chip talking behind his back to Catain? What was going on?

Chip said he had no idea—all he'd done was listen while Catain talked and try to get out of the office as politely as he could.

After a couple of minutes, Barry calmed down somewhat but still insisted on calling Catain immediately.

When he got Jack on the line, he started screaming, asking him why he was trying to talk "to *my* people behind my back."

Later Chip spoke to Catain, asking him not to put him in the middle of anything between him and "his boss" again. Soon after, Jack Catain stopped showing up regularly at ZZZZ Best.

— 11 —

WHEN BARRY MINKOW FOUND OUT that Jack Catain was marking up his points, he decided he had to get the man out of his life. *Imagine.* The fucking guy was already taking half the profits on the restoration jobs, getting three grand a month and a free office, and he was *still* marking up the points. It was just unbelievable.

Barry, who'd been paying five points (5 percent interest) per week to Rosario through Jack, had discovered that Catain, without his or Kay's knowledge, had been pocketing 1 or 2 percent of the interest money each week. Was the guy greedy or what?

It was at this juncture that Barry decided he had to cut Jack Catain out. So he picked up the phone, called Rosario, and told her what was happening. They talked some more, and over the following weeks, Barry became very close to Kay and, not incidentally, to her daughter too, whom he started dating regularly. On occasion, he even joked with Kay about one day becoming a member of the family.

But Barry had another, perhaps even more compelling reason for wanting to get rid of Catain.

As the year was drawing to a close, Minkow had found another investor named Robert Victor, who was willing to lend big money to him for restoration jobs. But the deal had to be a bit different from that with Rosario—in which he simply paid her and her group interest on the principal each week.

Victor was demanding to be an equal partner with a fifty-fifty split in the profits. As Catain was already getting 50 percent of the profits, however, giving his new investor 50 percent would leave nothing for Barry. He *had* to get rid of Catain.

Fortunately for Barry, there was at the time no love lost between Jack and Kay. Catain had allegedly sold her a trust deed that had been recorded to some other piece of property, and Kay didn't have the ownership she thought.

So when Barry proposed dealing directly with her and eliminating Jack, she was receptive, and the money between them no longer went through Jack Catain.

But Kay Rosario was no babe in the woods. As time went by she, like Catain, began to have doubts about the validity of the restoration jobs.

One day near the end of 1985, those doubts came to a head. She walked into John Miller's office with one of Barry's letters from Travelers signed by Padgett, and asked Miller how she could find out if the jobs were real. "The kid's into me for $345,000, and I'm worried. I'm getting paid, but it's coming slower."

Miller paused for a moment, asking himself why he should be involved, why he should take on any possible problems with Catain or DeNunzio. But then he thought, "Screw it," and picked up the phone and dialed Travelers. A woman answered and said that, yes, Tom Padgett was working for Travelers, as an auto damage appraiser.

"Well," said Miller as he hung up the phone. "What does *that* tell you? The guy's an auto appraiser out in the field, and he signed this letter? Come on. No way could a field appraiser for cars write this kind of a letter for this kind of money." The fact alone was enough to convince Miller that the jobs weren't real. And, he says, on that day Kay agreed with him.

Rosario, however, remembers the story differently, saying her attitude after the call was, "What are you talking about? Padgett works for Travelers, so that proves the jobs are good."

Whether Rosario was genuinely placated by the phone call or simply chose to ignore her doubts because the money was so good, by the late fall of 1985, Barry Minkow had moved at least halfway toward his goal of eliminating Jack Catain from his life. Barry was now dealing directly with Kay, not Jack, and was very close to her and her family. She wouldn't be asking too many more hard questions.

As Barry started growing more independent of Jack Catain, Catain grew less able to do anything about it. Not only had he alienated himself from Kay, but he'd done the same with Carmen DeNunzio.

Jack's ex-wife, it seems, was selling a condo through Jack to Carmen's brother, Anthony. Not surprisingly, Catain decided to hike the price by $13,000 or $14,000, which he would keep for himself. And not surprisingly, the DeNunzios found out about it. When they did, they showed up at John Miller's office—four guys, all in tank tops—and told Miller, who was serving as the loan broker, that they wanted to know the actual price of the condo.

"You're gonna leave here eventually," they said, "but whether it's in a vertical or horizontal position depends on what you tell us."

Miller told them the truth, and after that Jack Catain and his local muscle Carmen DeNunzio were no longer friends.

Meanwhile, Tom Padgett, who'd been given a $500 bonus by Barry before going home to Akron on a short vacation, returned and started verifying a steady stream of jobs at Travelers from individual investors, banks, and loan companies. The value of the restoration jobs Tom was now being asked to verify had grown from the $20,000 to $100,000 range to as high as $1 million.

And his rap was rapidly growing as smooth as Barry's as he replied to the surprisingly uninformed general questions he was asked.

"What's your relationship with Barry Minkow and ZZZZ Best?"

"We give them insurance restoration jobs."

"How's he doing?"

"Great," Padgett would reply. "You know, with damaged buildings it's necessary to get out there immediately to board up holes and dry out wet carpet after a fire. The first twenty-four hours are critical, and ZZZZ Best's available day and night—twenty-four hours a day. As long as he continues to display the capabilities to handle big jobs that he's shown us so far, we intend to give him more. I'm very strong on Barry Minkow and ZZZZ Best."

By the fall of 1985, Barry Minkow was pressuring Tom Padgett to start his own insurance appraisal service.

Padgett, who never thought of himself as an independent businessman, was reluctant to do so. But he felt that $1,600 a month was really an insulting salary for a man of his educational background and talent.

So he listened when Barry pushed the Debbie button. Debbie was the girl that Tom Padgett was in love with. But how could Tom Padgett expect to get anywhere with her—an LA lady—on $1,600 a month in a town where, as in New York, money talked and bullshit walked?

Finally, Padgett agreed. Barry had proposed vastly raising the $100 weekly salary he was paying Tom, allowing Padgett to continue working at Travelers, and paying all the expenses of setting up and running the new business.

Moreover, Barry was willing to agree to a stipulation dear to the heart of Tom Padgett. Tom could hire both Debbie and her

cousin Sandra (a good friend of Tom's) to work at the proposed
appraisal service. They would each get $10 an hour, and Barry
would pay. And as the money Barry made got bigger, so would the
money Tom got, including *big* bonuses that would enable Tom to
buy the beach house he'd always wanted.

Before finding a small office in the Transworld Bank Building
in Van Nuys, Barry and Tom spent days kicking around the name
of their new company.

Finally they settled on Interstate Appraisal Services. "Doesn't
that have a nice ring to it?" they asked each other. Interstate
Appraisal Services: serving the entire country. As their logo, they
chose a simple outline map of the continental United States.

Once they had decided on the name and logo, Barry and Padgett immediately had Interstate Appraisal Services stationery
printed and got down to business—Barry busily lining up bank
loans and investors, and Padgett confirming the existence of the
nonexistent restoration jobs.

In the course of the confirmations, Padgett, with his background in insurance to assist him, and growing more confident
daily, might purposely let slip a guarded fact or two that Barry
had already mentioned to investors, such as the growing number of
appraisers and adjusters that Padgett had working for him.

And if they asked what exactly he did for insurance companies,
he had his answer ready. After being notified of a fire- or water-
damaged building by one of his insurance company clients, he'd go
out, take pictures, ascertain the scope of the damages—a key
phrase—authorize any immediate repairs, and then come to an
agreement with the contractor on what needed to be done on a
permanent basis.

If the banks insisted on seeing the pictures—which very rarely
happened—he'd simply go to a vacant building and take some.

If they questioned why the restoration jobs—which would soon
run into the millions—cost so much, he had an answer for that also.
"You know how firemen are," he'd say. "They couldn't care less
about damage they do to a building. All they care about is putting
out the fire and stopping it from spreading. They'll knock gaping
holes in the walls and drench the entire building whether they need
to or not. That's just the way they operate."

If some potential investor wanted to go to a job site to verify the
work (most were now in far-off places like Arroyo Grande or San
Diego), Padgett would explain patiently why that was out of the
question. About eight months ago, it seems, he had let a loan

officer—at Barry's insistence and against Tom's better judgment—
go to one of the restoration sites. And sure enough, the guy tripped,
fractured his knee, and sued the insurance company that Padgett
was representing. And man, did he hear about *that*! It practically
cost him his business. There was no way he could risk another
situation like that.

And if an investor asked to speak to the insurance companies
directly, well that was another no-no. Some were back East, some
overseas, but in any case, they didn't want to be pestered with
twenty-five calls a day from people asking to verify jobs. That's
what they paid Padgett for. Tom Padgett, for his part, understood
the lender's concern for full disclosure, but, hey, what could he do?
His obligation was to his clients—the insurance companies—not to
ZZZZ Best or some lender.

If anyone insisted beyond *that* point, Tom Padgett would feel
compelled to lay it on the line. "Look," he'd say, "let me tell you the
facts of life. ZZZZ Best is just a little nothing company, and I'm
giving them this work because they're good and I like Barry." Then
he'd hit them with his favorite line: "But he's 20 percent of my
business and 80 percent of my problems. I don't make these rules,
but I have to live by them. I hope," Tom Padgett would add, "that
you'll respect that."

It isn't who you know, but what they'll do for you, and at this
stage of Jack Catain's life, people were prepared to do very little.
Not only had he antagonized friends like Rosario and DeNunzio by
shortchanging them, but he had the government, the courts, and
the cops on his back.

Barry, who knew all of this, had it reinforced for him in early
November when the FBI stopped by.

Buck Sadler, a veteran FBI agent assigned to the Organized
Crime Squad's LA office, had, it seems, some "very nebulous information" that a "Barry, last name unknown—who was in the carpet
business in the Valley—had a $150,000 juice or shylock loan from
Jack Catain."

That was all Sadler had to go on until early November, when he
read an *LA Times* article about Barry Minkow, highly successful
young carpet-cleaning entrepreneur.

Sadler decided to see if it was the same Barry, which, of
course, it was. But after talking with Minkow, he came away with
very little.

Barry told him that he didn't have a shylock loan with Catain but that he knew Jack, was impressed with him and his knowledge of business, and had, as a result, hired him as a consultant.

He also identified a picture of Carmen DeNunzio and one or two other alleged mob associates from a bunch of photos Sadler showed him.

And that was it—except for Barry telling Sadler and his fellow agent, in a somewhat "boastful" manner, according to Sadler, about his insurance restoration business and his plans to expand it soon into a publicly owned company. As the agents got up to leave, Barry offered them copies of his autobiography.

Although Jack Catain was no longer able to have one's legs broken if he was displeased, he was not about to walk away from the money to which he felt entitled.

He'd been cut out of his points with Rosario, and there was nothing he could do about that. But he had a signed agreement that proved that Barry Minkow owed him *big* money—half the profits on numerous restoration jobs. And what about the bank loans he'd helped Barry get—more than $150,000 worth? Sure, the loans were high, but the jobs were good—and if they weren't, well, that had nothing to do with him.

It wasn't as if Barry didn't have it to give him. The kid was playing the role and spending money all over town: a big, fancy house and a Ferrari for himself; furs, jewelry, and a car for his girl; picking up the check every place he went. No *way* should he be holding back.

So Jack Catain went to Barry Minkow and told him all this, and how unhappy he was that Barry was failing to pay him his half of the profits. And Barry agreed to pay him $350,000—the share of the restoration jobs he was currently owed—signing over three post-dated checks totaling $350,000 as proof of his sincerity. That, thought Jack Catain, was that.

But Minkow had other plans. Perhaps figuring that Jack couldn't and wouldn't do anything because of the FBI (which had called Barry to set up a second appointment), Barry Minkow put a stop payment on the checks.

Although Barry had told the bureau nothing during the first interview, the FBI still believed he was being shylocked and possibly extorted.

But when the agents met with him again in early December,

Barry's replies were essentially the same. There were, however, some subtle differences.

Jack Catain was no longer the businessman-consultant he liked and admired, but a partner in his restoration projects who was "pressuring" him "to come forward with money on the contract" they'd signed.

And when Sadler asked him if there was a possibility he was being extorted, Barry, accorded to Sadler, "nodded his head in the affirmative like that could be the case."

But he declined to say anything further, and the agents left.

It was unheard of, and retrospectively a lot of people were much amused by the specter of a con man and alleged mobster suing in civil court for what was owed him. But at the end of December, that was exactly what Jack Catain did. For $1.3 million.

Undoubtedly, Barry had thought that Catain, with all his legal problems and the FBI snooping around looking for more, would just swallow the loss and keep a low profile. But Catain not only sued, he listed the restoration jobs from which he was entitled money, including one for a startling $2.9 million in Santa Barbara. He also attached copies of the three stopped checks totaling $350,000.

With the lawsuit, Jack Catain, the old con man, had called the bluff of Barry Minkow, the fledgling, and left him with no alternative but to pay up.

For as Catain certainly knew, his suit couldn't have come at a worse time for Barry. He had outstanding loans totaling several million dollars, a high public profile, and, even more importantly, a commitment from his new partner, Robert Victor—with whom he had the fifty-fifty profit split—to assist Barry in making ZZZZ Best a publicly owned company.

Under no circumstances could Minkow afford to become involved in a public lawsuit with a man rumored to have mob connections and currently under indictment for passing counterfeit money. He was already dealing with banks, and serious money was about to be invested in ZZZZ Best.

Moreover, Catain had obtained a temporary restraining order prohibiting Barry from transferring any of his assets. If he didn't settle the lawsuit, this could significantly delay Barry's plans, since he would be unable to transfer his assets to the public company with which he planned to merge.

So Barry settled with Catain, agreeing to pay him $670,000

plus interest over a period of time (he eventually paid Catain about $500,000) and taking on another enormous debt.

On the other hand, in the seven months since he'd met Jack Catain, he'd also gone from a low-level con artist to a high minor leaguer.

Soon he'd be playing in the *big* leagues.

— 12 —

AS 1985 DREW TO A CLOSE, things appeared to be proceeding smoothly for Tom Padgett. Debbie and her cousin Sandra were working for him at Interstate, and Debbie was viewing him in action as *the boss*, taking calls, shuffling papers, and playing the role. With his salary from Travelers, the increased weekly money Barry was paying him, and the continued payments from Minkow on the loan, Tom Padgett was starting, at long last, to have some spare change in his pocket and to breathe a little easier.

But the Wednesday before Christmas, he received a most unwelcome call as he sat at his desk at Travelers. It was from a man named Berk, of Thomas Funding. Since he started working with Barry, he had received well over a dozen inquiries from lending institutions asking him in general terms to verify his relationship with ZZZZ Best, and he had verified between $2 and $3 million this way. But Berk was asking very specific questions as well as making a very specific request: "Hello, Mr. Padgett," Berk had said, introducing himself. "I'm calling because I need you to initial some job invoices you've given ZZZZ Best before we can proceed with our loan to them. Mr. Minkow is going to assign payment on the claim directly to us."

Padgett had no idea what Berk was talking about, for Barry rarely conferred with him about loan or investment deals that were in the works. Not knowing what to say, he tried stalling for time. "Well, usually we don't do that kind of thing," he said. "We just have too many clients. If we initialed every job or loan invoice for a subcontractor, I'd be doing nothing else all day."

"I appreciate that," said Berk, "but this loan request is for

$200,000, and Mr. Minkow's offering a job invoice of yours of $300,000 for collateral."

"Holy shit!" Padgett thought. "Look, I'm busy this afternoon," Padgett started to say, but Berk cut him off.

"I understand, but I'm just five minutes away from your office right now. It'll just take a minute; I really need you to initial these."

It quickly became apparent that Berk was not about to take no for an answer. If Tom wasn't going to be available, that would be fine; Berk would stop by in any case and get Padgett's boss or someone else to sign off on the papers.

That clearly being no option at all, Padgett reluctantly told him to come over, hung up, and immediately called Barry.

Padgett was scared.

Barry had always lied so big and so convincingly that nobody had ever questioned it. He'd just show a fraudulent set of books and photocopies of phony checks from Interstate, and that would be it. But now somebody was questioning Barry's story—or at least demanding further proof—and the whole scam now looked in danger of blowing up in their faces.

Luckily, Barry was in his office when Padgett called. Quickly filling him in, Padgett asked the essential question: "Barry, what the *fuck* are we gonna do?"

Remarkably calm, as he invariably was, Barry told him to just stall the guy, tell him not to come over.

"Goddamn it, Barry," Padgett said, trying to avoid screaming in the crowded office, "am I speaking Chinese or what? He's on his way here *now*. I'm an auto appraiser; what am I supposed to tell this guy about a $300,000 job?"

Barry had no answers. "You can do it, Tom; just say what you always do." Before hanging up, he added a little sweetener. "There is ten grand in your pocket," he said, "if you get the loan."

A few minutes later, Berk came in, asked for Tom, and was directed to his desk. He seemed pleasant enough, and after showing Padgett the papers, he asked Padgett to sign here, here, and here.

Then he asked to see Padgett's file on the job.

"You can't see the file on the job, you asshole," Padgett thought. "There is no fuckin' file because there is no fuckin' job."

But instead he said he was sorry, he'd sent the file back to Connecticut for review. Should he forward it to him when it was sent back?

"No," said Berk, walking out, "this should do it. Thanks a lot."

Relieved, Padgett immediately called Barry: "I think we pulled it off," he said.

The next day, however, Tom Padgett found out just how badly he'd misjudged the situation.

Still unsettled, Padgett called Barry early in the morning, hoping for some reassurance. Instead, he received a jarring piece of news. Berk had spoken with Dave Tengberg, Padgett's boss. Tengberg, appalled, told him that not only had Minkow and Padgett's story been a total fabrication but that Travelers didn't even deal in restoration work.

Almost as soon as he hung up, Padgett saw Tengberg approaching his desk and, feeling that old sinking feeling, knew exactly what was coming. "Tom," Dave Tengberg asked, "could you step into my office?"

As soon as they sat down, and before Tengberg could even open his mouth, Padgett had told him he didn't want any lectures, he knew what this was all about, and he was resigning effective immediately.

"I'm real sorry," he told Tengberg.

"So am I," his boss replied.

Within minutes, Tom Padgett was out the office door, shuffling down Wilshire Boulevard in a daze, crying like a baby.

His walking wasn't solely to relieve tension. He'd been required to turn in the keys to the company car. So he was now stuck in the middle of LA with no wheels, always an unnerving experience, given the city's appalling bus service.

Turning up Western Avenue, Padgett stopped at a pay phone, called Sandra, and asked if she would come and pick him up.

About an hour later, she dropped Tom Padgett off at the 7-Eleven by his Hollywood apartment and told him she'd call later. He then went into the store, bought a twelve-pack, went home, got drunk, and passed out.

Around five o'clock that evening, Padgett was awakened from a drunken stupor by the incessant ringing of his phone.

"Hey, babe," said Barry Minkow, "you getting ready for the party?"

Barry had just moved into his huge, new $700,000 home in a walled and gated community in Woodland Hills and that very night was throwing a Christmas party.

"Barry," said Padgett, still in a daze. "I don't feel much like going to a party. If you don't remember, I just got fired today."

"Don't worry about that shit. Look at it this way," said Barry. "You're now on my payroll for $500 a week, you're gonna run your own business, and I'm paying for everything. Come on to the party."

Which Tom did.

Sandra picked him up, and they drove to Barry's house in the swank, new private community of million-dollar homes called Westchester Estates. Passing through the guarded entrance that looked like the Magic Gates to the Magic Kingdom at Disneyland, they drove down the cobblestone streets—illuminated by wrought-iron, frosted-glass street lamps—and found Barry's red-tiled Mediterranean-style house. It was one of the more modest structures on the block, but easy to spot by the presence in the driveway of Barry's sleek new red Ferrari with its "ZZZZ Best" license plates.

About seventy people were there already, including several photographers Jeri Carr had hired for the occasion. Among the guests Tom recognized were Kay Rosario, Bob Victor, Jeri Carr, Elenora Madrinan, Dan Krowpman, and Chip Arrington and his young wife, Lulu.

Jeff Wayne was also there. Several weeks earlier, Wayne had received a call from Barry about the party. "You gotta be there, you gotta be there," Barry told him. "I want you to perform. Whatever they're paying you at the Cabaret, I'll double it!"

Wayne explained to the Boy Wonder that he couldn't possibly miss his regular house comic gig at the Cabaret, but that he'd drop by for a drink before heading to work.

Wayne liked Barry, and besides, the possibility of Minkow financing his HBO comedy special was still out there. After all, *Robin Williams* does specials on HBO.

"Lobster!" Barry said, greeting Wayne at the door. "We're having lobster!" Barry, who loved to impress people, seemed incredibly proud of what he was serving that night and pointed out his main course every few minutes. For a young man of his age and limited background, lobster must indeed have seemed the ultimate in haute cuisine and social status. But did he have to keep mentioning it every ten seconds as he showed Wayne the house and introduced him around? It was giving the God of Comedy a headache.

But the house *was* beautiful, with a terraced staircase that swooped down the center of its huge main room and was covered that night with some of the $1,000 worth of green garlands, wreaths, and floral arrangements that had been placed everywhere. All the rooms were somewhat bare because the professional interior-decorating project was far from complete. The plan called for a mixture of antique and modern furniture, some of which was custom designed and would not be delivered for months.

The backyard pool was wondrous to behold, with a large *Z* emblazoned on its bottom and two cascading waterfalls. Next to it was the Jacuzzi, that obligatory symbol of the Southern California good life.

But the house was more than just a big, new, expensive home. It was also the carrot Barry was showing to all those associated with him. It was the sign he'd *arrived*.

For Lulu Arrington, the party was "just like 'Dynasty'"— everybody "all dolled up," the big LA house, the people upstairs in a bedroom doing drugs.

She'd had about eight or nine vodkas with orange juice and was having a great time mingling when some guy told her Barry was offering $200 to anybody who'd go to bed with a ZZZZ Best secretary who badly needed a man that night. It was hard to believe, but, knowing Barry, it could well be true.

Tom Padgett, meanwhile, was circling around the food-laden tables set up in almost every room, eating, downing a few beers, and doing his best to avoid Kay Rosario, who would surely want to talk business. It was a cardinal rule of Tom's *never* to talk business with investors when Barry wasn't around. Who knew what the guy had just made up ten minutes ago?

Wayne, who was becoming familiar with Barry's ZZZZ Best employees through his role as host at various roasts and award ceremonies, noticed that the crowd and atmosphere at the party this evening were different.

The award ceremonies were mostly attended by Barry's employees—working and lower-middle class young people—and the themes were always the same: ZZZZ Best's new offices opening here, here, and here, and the adoration of the Boy Wonder.

But the people at this affair were mostly older—investors, supporters, and friends of Barry's. And the focus was not Barry. It was money. Money, money, money. It was driving Wayne crazy; it seemed that was all anybody could talk about. That and carpets. It was the most boring group of people Wayne could remember running across in a long time.

One guy was talking about how much his new car cost, another about his stocks. A kid—one of Barry's friends and devoted servants—started telling Wayne about his landscaping business and how he was sure to make a million. "Don't talk to me about your landscaping business," Wayne told the kid. "I could give a fuck less." Barry loved it.

Minkow introduced Wayne to a few more people, and Wayne talked for a few minutes to Barry's girlfriend, Joyce, who as usual looked good but was very quiet. Finally, bored, Wayne retreated into the kitchen just to get away for a few minutes.

Striking up a conversation with one of the caterers, Wayne was interrupted by Barry barging into the kitchen, "All right, let's get the lobster out there."

Shortly thereafter, Wayne left.

Tom Padgett remembers that night differently. Everyone really seemed to be having a great time, and no one more so than Barry Minkow.

And why not? Hadn't 1985 been his year?

He was, after all, a self-proclaimed multimillionaire widely hailed as such in the media.

The recipient of a scrolled commendation, complete with the Great Seal of the City of Los Angeles, for "obtaining the status of a millionaire at the age of eighteen years old."

He had four ZZZZ Best locations, and a fifth in the works.

He had a big, new house on which he'd put down almost $220,000.

He had $17,000 in furniture on order.

He had a condo he was renting out.

And a $55,000 red Ferrari convertible.

And a pretty, blond live-in girlfriend to wear the fur and drive the car he'd bought for her.

And a maid and a gardener.

And a measure of revenge.

For in the course of an article written about him in the *LA Times*, subtitled "19-Year-Old Founded Million-Dollar Business," he was at last able—although indirectly—to tell those small-time bankers with their condescending attitudes and cheap suits who'd refused him loans all those years exactly what he thought of them. "The jealousy comes out [in a loan officer]," gloated Barry, "because he's 42 years old, he's getting a salary of $30,000 or $40,000 a year out of the bank. Do you think he wants to help me earn more than him?"

But Barry really wasn't bitter, and watching him that night—the very epitome of the perfect host and life of the party—who would have guessed that he had used up almost every penny he'd taken in paying juice and living high while simultaneously engaged in a Ponzi in which he owed millions of dollars and that could explode at any moment?

Part II
Think Big, Be Big

— 1 —

AMONG THE MANY MYSTERIES of Barry J. Minkow was just where he found the hours in the day to do all that he did, and how he kept it all straight in his head.

From mid-1985 to the year's end, for example, he was—through Chip—running a carpet-cleaning business with several hundred employees while expanding into new territory and opening new locations; dealing with and conning Jack Catain, Kay and her investment group, and other investors, banks, and loan companies; constantly juggling the raising of money from one source to pay another; setting up Interstate Appraisal Services with Tom and trying to keep their scam and stories in sync; creating and forging phony documentation for the restoration loans; doing press interviews and making motivational and promotional speeches; closing on his new house; and—almost simultaneously—contending with a million-dollar lawsuit while the FBI was literally knocking on his door.

It was all the more amazing, therefore, that he managed in the time he had left to develop a whole new set of relationships that would lead him directly to Wall Street.

Maurice Rind was skeptical from the beginning. It was, he told Bobby and Richie, either the greatest deal or the biggest Ponzi he'd ever heard of.

But Bobby told him to butt out, that it wasn't any of his business, that he'd known Barry Minkow since the kid was fourteen, and that the situation was legit—he was sure of it.

So Maurice shut up. Hey, if it was none of his business, then forget about it. Let 'em do what they wanted.

Bobby, that is, Robert Victor, aka Robert Viggiano, aka Wide Load (because "he has an ass like this," says a friend, spreading his arms open), had met Barry in the early eighties when Minkow was working near the small San Fernando Valley vehicle maintenance/used-car lot owned by Victor.

They'd been casually acquainted for about a year and a half, when one day Barry wandered into his shop and traded in his '63 Chevy Nova for a '72 Buick.

Over the next several years, Barry kept in touch with Robert Victor (who had had his name legally changed from Viggiano) and would regularly stop by the shop to have his car checked and to play softball with Steve Viggiano, Victor's son.

Then, a month or so after Barry had met Catain in the summer of 1985, he began telling Victor about the rapid growth of his restoration business and the need for investment money up front. He was wondering if Victor might be interested in investing. When he heard the kind of big return Barry was talking about, Robert Victor decided to at least consider it.

So he set up a meeting with two of his friends and Barry for the first week in September. It was after this meeting that Maurice Rind would make his prophetic "greatest deal or biggest Ponzi" remark.

As they sat poolside at Bob Victor's rented Northridge home waiting for Barry to arrive, Victor told Maurice Rind and another old friend named Richie Schulman (who'd just flown in from Florida on a visit) all about Barry: about how the kid was a nineteen-year-old, self-made millionaire, about how he'd just published a book about his success, about the rapid growth of his carpet-cleaning business, and about how Barry wanted to talk about a joint venture restoration deal in which they'd put up the capital and split the profits fifty-fifty, doubling their money within a relatively short time.

Rind and Schulman nodded appreciatively as they basked in the sun and listened to Bobby. The proposal appealed to them, for they were, like Robert Victor, always looking for new "situations" and "opportunities."

For Maurice Rind, who was active in buying and selling shares of marginal companies on the stock market, there was the possibility, Victor had mentioned, of a stock deal involving the kid's company, ZZZZ Best.

The three, all in their late forties or early fifties, would later be portrayed in the press as high movers and shakers in the world of organized crime, but they were never that. Certainly by the time they were to become involved with Barry Minkow, any criminal activity in which they may have been engaged was of the quasi-legal, white-collar variety. It had not, however, always been that way.

Tough-talking street guys from working-class New York backgrounds, they'd grown up, like scores of other Italian and Jewish kids of their generation, on the fringes of the mob, on the corrupt streets of tough sections of New York picking up serious criminal records along the way.

When they came to Los Angeles with their rough New York accents and streetwise personas, it was inevitable they would stand out and be noticed.

This was of small consequence to the fifty-three-year-old Schulman, who lived in Florida, hated Los Angeles, and spent little time there, or to Robert Victor, who, while "you won't call him suave" (as one friend put it), could somewhat blend into LA by maintaining the image of the quiet family man he'd essentially become.

But for forty-eight-year-old Maurice Rind, with his quick temper, passionate manner of speaking, New York street accent, and liberal use of gangster jargon, there was no escaping his origins and the inferences that people in Los Angeles drew from them. To many of his LA associates, he appeared—in spite of his sharp intelligence—to be someone out of a Martin Scorsese movie— an East Coast ethnic character of unpredictable volatility.

To a Midwesterner like Tom Padgett, or to Chip Arrington, the native Southern Californian, Maurice Rind was the quintessential New Yorker, and Tom and Chip would often launch into an imitation of Maurice's high nasal voice at the mere mention of his name. The impersonations were amateurish, but they *were* unfailingly recognizable, consisting solely of repeating over and over the three questions that Maurice invariably placed at the end of almost every declarative sentence.

"You understand?" "Ya hear?" "Ya got it?" Maurice would shout, simultaneously punctuating the air with his index finger for emphasis. His stories, too, had their own distinctive ending. "And that," Maurice would say, "is the way that went down."

A brown-haired man of medium height and build who looks like a more boyish version of the sixties' rock promoter Bill Graham, Maurice Rind had grown up as a Jewish kid in the tough, Italian-American Bensonhurst section of Brooklyn, where his later

attitudes were undoubtedly formed. For it's unlikely that he acquired his style from living in middle-class Forest Hills, Queens,
where his family moved when Maurice was thirteen—a place more
famous for turning out the gentle likes of Simon and Garfunkel
than street-smart kids like Maurice Rind.

At fifteen, says Rind, he met Richie Schulman, "the neighborhood bully," at the Palladium Pool Hall on Queens Boulevard.
Although each went his separate way, they managed to remain
friends over the years.

In the early sixties, at the age of twenty-one, Rind became one
of Wall Street's youngest stockbrokers, doing so well that by 1972,
he says, he was virtually able to retire. Afterward, he "backed
Broadway and Off-Broadway plays."

But in 1975 he was indicted by the federal government and
convicted of eight counts, including conspiracy to violate securities
laws, violation of the antifraud provision of the securities laws, and
interstate transportation of forged securities. He was given a
$10,000 fine and sentenced to eighteen months in jail.

Then in early 1977, while still doing time at Allenwood Federal
Prison in Pennsylvania, Rind was again indicted and pleaded
guilty to two similar additional charges. As a result, his broker's
license was revoked. But as part of the plea bargain, he received no
further jail time, and after serving about ten months of his original
sentence, he was released.

"I had dealings with Caesar's Palace as well as with Mr.
[Jimmy] Hoffa and the [Teamsters'] pension fund," Rind complained later. "And the wonderful U.S. government put a tap on my
phones.

"They wanted to know about certain things going on at Caesar's, and certain loans and situations with the Teamsters' [pension]
fund. When I refused to talk, they tapped my phones. [And] when
they did that, they found out I was the undisclosed owner of a
brokerage firm, and they indicted me. That was all there was to all
this nonsense. I was told by the government if I go on the stand,
they'd drop the charges. [But] I refused." (When the LAPD later
identified Rind as "an associate of all five organized crime families," Rind was incensed. "All five! Can you imagine all five! Even
Meyer Lansky wasn't associated with all five!")

After getting out of jail, Rind says, he produced shows in Las
Vegas, and has "been trying to be a good businessman" ever since.

But in early 1985—about six months before he was to meet
Barry—Rind was again in trouble with the Securities and Ex-

change Commission and signed a consent agreement permanently enjoining him from "employing any device to defraud [or obtain] money by means of untrue statements" in connection with the sale of some Texas securities with which he'd been involved.

In signing the agreement, Rind didn't admit any guilt and continued "making loans and investments" and working at stock "sponsorship," advising people about stocks he liked and those he thought had potential—*sponsorship* being a word of Maurice's choosing, as he is barred from performing as a stockbroker.

Richie Schulman, meanwhile, was having his own troubles with the law.

Raised in the Williamsburg section of Brooklyn, Schulman, 5'8" and 275 pounds, was known as a *very* tough man. He had been arrested more than a dozen times before receiving seven years in Lewisburg Federal Prison for conspiracy and extortion in 1970.

Some of Richie's arrests were for minor crimes such as vagrancy, being a "common gambler," and possessing bookmaking records; others, however, were of a more serious nature like felonious assault with fist, foot, and iron bar; felonious assault with gun; burglary; and extortion. The LAPD has since stated that Schulman was a "reputed Genovese organized crime associate."

Paroled in 1974, Schulman told Barry Minkow when they met at Victor's pool party that he "used to be a street person, but had retired fifteen years ago" (after his last stint at Lewisberg). By 1985, he was "a sick guy," an overweight diabetic with high blood pressure.

It was while doing time at Lewisburg that Richie Schulman met Robert Victor. They were, in fact, cellmates. And although Victor, like Schulman, is 5'8" and now weighs over 250 pounds (hence the Wide Load street name), he was thinner then and needed Schulman's protection while in prison. "Victor's mother is Jewish, his father is Italian, and Bobby's wife, Rosalie, is Jewish too," says a former friend. "Bobby makes out like he's a hard Italian. But Richie had to protect him in jail. To outside suckers, Victor looked like he could handle himself, but to anybody with any balls, he was nothing."

Like Richie Schulman, Robert Victor also had an impressive record, having been arrested at least eight times for crimes like usury, forgery, extortion, and theft of interstate shipments. In 1971, along with Joseph Colombo, Sr.—the reputed head of the notorious New York Mafia family of the same name—he was also convicted of grand larceny for robbing the Long Island Diamond and Jewelry Exchange of $750,000 in jewels. But well before Robert Victor was talking about a deal with Barry Minkow, he was maintaining, like Maurice Rind and Richie Schulman, that he was now a legitimate businessman. It was a claim that all three would later have difficulty getting people to believe.

Once Barry settled in at the pool with the others, he started "talking fast," Maurice Rind recalls, while Victor proceeded to "sell the kid hard, trying to give him credibility." "Oh, yeah," Victor told Rind and Schulman again, "he's a legit millionaire; he's written his own book; the joint venture would be great," and so on.

And then Barry would pick it up, once in a while playing a little hard to get, but most of the time being more than a little obvious as he talked about his carpet-cleaning business and how he owned 100 percent of it, and about how well it was doing. He had a press kit, he said, all about his business and himself, which he would give them later.

He talked as well about the growth of his restoration business, and how he desperately needed capital to stay abreast of all the work he was getting. He had, for example, a contract from Travelers Corp. for $1.5 million to restore a water-damaged building in San Diego, and excellent contacts who would get him further jobs. But he just didn't have the cash flow to handle more than one job at a time. (The San Diego job and others he would sell to Victor, Rind, and Schulman were the same ones he was selling to Catain and Kay Rosario.)

A really big job like that in San Diego, Barry continued, would tie up all his available cash and *still* leave the project grossly underfinanced, what with ZZZZ Best having to purchase materials beforehand, and with almost everything in a water-damaged building having to be replaced.

Barry's and Victor's sales pitch that day was directed mainly at Richie Schulman. For although Maurice Rind would later have his own pivotal dealings with Barry, he was not there to invest, but rather to tell his friend Richie what he thought of the kid and the proposal, and to feel Minkow out on that possible stock deal.

But Barry wasn't just concentrating on Richie Schulman because he was a potential investor. Schulman also had access to a great deal of *serious* money through one of his closest friends, Jay Botchman, the owner of a major New Jersey factoring company.

Factoring companies, which make high-risk, high-interest, short-term loans to businesses or individuals who can't obtain more conventional financing, were to become for Barry and Tom Padgett a major target for obtaining investment capital, and Barry was keen to develop a relationship with anyone who, like Richie Schulman, could provide entrée to them.

For the present, however, Barry proposed a joint venture with Victor and Schulman on the San Diego job. In return for a loan of $350,000, he would, when the project was completed, return their principal and give them an additional $350,000, thereby offering them a chance to double their money.

The joint venture would have its own name and office—through which all purchases and revenues would flow—and be independent of ZZZZ Best Carpet and Furniture Cleaning Co. Victor and Schulman would, in addition, immediately go on salary at a $1,000 a week, the money to pay them coming "off the top" of the San Diego job.

Then Barry brought up a subject that—while it didn't seem to disturb Robert Victor—cast a shadow, for Richie Schulman, over what otherwise seemed like a tempting deal. There was a guy named Jack Catain, Barry told them, who was shylocking him, and he just couldn't get him off his back. Could they help out?

Almost before Barry could finish, Richie gave him his answer: No.

There was no way. He understood, said Schulman, that Barry was "caught up in a loan-sharking Ponzi," but Barry had to understand the rules of the game. And one paramount rule was that "a sucker doesn't jam another sucker." And even though he was now "retired," if there was another "street person" in the picture, he still had to follow the code of the street and not become involved. Richard Schulman, after all, had his ethics.

Barry would have to disengage himself from Jack Catain, Richie told him, before they could do any business. "Either you are a businessman or a street person," Richie said. "The two don't mix." The last thing Richie needed was to get involved in a dispute with Jack Catain, who might still be able to call on some mob muscle and make trouble for him if Catain decided Shulman was trying to co-opt someone with whom Jack was already doing business.

Determined to make the deal, Barry told Richie that he understood and was so impressed with the way Schulman spoke and carried himself that he'd do whatever he had to to conclude his dealings with Catain. Schulman, he added, had nothing to worry about.

After Barry left, Victor continued hard-selling Richie, presenting him with what Maurice Rind later described as a "riskless deal." First, Victor told him he would personally check out the validity of the San Diego job and ensure that Barry fulfilled his commitment to sever his ties with Jack Catain.

Further, said Victor, he'd put up $260,000 of his own money, plus another $40,000 he owed Richie. All Schulman had to do was come up with the remaining $50,000. And, Victor added as the final sweetener to nail down the deal, he would *guarantee* Schulman his full $90,000 investment. "Richie thought," said Maurice Rind, "that it was the perfect deal—that he couldn't lose." And that might have been the case, had Victor done what he promised.

But, in fact, Robert Victor did not, taking Barry's word for it that he was no longer dealing with Catain without actually talking to Jack; and he was stymied, stalled, and talked to death by Barry and Tom Padgett when he asked to visit the San Diego restoration site.

And having done neither, Robert Victor told Richard Schulman he'd done both. Richie, pleased, said, "OK, then go ahead with the deal." And Victor and Schulman put up their money. "It was the old story," says Maurice Rind. "The easiest person to con is another con man."

So in September 1985, Richie Schulman, who was to become a silent partner, flew back to his Florida home, and Barry Minkow and Robert Victor opened B & M Insurance Services.

Barry, who had other tasks with which to busy himself, was rarely at B & M's new office. But Victor showed up with some regularity, at least initially, "to watch our investments," as he put it, and to extract his and Richie's profits. As there was no restoration work to oversee, and the paperwork generated for the alleged jobs by Barry and Tom was always minimal, it can only be assumed that Victor used the offices for his other business activities, which included his considerable stock trading.

Maurice had also been hired by B & M as a "consultant" for a fee of $1,000 a week. His primary functions were to "look after Richie's interests" (it was feared Victor and Barry were too close), to help Minkow clean up his TRW record, and, most importantly, to help Minkow make ZZZZ Best a publicly owned corporation, something Maurice had done with other small private companies in the past.

Rind's purpose in making ZZZZ Best a publicly owned corporation was simply to buy the stock early and dirt cheap, help create a demand for it, and then, once the price had risen enough to make a substantial profit, sell it and move on.

Minkow, for his part, wanted ZZZZ Best to become a public company so that he could pocket money by selling some of his shares, and make ZZZZ Best appear more attractive to potential investors as the value of its stock went up. Shortly after the formation of B & M, Maurice Rind set to work on the initial stages of the process.

It wasn't too long afterward that Barry informed Victor and Richie that the insurance restoration job in which they'd invested their $350,000 was going to cost far more than the $1.5 million that had been anticipated. The damage was more extensive than originally thought—about $2.7 million—and he needed an additional $250,000 up front to pay the increased costs of material and labor.

But he was stretched thin, Barry continued. Would Victor talk to Richie Schulman and see if Richie could arrange a loan through his friend Jay Botchman's factoring company? Amazingly—despite Maurice's initial suspicions—the request aroused few doubts in three men not known for their innocence. But their blasé reaction was typical of all Barry's investors, whether men with a past on the fringes of the mob, bankers, or little old ladies turning over their life savings. They were all taken in by Barry, who lied so convincingly, perhaps because he *truly* believed it would all work out and he'd pay everybody back, and by the enormous profits to be made.

Victor assured Barry that raising the additional money would be no problem, that he'd talk to Richie and see what they could do, and in the meantime Barry should go ahead and take the expanded contract.

Victor then called Richie Schulman, who agreed that Jay Botchman, through his factoring company, probably would make the loan. But he was going to wait to call Jay until Victor had again checked out the job. Victor told him he'd get to work on it.

Soon Barry was back with yet another loan request. He'd gotten a contract on a $1.9 million restoration job in a tiny California town called Arroyo Grande, but he couldn't take it unless Victor—through Schulman—could persuade Jay Botchman to advance him money for that job as well. All told, counting the increase in the San Diego project and the new Arroyo Grande contract, he'd need $1 million from Jay.

When Victor called, Richie Schulman agreed he'd talk to Jay Botchman about the Arroyo Grande job at the same time he spoke to him about San Diego, and said he thought Jay might go for the million-dollar line of credit. But he had no intention of calling before Victor had checked out the jobs. Had he taken care of that yet? No, said Robert Victor, but he would.

At about the same time, Barry called Chip Arrington into his office. "We're going to become a public company," he said, "and I wanna have a meeting." Arrington, who at the time didn't even know what a public company was, paid little attention to the rest of what Barry had to say. It was, he thought, just another in a long line of Minkow pipe dreams to be listened to with half an ear and then forgotten.

But Barry was serious, and in late November, the meeting took place. Attending were his mother; Vera Hojecki, a telemarketer, longtime friend of Mrs. Minkow's, and a kind of surrogate mom to Barry; Chip, of course; and most of the managers of the carpet-cleaning locations.

The company was going public, Barry told them, and they were going to have the opportunity to get in on the ground floor—purchasing stock early on and experiencing the thrill of watching it rise daily when they picked up their newspaper.

"We're all gonna be rich," said Barry. He also touted Maurice Rind as the Wall Street genius who was going to make it possible. Maurice came by soon afterward and gave a little rundown to the group about the process of becoming a public company.

After that, Maurice began appearing at the office with some regularity. Barry was his worst on these occasions, as he was when any business associate he deemed important arrived.

"Everybody out, everybody out," he would shout at any unfortunate employees who happened to be in his office at the time. "No phone calls! We've got *serious* business to discuss here." And if, later on, Chip or any other underling would dare interrupt one of the meetings, Barry would inquire in the rudest manner what that person thought he or she was doing and if that person was a fuckin' idiot or what? After all, the pressure—and contempt—he kept so well in check so much of the time had to come out somewhere.

It was during one of the meetings at Barry's office that Maurice Rind first met Tom Padgett.

As with Tom's initial introduction to Jack Catain, Barry and Padgett had worked out a little scenario beforehand.

Barry, for his part, told Maurice about how Tom Padgett's father, like Tom, had also been an insurance appraiser and about how, as a result, Tom Padgett not only knew the restoration business but, even more importantly, possessed extraordinary business contacts handed down from father to son.

It was, of course, an integral part of Barry's nature to exaggerate, especially when he was selling. And on this day he *was* selling. The product was Tom Padgett, the buyer Maurice Rind, a man in the middle of a million-dollar loan who was also about to bring ZZZZ Best public. So it was understandable that, as Barry talked, Tom Padgett, the ne'er-do-well bump-and-dent guy, was transformed into the dynamically successful insurance appraiser-businessman who was on his way to big-time riches and success and was fortunately taking Barry along with him.

Tom Padgett's assignment at the meeting was to play the person Barry had described, to talk knowledgeably about the restoration jobs, and—in what was later to become standard procedure—to set the stage for a little breathing room in case, when the time came to make the payments due, they didn't have the cash. Given his growing experience in the insurance industry as well as in conning investors, that was no problem. They'd decided that Tom would recite the typical payment schedule for a restoration job. When 30 percent of a job was done, Padgett told Rind, the insurance company would pay 20 percent. When 50 percent was completed, they'd pay another 20 percent, with the balance coming at the end of the job.

However, Tom said—addressing the "breathing room" concern—the payments were contingent on the approval of the insurance company inspectors. If the electrical work had not been inspected or the plumbing was not finished, well, then the payment would be delayed. "This gave us an out and more time for the Ponzi," Padgett was to say later, "in case the money wasn't there."

Whatever doubts Maurice might have harbored were assuaged by the meeting, and he plunged ahead with the plans to take ZZZZ Best public.

Barry became consumed with the plan as well. "That was

when Barry stopped paying any attention at all to carpet cleaning,"
says Chip Arrington. "Now he was a big-league hitter."

By mid-November, Barry Minkow was pressing Robert Victor
on the loans. Bobby, after all, had told him to go ahead, and now he
needed the money.

Victor, in turn, began urging Schulman to contact Jay Botchman.

But Schulman was refusing to move. He was still waiting for
Victor's guarantee that the jobs were real. The assurance was
forthcoming by December.

Unfortunately, it was a lie. Robert Victor never saw the restoration jobs. Instead, he allowed himself to be stalled to death by
Barry and Tom Padgett. In fairness, Victor *had* tried to get to the
restoration sites, but Tom and Barry's delaying techniques proved
too sophisticated for him.

To discourage him, Padgett had told Victor that before he
could visit the sites, he'd have to be bonded. This was to ensure that
if Victor or anybody else was injured during a visit ("as had
happened before"), the insurance companies that Tom Padgett
represented would not be held responsible. Of course, it would take
some time before the bond could be obtained, Padgett explained.
He'd need Victor's social security and driver's license numbers and
a few other facts, and would give him a call when the bond came
through.

Robert Victor's failure to confirm the validity of the restoration jobs would later cost Rind, Schulman, and himself not only
heavy financial losses but big problems with the local cops.

Had Rind and Schulman known at the time that the jobs didn't
exist, they would have bailed out immediately. Rind had no money
as yet invested, and Schulman $50,000—not small change but
certainly not worth a long jail sentence. And that is exactly what
Rind and Schulman—with their prior felony convictions—would
face. It's one thing to be involved in a Ponzi like the one Barry and
Tom had devised when you're twenty or even thirty-five and have
no prior record. But to be over fifty and a two-time loser with a
family, *knowing* any judge is going to throw the book at you, is very
different. *That* just didn't make sense. Eight or ten years in jail out
of the twenty or so one might have left at that age simply wasn't
worth it. Not when it involved a crude Ponzi that nobody but a kid
and heavy-drinking, fog-brained outlaw neo-Nazi would have
thought could ever succeed. A shot at a little low-profile, hard-to-

prove stock manipulation—trading penny-ante stocks like ZZZZ
Best back and forth before selling their shares and getting out—
perhaps. But to get involved in a Ponzi out there for anybody really
looking hard to see, and to jeopardize their connection with a big-
money, high-rolling financier like Jay Botchman over fifty grand,
well, that, as Maurice himself might have said, would have been
"retarded."

Why, then, given the stakes, hadn't Robert Victor been more
diligent in protecting not just Richie and Maurice but ultimately
himself as well?

The almost certain answer is that Robert Victor *did* eventually
check the jobs out. And when he did, he discovered they were bogus.
By then, however—in December—it was too late. He and Schulman
had already given Barry their $350,000. If Victor had told Schul-
man then that the jobs didn't exist, Richie would have demanded
that Victor give him back his $90,000 investment.

Victor, moreover, would have lost *his* $260,000 investment as
well. For had he told Schulman and Rind the jobs were phony, they
would not have recommended the additional loans to Jay Botchman
and the Ponzi would have been stopped dead in its tracks. *And*
Victor would have lost any chance of ever recovering his money. His
only option was to keep his mouth shut and to hope that the loans
from Jay went through, that Kay and her investors kept coughing
up money, that Maurice could bring ZZZZ Best public so that the
company looked good, and that Barry could attract additional new
money. Then he could get *his* money back and eventually hop off the
pyramid.

Robert Victor has denied all this, maintaining, like all the rest
of the investors, that he never knew that the jobs were fake, going so
far as to tell the police that he inspected the San Diego and Arroyo
Grande sites—but only their "exteriors." This is impossible, of
course, since they did not exist. Additionally, neither Barry nor
Tom had ever been in Arroyo Grande, so they couldn't have
matched a building being renovated with a phony address if they'd
wanted to.

Instead, according to Barry, what happened was that Victor
did indeed find out the jobs were nonexistent but, because of his
situation, could do little about it but rant and rave, shake Barry
down for some cash, and keep his mouth shut.

As with so much that happened during those years, it was
fortunate for Barry that it was Victor and not Maurice or Richie
who found out about the scam, for Barry's and Victor's interests in

keeping it secret coincided. Their mutual interest was yet another mini-cure for Barry Minkow.

So on December 31, 1985, Maurice Rind—anxious that nothing interfere with his efforts to bring ZZZZ Best public, and assured of the validity of the restoration jobs by Robert Victor—flew from Burbank Airport to Caesar's Palace in Las Vegas and presented the loan deal to Jay Botchman. "Jay says," Maurice reported, "that he likes what he sees, and that he'll, you know, let us know, but that it looked good."

In mid-January, Jay Botchman apparently felt that the deal did indeed look good, for he sent word for Barry, Maurice, Chip, and one or two others involved in ZZZZ Best to fly to New Jersey to sign the papers, as he was not a registered lender in California. Then on back-to-back days, he wired a total of $1 million into B & M's account for the San Diego and Arroyo Grande jobs. The interest rate was to be 24 percent annually.

"We felt the jobs were real," Maurice Rind said afterward, "and when Jay asked if Richie and I stood behind them, I said, 'Yeah, we stand behind them. Absolutely.'"

For Barry the money was a godsend, for it allowed him to continue the Ponzi and buy his way out of his deal with Jack Catain.

— 2 —

NOT LONG AFTER BARRY MINKOW RECEIVED his $1 million line of credit, a pretty, hazel-eyed blond named Joyce Lipman was placing an ad in the Help Wanted section of the *Los Angeles Times*.

The ad was for a houseman/chef, someone who could help her run the household she was setting up with Barry Minkow in Woodland Hills.

At just seventeen, the slim, 5'8" Lipman, whose hair and nails were always just so and whose major passion was said to be shopping, was hardly prepared to take on alone the burdens and responsibilities of caring for a large home, cooking, and entertaining on the scale that Barry Minkow felt was necessary for his business.

Joyce Lipman was not just the perfect blond bimbo, ultimate

JAP, or vacant-headed Valley Girl that unkind and jealous acquaintances made her out to be. In spite of Barry's newfound wealth and free-spending ways, she still held down a job as a salesgirl in a local department store and was, by all accounts, truly devoted to Barry, for whom she was always there when needed.

And just out of high school, Joyce really *did* need help in that house, and God knows, with the way Barry was making money, it certainly seemed like a small enough expense.

So the ad was placed.

Among those who responded was a thirty-one-year-old ex–New Yorker named Arthur Uhl.

If one wished to cast Uhl in a movie, you'd need look no further than the actor Mickey Rourke, to whom Uhl bears an uncanny resemblance—if, that is, Rourke were obviously gay, stood about 5'2", and weighed in at no more than 110 pounds.

Before answering Joyce's ad, Uhl, who wears his fey persona on his sleeve as a badge of pride, had worked, he says, as a majordomo in households in New York, Paris, and LA.

Cultured and articulate, Uhl also claims to have grown up in New York's exclusive Gramercy Park, to have attended Mt. Vernon Academy, to speak fluent French, and to have graduated from the famous Paris school for chefs, the Cordon Bleu.

When Uhl first met Joyce and her parents at a local Valley deli to be interviewed, he was confused. The Lipmans kept referring to "Barry"—Barry likes this, Barry doesn't like that, Barry likes to do such and such—as if they just naturally expected that Uhl *knew* who Barry was. And Uhl thought he did. He was that singer, right? Barry Manilow. The guy who did those sappy love songs.

But the faux pas obviously proved of no consequence, for the next day Joyce called and said he was hired. His salary was to be $350 a week in cash, and he'd live in and thus wouldn't have to pay for a thing—terms that well satisfied Arthur Uhl.

About a week later, Arthur moved in. While duly impressed with the neighborhood—although it *was* nouveau riche—Uhl also noted that the Minkow residence was one of the smallest, least imposing structures within the wealthy new complex.

Meeting Arthur at the door, Joyce showed him his room on the ground floor and then led him off to meet Barry.

Up they went to the master bedroom, where Barry Minkow, clad only in Jockey shorts, lay sprawled across his bed, watching cartoons. ("Barry always liked simple entertainment," says Arthur

Uhl.) Upon introduction, Barry looked up, said a quick hi, and reached for his ever-present Ding Dongs. Ding Dongs and cartoons, along with Twinkies, Oreos, and "The Rockford Files," were Barry's favorite pacifiers, a way for Barry—who didn't drink and rarely used recreational drugs (except steroids)—to cool out and relax.

In spite of Barry's disdain for alcohol, one of Arthur's first tasks was to go to the neighborhood store and buy a big supply of liquor to stock Barry's bar so he could entertain properly. Barry and Joyce were both under twenty-one, too young to buy liquor in California. "Jesus," joked Arthur to Joyce and Barry as he left to purchase the liquor, "I'll probably be the first guy to get busted for serving alcohol to minors because they're my boss."

But, of course, the liquor really wasn't for Joyce or Barry; it was for their guests. Barry Minkow *loved* to entertain and impress people. On the weekends, there would be a constant parade of people—old high school chums, to whom he was always a very generous soft touch, and new business associates. Barry thought nothing of inviting dozens of people to huge, expensive parties. At his 1986 Fourth of July bash, Arthur recalls, Barry served well over sixty lobsters and easily as many steaks.

Such affairs always brought out the best in Barry, who invariably invited Arthur, once his chores had been attended to, to kick back and join the party. These invitations were also usually followed up with a $100 tip and a thoughtful proposal that Arthur take the next day off.

Money was no object on these occasions, but then again, money was rarely of concern in anything Minkow did. "Barry always had to have a pocket full of hundreds with him," says Chip Arrington. "If we went to dinner, and the bill was $120, he'd just throw two $100 bills at the waiter and tell him to keep the change." Arrington's role was to be always ready with extra cash. "I had to keep a minimum of $100 in my pocket at work," says Chip, "just in case he needed it. That was a *rule*."

Barry never carried his money in a wallet. Usually, he just stuffed a couple thousand dollars into his pocket.

At times, this caused problems. One day Barry left for work and several hours later called Arthur at the house. He'd misplaced a check for $650,000. Look in my pants pockets, he told Uhl, see if it's there. Sure enough, Arthur found the check in a pair of walking shorts that Barry had thrown in the hamper. "Things like that happened more than once," says Uhl. "In the time I was there, there was money all over the place."

One evening, Kay Rosario came to the house for dinner, bringing with her as a gift two cloisonné vases valued at $1,800. (Arthur knew the value because he'd noted with disgust that the price stickers were still on the bottom.)

Placing the vases on the table, Rosario mentioned to Arthur that she'd left a shawl in her car and asked him to run out and get it. Later, when Arthur was serving coffee, Kay opened the shawl—which she had been using as a sort of wraparound carryall—and took out stacks of money, which she started counting before passing them on to Barry.

With that kind of cash floating around, it was not surprising that Barry would occasionally indulge himself with an impulsive purchase. For example, he bought an expensive cigarette racer—a sleek, high-powered speedboat—even though he had nowhere to store the craft and little time or inclination to use it. On another day, when Joyce was out of town, he went shopping at various flea markets, spending $5,000 in a couple of hours on junk. "It was very strange," says Arthur Uhl, "how money meant nothing to him—and everything."

Barry also particularly liked to use his money, or at least the lure of it, to indulge a passion not uncommon among young men: young girls. Barry *loved* young girls, that is, at least until he could bed them. "He just wanted to get them once," says Chip Arrington, "to add another notch on his gun. And they *had* to be young. He rarely dated older women."

"I never saw such a parade of more underage good-looking girls in my life," says Arthur Uhl. "But I never saw the same one twice."

"I just wish you were single so we could run around," Barry would tell Chip Arrington. "We'd be great together."

But with his charm, physique, fancy car, and pocket full of money, Barry didn't really need Arrington in order to do well with the ladies. "Barry wasn't the best-looking guy in town," says Chip, "but he had that car and all that money. And he really knew how to act big-time. When the show was on, the dough was there."

While the key to Barry's success in philandering may have rested on his money and charm, the key to his philandering *opportunities* lay in his getting rid of Joyce. Not permanently, of course, for Joyce Lipman undoubtedly provided Barry with the structure, the consistency, and the status (as the daughter of a man with a sterling reputation as an associate superintendent of a nearby school district) that Barry surely found comforting.

But Jesus *Christ*, was it fair to ask a high-spirited young man, already proclaimed by the press as a millionaire Boy Wonder, to pass up all those Valley Girls just ripe for the taking?

So on occasion Barry would suggest to Joyce that she take a trip to Palm Springs, or to Hawaii, with Barry naturally footing the bill. When Joyce would protest, as was understandable, that she didn't want to go alone, Barry would say, fine, take a girlfriend with you, it'll be on me, too. "Then," says Chip Arrington, "it would be party time!" And Barry would reach into his wallet, pull out fifty or a hundred bucks, and tell Arthur to get lost for the night. "Take Joyce's car," he'd add.

— 3 —

IT WAS ANOTHER OF THE MYSTERIES of Barry Minkow just how, at such a relatively young age, he could absorb so much of what he needed to know, evaluate it, and use it for his advantage.

But he could. And it was this—even more than his charm, charisma, and talent for homing in on a person's weakness and using it to his advantage; even more than his energy; even more than his ability to believe utterly his own lies—that would turn out to be his genius.

He was able to go into a situation, absorb the jargon, the language, the inflection, the attitude of those around him—and make them his own.

Even more importantly, in the things he cared about—that is, money and finance—he was also able to quickly pick up the infor-mation he needed. And in Maurice Rind, he found a teacher who would explain the concepts, and guide him through the process of making ZZZZ Best a public company.

Even before meeting Maurice, Barry understood the whole purpose of becoming a public company: to have shares that are acquired cheaply and then sold at a high margin of profit or kept to rise in value as other investors are attracted to the corporation.

And he surely understood that advertising and PR can be as

*important in raising the price of a stock—and thereby its worth—as
they are in selling a product.*

*But it was Maurice who would show Barry Minkow the ins and
outs and provide the expertise that would take him to Wall Street.*

It was clear to Maurice Rind after one look at Barry's best
doctored paperwork (which Maurice probably did not know had
been doctored) that the *only* way that ZZZZ Best could be brought
public was through a kind of backdoor method called a shell route.
There were just too many problems—even with the restoration
jobs—to consider anything else. Carpet cleaning was not a fast-
growth industry; the company was too young, and so was Barry;
ZZZZ Best had no track record to speak of and no hard assets.

Besides, ZZZZ Best's current books and records would never
survive the lengthy, complex screening process required by the
SEC to become a public company. Rind was familiar with the shell
route, however, and decided to try it.

A shell corporation is a company that is already public, whose
stock can be bought and sold, and that is currently registered with
the SEC. For a variety of reasons, however—usually because it has
lost money over a period of time—the company, although still in
existence, has ceased doing business.

A private company like ZZZZ Best wishing to become a public
one can seek out such a shell corporation and, by merging with it or
simply buying it outright, can acquire the corporation's rights as a
public company. It's a common, perfectly legal practice, a simple
way for a private company to quickly become a public one.

In the case of ZZZZ Best, it just might work, reasoned Rind.

So Maurice Rind got in touch with Harold Fischman, a New
York attorney and longtime business associate, who specialized in
the kind of shells in which Maurice was interested.

Rind then flew to New York, met with Fischman in his Manhattan office, and showed him a "due diligence package" compiled
from some records Barry had provided. Among them were a phony
financial statement of ZZZZ Best's last financial quarter and some
bank statements. "Everything," said Rind, "that's normally in such
a package."

Fischman looked the package over, and his immediate reaction
was that it wouldn't work, that carpet cleaning wasn't "dynamic,"
was in fact just a small-time, mom-and-pop industry that was
highly competitive and filled with bait-and-switch artists.

But Rind told Fischman—a man in his fifties, who, according

to Maurice, is a "connoisseur" who wears ascots and knows wines—
that the difference between other carpet-cleaning companies and
ZZZZ Best was that Barry had these big restoration jobs, jobs that
meant tremendous earnings for the company. Maurice even showed
him copies of the San Diego and Arroyo Grande jobs.

"Everything that happens after this is a fluke," says Rind.
"Harold knows me and thinks me and Richie are pros. If we're
putting up the money, he thinks we checked the jobs, made sure the
jobs are real 'cause we're sophisticated. We got credibility. Nobody
had any idea the jobs were unreal."

Fischman told Rind he wanted to take a closer look at Barry's
papers and would let him know.

So Rind flew back to California and a few days later called
Fischman, who was still undecided. Fischman wanted, he said, to
talk to Barry personally before he made up his mind.

When Harold Fischman called Barry Minkow, Fischman was
obviously impressed, for he informed Maurice that he intended to
go ahead and arrange the shell. "Barry," says Maurice, "was *very*
good on the phone." Fischman was hired to file all necessary
papers and was paid between $2,000 and $3,000 a month. The rest
of the arrangement to acquire the shell corporation took place,
according to Rind, between Barry and Fischman.

What was done, by Fischman, Rind, or both, was to acquire
Morningstar Investments, Inc., an inactive Utah mineral explora-
tion firm. Morningstar had all but collapsed, and Fischman and
Rind, acting for Barry, were able to buy its publicly owned shares
and subsume the company under ZZZZ Best. In return, Morningstar shareholders received stock in the newly merged company.

It was a slick, swift stroke that allowed ZZZZ Best to become a
publicly listed company without having to file a lot of papers and
meet a lot of SEC requirements.

In late December 1985, it was announced that ZZZZ Best was
buying Morningstar.

Barry was to gain the most from acquisition, receiving 76
percent of the shares (none of which, however, could be sold for two
years due to insider-trading laws), with the remaining 24 percent
to be offered for sale.

Many of those "free trading" or "unrestricted" shares were
quickly bought up by Rind, Victor, and Schulman for about a nickel
a share. In all, the three bought about a million shares, which were
divided in quarters among the three of them and Barry.

Unlike Barry's shares, however, these could be sold at any time.

But because they were worth so little, the only way Maurice and the others could make their killing was to puff up the stock, hype it all over town, tell all those would-be Ray Krocs out there how great Barry and ZZZZ Best were, how the company was about to set the world on fire, and how, if they were smart, they'd start buying in.

It was later said, never proved (in fact, heatedly denied) that Rind and the others went beyond the process of legal hype and created a false demand for ZZZZ Best's stock, that they traded it back and forth among themselves in order to raise the price and disseminated false information about the stock and its value. This is easy to do with a small company like ZZZZ Best, as the volume of the stock traded is so limited.

Whatever the case, Barry, Maurice, and Fischman (whom Rind called over 600 times between November 1985 and July 1987) were soon able to hype the stock to a dollar a share. That price was not, however, all that it appeared to be.

ZZZZ Best wasn't listed on any national stock exchange, but traded directly between individuals and brokers—there being no regulating body setting prices in this system of stock trading, known as trading in the pink sheets, as there is, say, with the New York Stock Exchange. So the stock is really worth whatever its market maker (who is hired by its owners) says it is, even if nobody is willing to buy it at that price.

But it was good for Rind and the boys, particularly for Barry, that the stock was at least being *quoted* at $1 a share. It enabled Barry with his 12 million shares of ZZZZ Best stock to say that he was worth $12 million, even though it was only on paper.

Although SEC regulations prohibited him from selling his stock before January 1988, Barry could still use the stock—with its puffed-up value—to attract investors to his restoration jobs, thereby showing increased business activity and further raising the value of the stock he held. This in turn would enable him to borrow additional money, using his increasingly high-priced stock as collateral.

Jeri Carr would have her work cut out for her in the next several months.

Before plunging into his PR campaign, however, Barry, along with Chip, Maurice, Victor, Dan Krowpman, and a few others, flew to Las Vegas to meet Harold Fischman and sign the papers finalizing ZZZZ Best's takeover of Morningstar.

They landed on Saturday afternoon, and the weekend turned

out to be one long gambling spree. "Barry *loved* craps and was obsessed with Vegas," says Chip Arrington. "The minute we got off the plane, Barry started gambling, and he gambled all day Saturday and all day Sunday."

Then on Monday, Barry was in the lobby with Chip, Victor, and Krowpman waiting to go sign the papers at a nearby hotel where Fischman and Rind were staying. Having a couple of minutes to spare, Barry decided to shoot a little craps and got on an ill-timed roll. "Chip," said Barry, "go up and tell them we've been delayed but we're on our way."

When Arrington conveyed this message to Fischman and Maurice, who were sitting there with some other lawyers involved in the deal, Maurice "nearly had a fit," Chip recalls. Barry had a check for $20,000 or $30,000 waiting for him, representing the cash assets of Morningstar, yet he was seriously late. Finally, growing impatient, Maurice put the question to Chip: "Where the fuck are they? Are they coming or what?" And Chip had to tell them, "Well, they're downstairs playin' craps." "Harold Fischman," recalls Chip, "couldn't believe it."

Sometime in February or early March, Arthur Uhl received a call from Ana Madrinan. Ana, the sister of Barry's adoring employee Elenora, as well as the Jeri Carr executive in charge of Barry's PR account, was calling to arrange a television interview.

Over the preceding month, Carr's agency had contacted more than fifty newspapers, magazines, and radio and TV shows regarding Barry's "new business ventures." The list included everyone from *Playboy* to *U.S. News and World Report*, from "20/20" to Johnny Carson, from the *Wall Street Journal* to *People* magazine.

Madrinan told Arthur that "PM Magazine," a local lifestyle or newsmagazine show similar to those featuring bikini bottoms and exotic travel that usually follow the network news, was coming to Barry's house to shoot him relaxing at home. They'd be taping at the office first, she explained, before coming to the house for the shooting, which was expected to take about four to five hours.

Several days later, as arranged, a van filled with TV equipment and cameras pulled in the Minkow driveway. With Barry still at his office being taped, and Jeri and Ana assisting there, it was left to Arthur to greet the camera crew, which quickly began discussing which room would be best to shoot in and where the lights should be placed, before setting up their equipment.

After several hours, Ana, Elenora, and Jeri Carr (whose monthly fee had recently been raised to $2,500) arrived, highly excited, to make sure everything would be just right when Barry and the reporting crew got there.

When Minkow and the others came in, Barry, says Arthur Uhl, was wearing "his usual schlepp clothes." The producer, seeing the formality of the living room in which the camera crew had decided to shoot Minkow, quickly called Arthur aside and asked if he might lay out two or three outfits for Barry that would coordinate with the living room backdrop.

Arthur readily agreed; he or Joyce usually had to dress Barry anyway whenever a special occasion arose. Otherwise, says Uhl, he'd "just grab anything."

Barry, meanwhile, was busy applying his magic touch to the camera and reporting crew. Although at his office he was *the boss*, whenever he was dealing with the press, Barry was savvy enough never to try to run the show. "He understood the media enough," says Jeri Carr, "to let them do what they wanted."

And, of course, Barry—no longer shy before the camera—had no trouble charming the newsmagazine TV people, whose specialty was superficial charm. "He had a way of building rapport with the media in less than thirty seconds," remembers Carr. "Whoever was interviewing him just automatically fell in love with him, or really got a kick out of what a high-strung, hyper individual he was."

Barry was also astutely solicitous of the camera crews, taking care to ensure that they were provided with cheese, crackers, and soft drinks, joking with them, and going out of his way to acknowledge their importance. But he was also wise enough to be smoothly professional when it was showtime.

As Barry dressed for the shooting, friends, neighbors, and family members began appearing, and soon, if one included the camera crew and Jeri Carr and her entourage, about twenty people were milling about.

After he'd changed, Barry was shot in the living room, out by the pool, in front of the house standing by his Ferrari, and finally at the dining room table, talking nonchalantly, as he'd been asked to do by the producer, while being served pasta by the chef of a local restaurant he frequented. This last scene Arthur thought a poor idea, for Barry's atrocious table manners were legend, and Uhl found himself inwardly wincing with each "fistful of pasta that Barry shoved in his mouth."

But the pasta sequence was never shown. Instead, the story on "PM Magazine" was to prove remarkably similar to others about Minkow that appeared on equally indistinguishable newsmagazine shows like KCBS's "Two on the Town" or KABC's "Eye on LA"; or on any of half a dozen local news broadcasts. Basically the stories were much alike:

1. A cute introduction centering around Minkow's tender age
2. Details of Barry's net worth and meteoric rise
3. A shot of Barry working out ("The Rambo of Carpet Cleaning," said "Eye on LA.")
4. Mention of his Ferrari
5. Characterizations of ZZZZ Best, using Barry's new self-promotional line: "The General Motors of Carpet Cleaning"
6. A Chamber of Commerce pitch by either Barry or the journalist ("Barry Minkow is proof," enthused KABC reporter Joe McMahan, "that if you've got the right idea at the right time and you're willing to work, you can still make millions of dollars in this country!")
7. A few modest words from Barry (to "Two on the Town" on his new house: "This is only a $900,000 or million-dollar house. In Beverly Hills, a million-dollar house is a dump.")

The PR campaign, which had always been designed to promote ZZZZ Best's carpet-cleaning services and lure new investors, now took on the additional mission of hyping ZZZZ Best stock, occasionally assisted by Maurice Rind, who came up with "The General Motors of Carpet Cleaning" motto.

Six women worked full- or part-time on Barry's account—updating the press kit; booking him for speeches at places like the University of Nevada at Las Vegas, Arizona State University, UCLA, and the Los Angeles Chamber of Commerce; making calls to newspapers, magazines, and radio and TV stations; pushing Minkow's book; and churning out press releases on each of Barry's latest phenomenal accomplishments or selfless acts of charity. Thanks to these efforts, the media blitz began to pay off.

In addition to the TV coverage, there were stories about Barry in the *LA Times*, the *LA Herald-Examiner*, and other local papers, and then nationally in *Newsweek*, *Barron's*, *USA Today*, and the *Washington Post*. Typical of the tone was the headline of an article in *Entrepreneur* magazine: "18-Year-Old Cleaning Mogul Makes the Rules and Plays by Them."

More often than not, the stories' content would describe a young, hardworking teenager from a modest background, on his way to becoming founder and chairman of the board of "the General Motors of the carpet-cleaning business." Later articles would tell of Barry Minkow, the soldier and crusader in the President's War on Drugs, or of the young lover of the free-enterprise system who, in the Age of Ronald Reagan, caught the entrepreneurial spirit and ran with it.

"The last five or six years," says Ana Madrinan, "were the Reagan years—having your own business, being an entrepreneur was a big story. Now if you were to try and push a client with that angle, it's not going to sell because the media is burned out on it. But at that time they liked it."

The extensive, almost exclusively favorable coverage given to Barry proved invaluable in promoting both his business and himself, and in enhancing his credibility with would-be investors.

Later, the press was criticized for not checking out Barry's story before printing it. But reporters on deadline had neither the the time to do so nor the grounds for suspicion.

If the press is to be criticized, however, it is for a failure of a different magnitude: allowing itself to be used as a willing tool in the selling and promotion of Barry Minkow, ZZZZ Best, and all that the media thought he stood for, and for taking the PR release and simply and uncritically going with it because it was the easy thing to do and because Barry was good happy-talk copy in an era that encouraged precisely that.

Some thought it was stealing his grandmother's jewelry. Others the time he flew out a loan officer from New York, wined, dined, and romanced her—got the loan—and then bounced the check he'd written as reimbursement for her airfare. But Barry himself always says that the "worst conduct [he] ever displayed as a human being" was a relatively minor incident in which he urged Dan Krowpman, Jr.—Danny's son—to stomp on the glasses of Bill Swanson.

Early in 1986, Swanson's wife had bought about $25 worth of flowers from a small Valley shop called Floral Fantasies, using her credit card for the purchase. The next month, the Swansons received the bill. It was for over $600—a bit higher than they'd anticipated. It would be several months, however, before Bill Swanson was to meet Krowpman's son and Barry. Or to discover that

Barry Minkow was once again working a credit card scam.

Ever desperate for cash to pay his past loans, Barry had secretly bought Floral Fantasies, and almost immediately started overcharging credit card customers.

Anxious to avoid the appearance that he was diversifying just as ZZZZ Best was taking off, he had talked the ever-faithful Chip Arrington into putting the shop in his name. It wouldn't be a problem; they'd sign an agreement absolving Arrington of any financial responsibility should anything go wrong, Barry assured him.

As an added sweetener, Barry also offered to make Chip's wife, Lulu, the shop's manager. Arrington had never been able to say no to Minkow, and now that Chip was driving around in a new car leased by ZZZZ Best, making payments on a new house, being CEO of Barry's company and in a position to make really big money, he found it even harder to refuse. So he agreed.

Then, in January, customers like Swanson started coming into the shop complaining to Lulu about the overcharges.

When Chip told Barry, he got annoyed. What was he worrying about? They had an agreement, didn't they? It wasn't Chip's problem even if something *was* wrong, so why didn't he just forget it?

As the volume of complaints increased, however, Chip, whose name was on the merchant credit card account, finally got up the nerve to demand that Barry transfer the shop and the account out of his name. And Barry did—but not before he'd run up about $90,000 in false charges. (Some of the same credit card numbers were also run through Robert Victor's gas station. It was never clear, however, if Victor, who had been convicted of credit card fraud in the past, was a willing participant or just running them through as a favor to Barry. But when the flower shop was sold, it was Victor who bought it.)

In any case, this time the merchant credit account Barry was using was from California Overseas Bank, an institution without a kindly Robert Turnbow, and one that—unlike West Valley Bank— was not about to go out of business.

Barry therefore had to make the charges good, paying back the bank, which had originally honored them, but also getting his needed forty-five days' to six months' float time in the process.

He didn't reimburse the bank for *all* the money, however. A few of those bilked had been told by Barry that he'd ensure that they received a credit on their bill from the credit card company.

One of them was Robin Swanson, Bill's wife. But Barry did nothing, and eventually the Swansons were told by their credit card management that the problem had been reported too late, that *they* would be responsible for paying the charge.

Irate, they filed suit against Barry, and Bill Swanson went to Barry's office to serve him with a subpoena. It was at that point that Barry exhibited his self-described worst conduct.

After first trying to serve Barry's father, Swanson encountered Barry in the parking lot with Dan Krowpman, Jr., and a couple of other friends.

Handing him the subpoena, Swanson said, "You're now served." Barry took it, crumpled it up, threw it to the ground, and told the forty-eight-year-old Swanson not to bother him about "chump change."

Then, as Swanson started walking toward his car, Danny Jr. popped him a couple of times in the head, sending his glasses flying. As Swanson bent down, trying to retrieve them, Krowpman picked them up, gestured as if he was going to hand them to Swanson—who was saying over and over, "Please give me my glasses, please give me my glasses"—and instead, threw them to the ground, stomped on them, and, as Swanson retreated into his car, started kicking it.

All the while, Barry, a con man but no thug, stood on the sidelines enthusiastically cheering Danny Jr. on. "Get him, get him!" Barry shouted. "He deserves it. He deserves what he's getting."

Nothing came out of the incident, nor, for the time being, did Barry face any problems as a result of the $90,000 fraud. When a security firm employed by the bank told him they were preparing a report for the Secret Service, Barry quickly agreed to reimburse the bank, and the bank told the security firm to back off. They, in turn, called the Secret Service and said they no longer had a victim, and the case was dropped.

Once again, it appeared a mini-cure had been found. But *this* scam, whose benefits in light of the big events to come might truly be thought of as "chump change," would come back to haunt Barry Minkow.

Simultaneously with the Floral Fantasies credit card fraud, Barry was reviving yet another old swindle, this one a variation of his earlier stolen-phony-equipment insurance fraud. Like almost every Minkow con, its chief purpose was to get money to keep the float going, pay off his most pressing debts, and continue making all those monthly payments.

Using his Ferrari, his house, ZZZZ Best trucks, his new, re- vised phony financial statements and tax returns, and other more complex forms of collateral (he would use the Ferrari's pink slip dozens of times as collateral for loans, frequently pledging the same collateral to four or five lenders simultaneously), Barry would borrow money from loan and leasing companies to buy cleaning equipment.

He needed the equipment, he would tell the loan officers, to expand his carpet locations (eight or nine were to be opened in 1986) and to handle ZZZZ Best's rapidly increasing volume of restoration business. As usual, he needed the money up front to buy the equipment before opening the locations or starting the restora- tion jobs.

Then he'd negotiate a loan to purchase the equipment. On the average, the loans were for about $100,000, with Barry exaggerat- ing the price of each machine to be purchased. An industrial steam cleaner, for example, typically costs about $575 and at most $900, but Barry's fictitious steam cleaners were listed on the loan as costing $4,500 each.

He even got a loan for a nonexistent drapery-cleaning machine. The machine was big and efficient, Barry said, and able to clean the drapes for all of ZZZZ Best's jobs—that's why it cost *$61,000*.

Starting about February 1986, and over the next year and a half, Barry borrowed more than $1 million in this fashion.

The high interest rates he was willing to pay, as always, accounted for much of the relative ease with which Barry was able to get the loans. And Barry was also his usual believable, seem- ingly reliable self, quick to return phone calls and come up with an answer to any question or with paperwork to match any request.

Leasing and loan companies, moreover, rarely inspected the equipment to be bought. "I'd never see my wife if I inspected all the equipment we lent money on to be leased," one loan officer said.

And if, as was the case with Linna Currie (a manager in the leasing division of an Encino thrift and loan association), a loan officer *did* decide to take a look around and check things out, well, they'd see what Currie saw: a bustling office with carpet cleaners coming in and out, Barry on the phone talking with his stock- broker, and the appearance that everything was as he had said.

On the particular day that Currie visited ZZZZ Best, she also saw that Barry "was impressed, really impressed" with the fact that he was getting ready to be taped for the TV newsmagazine "Eye on LA." "*I* was impressed, too," says Currie.

But the biggest factor in putting the minds of loan officers at ease was the fact that their money was going to be used exactly as Barry had said, for the purchase of new equipment, and would be paid directly to the equipment vendor. Barry would then "buy" the equipment from the lenders with his monthly loan payments. *He*, theoretically, would never touch the loan money.

The loan officers, however, had no idea that Cornwell Quality Tools and Equipment—which was allegedly selling Barry the machines—didn't make carpet-cleaning equipment and had nothing to do with the deals.

Rather, it was Dan Krowpman, working independently of his hand-tool supplier, Cornwell, who would sign the forms stating that he'd sent Barry the equipment, and who would receive the checks from the loan companies for the nonexistent equipment. Danny would then cash the checks and turn the money over to Barry, usually keeping about 25 percent for himself, making $25,000 for a few minutes' work on a $100,000 loan.

In addition to financing the float and Barry's standard of living, the arrangement also added another tier of paperwork to prove the reality of the restoration jobs.

But despite all the invoices from Cornwell and other bogus suppliers, paperwork was still Barry's weak suit. Barry was a con man, and a superb one—glib, charming, audacious, amoral, fast on his feet, able to read people quickly. But a forger he was not. A lot of the documents created thus far had been his handiwork, but he certainly wasn't first-class. At times, in fact, Barry could actually be quite sloppy, lacking the skill and patience to visualize and produce truly creative documents like the phony bank statements, cashier's checks, and completion bonds he needed. Tom Padgett was even less suited to the task, as was Dan Krowpman, who in any case was only marginally involved in the scheme.

From the beginning, lack of good, convincing documents had been a problem for Barry. Not with investors like Kay, but with banks, particularly the big ones in a position to make the kind of big loans Barry craved.

He had had some success, however, with the set of tax returns Jack Catain and John Miller had prepared for him back in the summer of 1985, and shortly thereafter he made a call to their creator, and arranged for him to start working for ZZZZ Best one day a week, doing some bookkeeping and assembling a loan package for banks. Six months later, the man would go to work with Barry full-time. Like Jack Catain bringing in big money from investors, and Maurice Rind bringing ZZZZ Best public, this man would raise the scam to a new, far higher level than he'd found it. Unlike them, however, he would be precisely aware of what he was doing.

His name was Mark Morze, and with him Barry Minkow had found the vital link to put it all together.

— 4 —

IN HIS MIDTHIRTIES, broad and stocky, with a blond beard, thinning hair, and a body that was turning to fat, Mark Morze perfectly projected an LA postcollegiate style: sports car, sports clothes, success. He was the power-breakfast man on the move known for doing everything fast. He drove his Mercedes 450 SL convertible fast. He talked fast, moved fast, and made decisions fast. Arriving for a meeting in full stride, he would immediately excuse himself to get to a phone and readjust his overbooked schedule. Then, with the meeting hardly begun, he'd jump up and announce how sorry he was, but he really *did* have to get on to his next appointment. "Mark was the kind of a guy," says Tom Padgett, "who'd read the paper, shave, and drive his car at the same time."

At UCLA in the early seventies, he'd known the school's famed football coach, Terry Donahue, on a first-name basis, won a letter as a linebacker on the varsity football team, and pledged Sigma Alpha Epsilon. Later, as a graduate student, he worked as an assistant football coach and as a player-coach on one of the intramural rugby teams, and never hesitated to buy the round of beer after a practice. Along the way, he picked up a degree in history and joined the Football Alumni Club.

He was a loyal Bruin, a university man, known as a good but not great player—solid on and off the field, with a gutsy quality that at times enabled him to explode and go beyond his physical limitations.

He'd grown up poor in suburban Detroit. His father, a physicist, had died when Mark was five. His mother struggled to support him, his two older brothers, and a younger sister, but the family suffered hardships and was often evicted for nonpayment of rent. They moved to Los Angeles when Mark was twelve.

His first day at LA's heavily black and Hispanic Virgil Junior High, he was lying on the steps, getting a tan when a bunch of Hispanics, spotting his blond hair and blue eyes, walked up and asked if he was a surfer. "What's a surfer?" replied Mark, who'd just moved into a downtown hotel frequented by hookers and truly didn't know. The Mexican guys kicked the shit out of him.

After school and into the evening, he sold the *Herald-Examiner* on Third and Vermont in the old streetcar zone, working the same corner with half a dozen prostitutes, who'd tip him a buck for serving as an intermediary with their customers.

By the time he was old enough to enter high school, the family had moved to the Valley suburb of Van Nuys, where Mark worked his way through school and ran track and played on the football team before going on to UCLA.

After graduation, he had no definite plans. But with his ambition, charm, and intelligence, it seemed likely that Mark Morze would one day scale the heights of Southern California's corporate hierarchy.

But Mark Morze was no company man, and he opted for a more independent lifestyle. Perhaps his love of long-legged cocktail waitresses and the action in Vegas had something to do with it. For Mark Morze, Valhalla was not a castle in the clouds but a penthouse suite at the Imperial Palace Hotel right across from Caesar's Palace on the strip. And over eighteen months, on at least forty-seven different weekends in 1986 and 1987—when the money was good and he and Barry and Tom were riding high—a penthouse suite at the Imperial was exactly where one would find him.

There he was known and loved by the craps dealers as Mr. M because of his big-tipping ways. "Hey, Mr. M!" they would shout, "when you gonna come down to my table?" And those cocktail waitresses cut into those little blue outfits, Mark must have dated a dozen of them.

Mark loved the shows, too. Nudes on Ice, Folies-Bergère, Tom Jones, Rodney Dangerfield, Cher—and all on the house because he was such a high roller. It was just like "Love Boat" or "Fantasy Island." The decadence, the escape, it all appealed to Mark Morze.

And so did the freedom from the constraints of a regimented corporate lifestyle. In the midseventies, wanting to maintain his independence, Morze took what he describes as "an H & R Block type of class on how to do taxes," and founded a small bookkeeping firm. He prepared tax returns, profit-and-loss statements, and loan applications for small businesses, occasionally inflating figures, and now and then preparing some phony paperwork as he'd done for Barry, but for the most part running a legitimate business.

By the time he met Barry, Mark had built a clientele of about one hundred mom-and-pop customers in the Valley: liquor stores, dry cleaners, auto-repair shops, and other small businesses. He wasn't a CPA, but he'd give his clients advice and do their paperwork, charging them about $100 a month for a profit-and-loss statement and $200 at the end of the year for doing their taxes.

He made a good living that way, but it was beer money for a man with champagne taste.

Moreover, when Mark first started working with Barry, his attempt at opening a health club had just failed, and he'd been forced to declare bankruptcy, losing $10,000 as a result.

So he was more than receptive when Minkow proposed he go to work for ZZZZ Best one day a week. Mark needed all the money he could get.

Barry also needed Mark. He'd heard about what a good bookkeeper Mark was and that he also knew a lot about the loan situation in the Valley, things like which banks wanted to see tax returns, which would just settle for an adjusted statement, and the best way to approach bankers. Barry needed someone with that kind of expertise to help him assemble financial packages, as well as find a CPA who would sign off on an audit statement.

After starting work, Morze initially spent most of his time trying to line up loans and a CPA.

But finding a CPA initially proved impossible. Mark contacted about a dozen, but none were willing to sign their name to an audit without all the necessary documentation—documentation that Barry was unable to provide. Some documents had been stolen, Barry told Mark, much of the rest had been water-damaged.

At this stage, says Morze, he suspected nothing. ZZZZ Best's monthly bank statements showed a lot of money passing through the company's accounts, and Mark was impressed. (Much of that money, he was later to learn, was from loans made by Kay Rosario and her investment group.)

True, there were some papers and cancelled checks that Mark found baffling—for example, the quarter of a million dollars that seemed to fit nowhere within the income and debit categories he'd been establishing for ZZZZ Best's books. When he questioned Barry about it, Minkow casually told him not to worry but just to go ahead and record the money under "San Diego Job."

There was also the check for $5,300 that had to be paid out every week but seemed to have nothing to do with the rest of ZZZZ Best's expenses. Barry explained that, however. The check was the payroll for the San Diego job. (In reality, it was the juice for Kay, that is, the weekly interest check that Barry had to pay to Rosario and her investors.)

Mark took these explanations at face value, he says, and set to work putting together the semblance of a "financial package" from whatever records Barry *had* maintained. He retyped the job invoices, the bank statements, and the phony equipment and material purchases and leases from Dan Krowpman, and then had them bound so they'd look more professional. "Bankers like that," Morze pointed out.

Later, with the help of a loan broker he knew, a bound ZZZZ Best "bible" would be assembled, consisting—in addition to the invoices, bank statements, and equipment leases—of financial projections, tax returns, newspaper clips, and letters from movie stars and celebrities attesting to what a good job ZZZZ Best had done cleaning their carpet. "Ninety percent was easy to get," says Morze. "The carpet cleaning was all real—so when we put it all together, it looked just like a prospectus. If they [the banks or investors] had any questions, we'd hand them the 'bible' and say, 'Here're the answers.'"

With the initial financial papers bound and assembled by Morze, Barry managed to get two short-term bank loans, one for $50,000, the other for $35,000.

Barry also showed the bound statement (which, says Morze, "really looked good") to Victor, Rind, and Jay Botchman when he was attempting to get his first $1 million line of credit from Jay's J & B Equity factoring company.

As the weeks passed, Mark Morze became indispensable to Barry Minkow and ZZZZ Best. "Barry couldn't seem to praise Mark enough," says Tom Padgett, "how good he was, how ambitious, how brilliant. I never saw him so high on anybody."

So it wasn't at all surprising when Barry asked Mark in early

1986 to sell his bookkeeping practice and come to work for ZZZZ Best full-time. Barry offered him $100,000 a year plus bonuses and a finder's fee for bringing in new investors. Morze immediately took Barry up on his offer.

"I saw the excitement Barry was generating," Morze says, "and really believed his shtick. I bought the 'General Motors of Carpet Cleaning' routine, the 'one [carpet-cleaning location] on every corner' bit, the 'more outlets than McDonald's.' The ideas Barry had were really great. I could see myself making $200,000 to $300,000 within a year."

"And there was [also] a *lot* of work getting done," Morze recalls. "There were cleaning crews downstairs [from Barry's office]—dozens of guys going out every day and cleaning carpets.... It was all very impressive."

Whether Mark was indeed that innocent or on to the hustle from the beginning, his hiring was Barry's master stroke. For Mark Morze turned out to be a genius at cooking the books: coming up with paperwork that didn't exist, projecting bogus future earnings to investors, detailing the alleged expenses for the restoration jobs, making out phony insurance company payment schedules, and fixing that which *was* real so it read any way you wanted it to.

But of almost equal importance, he also had a rare ability to talk to people face to face in a quick, sharp, believable way, acting likable, looking presentable, sounding logical, and always coming up with the right excuse when needed. Mark would, in fact, have everything going for him except one thing: all that he would say was a lie.

— 5 —

IT WAS MARCH 1986, the day after the Hagler–Mugabee fight, and Tom Padgett was not happy. Much to his disgust, the TV reception in the Valley had gone bad during the bout, and Padgett, who'd been worked up for the match, had missed most of it.

But Jay Botchman had been at ringside that night and was able to tell Tom some of what happened. Not much, of course; they'd only just met and were together in any case on business.

They were at the Beverly Wilshire—along with Barry, Maurice

Rind, and Robert Victor—to discuss a new loan for $2.1 million. Barry had told Rind and Victor he needed that much to proceed with a staggering $7.5 million restoration job in Sacramento. (The highest-priced *legitimate* restoration job ever done was for about $2 million after the MGM Grand fire in Las Vegas.) They in turn prevailed on Richie Schulman to call Jay Botchman for the additional loan.

Before loaning *that* kind of money, however, Botchman wanted to talk to Barry personally, meet Tom Padgett, and find out more about Interstate Appraisal, which was, after all, giving ZZZZ Best the job. Despite any misgivings, Botchman was attracted by the terms Barry was willing to pay: 2 percent interest per month on a loan due for repayment in 120 to 200 days.

The meeting began with Jay asking Tom a few questions between puffs on his cigar. Tom, by way of reply, went into a variation of his standard rap: The water tank on the building had collapsed, he told them, soaking everything and ruining the plumbing. With the cost of drying the new carpets and replacing the drywall and the plumbing, the expenses were going to be unbelievable.

As Tom went through his routine, he felt fairly comfortable, and was made even more so by Jay Botchman, "a polite gentleman" who insisted that Tom please call him Jay, not Mr. Botchman. Botchman, however, was no innocent and later that year would be closely linked to—but never charged in—a massive $80 million Atlantic City, New Jersey, development fraud. In addition, Barry was later to claim that, as part of the deal he would make with Botchman, he had to give him back between $300,000 and $400,000 off the top and under the table when the loan money came through. That claim, however, was also never substantiated.

But apparently Tom Padgett's rap wasn't quite as good as he thought, for Jay Botchman flew back to New Jersey uncommitted. Several days later, after Barry had called Jay pretending to be Padgett—because *nobody*, says Padgett, "had Barry's gift for talking when it came to money"—Jay Botchman phoned back and told them he'd make the loan. It was the biggest restoration job they'd ever gotten, Barry told Botchman, and he was grateful that Jay was coming through with the capital. Otherwise, Padgett would have had to give it to someone else. When the conversation ended, Barry and Tom were beside themselves with glee. "The Sacramento job! $2.1 million for the Sacramento job! How about

$180 million for a job in Boston! How about a couple of billion to restore the Sphinx!"

But as things turned out, it wasn't quite so easy.

Botchman was still uneasy and later called back to say he couldn't make the loan until Minkow had first paid off the remaining principal on the original $1 million loan from Jay. Barry had already reduced that loan considerably—getting it down to a couple of hundred thousand dollars—but he had to make it all good, he was told, before the new loan would be approved. Having no other choice, Barry agreed to meet the stipulation. To do so, however, he was going to have to "hustle around like a maniac," as Mark Morze put it, to get the money to pay off the remaining debt.

One possibility was a Burbank factoring company called California Factors and Finance (Cal Factor) that had recently made a high-yield, short-term loan to Barry, which he had managed to pay back on time and in full. It seemed logical, therefore, that they'd be willing to make another, similar loan.

So Barry called Tom, and they made an appointment to go to Cal Factor.

On the way to the meeting in Burbank, Padgett was in an expansive mood and told Barry about how he'd recently been thinking about owning his own insurance company. They could start first, he explained, with a small insurance agency, expand into underwriting, and later even add an appraisal service. "That's a great idea, Tom," said Barry as he drove. "Who we gonna rip off, ourselves?"

At Cal Factor, things did not go as well as anticipated.

Tom was spouting his usual rap, and Barry was waving around a bogus but sufficiently real-looking job invoice from the Arroyo Grande restoration site. But Tony, the loan officer who'd approved the previous loan, and Dale, his partner, were not buying.

Dale in particular, was skeptical. In his early forties, with short hair, K mart business clothes, and a small, trimmed cop mustache, he was the kind of guy Tom Padgett instantly loathed: as square, humorless, and straight in his thoughts as he was in his appearance, with that cold and sober cop attitude that set Padgett's teeth on edge. Mark Morze had a phrase for men like Dale. "Deal busters," Morze would call them.

Dale was asking all the wrong questions, and not in a really friendly way. Tony, however, was more conciliatory, explaining that while they'd been delighted that this first loan had been repaid in full and on time, they nonetheless were *still* a little nervous. When they'd made Barry the loan, he'd agreed that the payments were to come *directly* from the insurance firms in the form of company checks made out to ZZZZ Best and signed over to Cal Factor. But instead, they'd received cashier's checks without even a letterhead, signed by Tom Padgett. *That* made them nervous.

It was nothing personal, Tony continued, but they'd rather do business with a major insurance company. Padgett's Interstate Appraisal Services just wasn't strong enough for them to bank on, particularly since Padgett had stipulated that they could neither directly contact the insurance company nor visit the job site. The "comfort factor" wasn't there with a small, new company like Tom's, said Tony.

On the other hand, Barry *had* paid off the previous loan and was willing to pay the maximum interest allowed by law for the new loan, which was not some nickel-and-dime auto loan, but one that would involve serious profits on interest.

It was agreed, therefore, that both parties would see what they could do to make the loan happen. Cal Factor would start to process it, and Tom and Barry would see if they could find a way around the insurance company's desire for anonymity and show them an insurance company check they'd received in payment for the first loan.

Unhappily, over the next several days, Tom Padgett started getting calls from Dale with questions that he *did not want to hear*. "Tom," Dale would ask, "what's the address of that job in Arroyo Grande? I'm going up there this weekend with my family, and I'd like to take a look at it." And Tom Padgett, who was *never* in when someone called his office precisely because he didn't want to answer questions like that, had to hem and haw before telling Dale he was at a meeting and would get back to him, which, of course, he never did.

But Dale was not to be put off, and when he couldn't reach Tom again at the office, he called him at home, again asking for the address of the Arroyo Grande job site. All Padgett could do was stammer that he didn't have the file at his apartment and that he'd call him when he got to his office. "Christ," thought Padgett as he phoned Barry to find out what to do, "something is really not ringing true to this guy." When Tom got ahold of Barry and told him about Dale's latest call, Minkow told him to sit tight, that he'd thought of a possible way to cool the guy out.

That same April week, Barry called Mark Morze into his office and announced that he had a serious problem.

The final payments on his loan from Jay Botchman had to be paid before Jay would make the new loan, he told Mark, and it looked like he was going to have trouble finding the money. He had intended to pay Jay by obtaining a new loan from Cal Factor, but Cal Factor was busting his ass, wanting to see an insurance company check or inspect the Arroyo Grande job site before making another loan. Normally, Barry explained, he'd just tell them to forget it, that it was Padgett's policy never to pay in that way or to allow such visits. But he was tapped out and didn't know how he'd be able to pay Jay without the money from Cal Factor, so he *had* to deal with them.

"So what's the problem?" Morze asked. "If they really want to see the job site, let 'em see the job site."

"Look, Mark," Barry finally said, "*here's* the problem. There is no Arroyo Grande job. It doesn't exist and never has. I made it up to get some cash to tide us over until we got Jay paid off; I just picked the name off a map."

Located a six- or seven-hour car ride north of LA, Arroyo Grande was far enough away, explained Barry, that nobody was likely to check up on it. But with Cal Factor now demanding to see a site or an insurance company check that didn't exist, he'd have to come across with *something* to appease them. He needed Mark to go up to Arroyo Grande, find the biggest building in town, and take some pictures of it that Barry could use at an upcoming meeting at Cal Factor.

Morze knew that the $2 million–plus loan from Jay Botchman depended on this loan from Cal Factor and that, if the deal fell through, it was going to be extraordinarily difficult to come up with any other money.

More importantly to Mark, Barry already owed him at least $50,000 to $60,000—money that Morze would never see if Minkow's elaborate Ponzi started to unravel.

As he later said, it seemed "a stupid way to try to float money," but, considering that Cal Factor had already been repaid, "a rather harmless lie." And even though he knew what Barry was asking was illegal, it certainly "didn't seem monumental." In any case, it appeared to be the only way out.

So he agreed.

Wednesday, Barry called Padgett and told him that he'd scheduled a meeting at Cal Factor for Friday, but that the news wasn't good—Dale and Tony were still insisting on seeing an insurance company draft.

Trying to come up with a solution—any solution—they continued endlessly kicking around ideas. The only one that seemed remotely feasible was to wire $100,000 into Travelers Corporation's bank account (Tom knew the account number), call Travelers immediately afterward, say they'd made a terrible blunder, and ask the insurance company to return the money in the form of a check made out to ZZZZ Best. Then, with check in hand, they'd be able to go to Cal Factor and show Dale and Tony what they'd asked for: a major insurance company check made out to Barry's company.

But it was too complex, too iffy, too fraught with problems, and they decided against it. If Cal Factor was going to insist on an insurance check, they'd just have to take their chances. And who knew, maybe Morze would come up with something.

Mark's Mercedes had been in an accident, so he rented a little Escort for the trek up to Arroyo Grande. He had no idea what to expect when he got there, but he certainly wasn't expecting the sleepy little town that he found. "It made Santa Barbara look like a throbbing metropolis," Morze said later.

The restoration job was supposed to be on an eight-story building, but as Mark drove around, it began to dawn on him that there was no eight-story building in the entire town. In fact, there wasn't a building over three stories.

So Mark Morze decided to make the best of it and do what he had to.

Stopping at the local Thrifty's, he bought a Polaroid camera, selected a building—a two-story building—went inside, told the management he was thinking of renting an office and needed to take a few pictures for his boss, got permission, and snapped away.

Then he went outside, laid on his back in the hope of finding an angle that would make the two stories look like eight, carefully aimed his camera so as to cut off the building's top, took a half-dozen pictures, got up, and headed back to LA.

Friday morning, Barry and Tom arrived at Cal Factor, and it immediately became apparent that something was wrong.

Barry, as usual, was going around flirting with the secretaries, pimping them along, laying on his typical rap: "Hi, babe," "Hey, babe, love you," "Wow! Are *you* looking good; let's get married"—the little goofs and snaps Barry always did that were as funny and charming as they were obvious.

But on this day nobody was responding.

Blithely ignoring the cold shoulder, Barry then floated over to Tony, told him Tom had a number of appointments to go to, and asked if they might have the meeting right away.

Tony, who'd always been the friendly member of the loan team, took Tom and Barry aback with the harshness of his reply: "No," he said, "we're going to wait for Dale."

"Jesus, Barry," Tom whispered after Tony walked away, "something's real wrong here. How much money do we owe them?"

"Nothing," said Barry. "Everything's paid, relax."

Finally Dale came in and went to the rear of the office to get some coffee. "God," thought Padgett, "let's get this *over*."

Coffee in hand, Dale walked into Tony's office, followed by Tony, Barry, and Padgett. After closing the door, Tony sat down, looked at Minkow and Padgett, and told them their line of credit had been pulled, and the new $400,000 loan they'd asked for would *not* be forthcoming.

"We understand," said Tony, "that the [restoration] jobs you've been using for loans either don't exist or don't exist with the insurance companies you say they do."

As Padgett listened, horrified, he realized that as a result of being too slick, they'd been found out.

To placate Cal Factor about the cashier's checks, Padgett had taken one of the letterheads he'd stolen while he worked for Travelers and typed the following letter for Tony above the forged signature of David Tengberg, his former boss. Addressed to Padgett at Interstate Appraisal, it read:

Dear Mr. Padgett,
    I wish I could be more helpful to you in this matter, but as you well know, claims of large dollar amounts are paid

by wire or cashier's check [only]. . . . [The reason is that] anything that amounts to more than $25,000 requires us to use a reserve account for payment.

Padgett and Barry had thought that the letter, which looked very official, might be enough to satisfy Cal Factor and get Tony and Dale off their backs. Instead, it had provided Tony and Dale with what they'd been looking for: a way to verify Barry and Tom's stories. True, they weren't supposed to contact any of the insurers, but Minkow was asking for $400,000.

Tony unfolded the story of how he had called Dave Tengberg, and how Tengberg told him that Padgett was an ex-employee, *not* a business associate, and that Travelers did no work with Interstate Appraisal or ZZZZ Best. As he listened, Tom Padgett mournfully thought about how obtaining a loan under false pretenses was a felony. And as Tony droned on, he mentally calculated the number of felonies they'd committed and the number of counts they were liable for. "All I want to do," thought Padgett, "is get out of here without wearing handcuffs."

When Mark Morze got back to LA, a message from Barry was waiting for him on his telephone answering machine. "We've got big problems at Cal Factor," the message said. "Get over there as soon as you can."

Morze, who'd known about the meeting before going to Arroyo Grande, arrived at Cal Factor about a half hour after the meeting had started. His heart was pounding, he remembers, as he pulled up just short of the building and looked around, half expecting to see police cars parked outside.

He waited for a few minutes, hating to go in but knowing he had to. Finally, he decided, "What the fuck, we've already paid them; what could happen?" and got out of his car and went inside.

As soon as Mark walked in, he could tell that something was wrong just by looking at Tom, Dale, and Tony. Barry, however, appeared perfectly normal as he held center stage and spoke with his usual high energy and utter conviction.

Quickly filled in as to the problem, Morze sat down and, with something between awe and amazement, listened as Barry continued talking.

"Of course, Dave Tengberg told you he wasn't doing business with ZZZZ Best," Barry was saying to Tony. "He was under orders to deny any knowledge of those claims."

"Wait," said Tony. "Are you sure you're talking about Dave Tengberg at Travelers?"

"Yeah, Dave Tengberg," Barry replied. "Big, tall Mormon guy. I know Dave real well. In fact, we had dinner together last night, but if you call him, he'll deny that too!"

Tony turned toward Tom and Dale and shrugged as if to ask, "Do you believe this guy?"

There was nothing Padgett could say. Given the situation, he was as amazed as Tony at Barry's explanation.

Barry, now wound up, apparently felt secure enough now to go on the offensive, and he demanded that Tony *prove* the jobs didn't exist.

This turned out to be the wrong tactic to take with Tony, a tall, fit martial arts instructor and ex-cop, who was beginning to strain to stay in control.

Furious that he'd been duped and insulted by the unabashed lies Barry was telling, Tony was now convinced that what Barry and Tom had really been trying to do all the time was set him up for *the big one*. By borrowing a couple of hundred thousand dollars, quickly paying it back, they'd get him feeling secure, then borrow some *big* money and get lost somewhere in the Yukon. That was what they had in mind, wasn't it? Tony wanted to know.

Barry told him not to be ridiculous, and again proceeded to babble away, with Tony all the while growing more furious. Padgett became convinced that if Barry didn't shut up, Tony was going to "ask them out in the alley."

Mercifully, Morze broke the tension by asking if there was anything they could do to salvage the situation.

The question seemed to calm Tony down, and after several minutes of further conciliatory remarks from Tom and Mark, he finally said that there was nothing they could do about *this* deal, but in the future, if they wanted a loan, Cal Factor would have to be permitted to see the jobs.

"In the future . . ."—the words swept over Tom Padgett with the uplifting force of a six-pack of Dos Equis. "In the future" meant they weren't going to press charges. "In the future" meant they weren't going to call the cops. Tom Padgett had heard all he needed to and could now just tune out the rest of the conversation and focus on that comforting thought: no charges, no cops. After awhile, he began to relax and wondered why he'd been so worried in the first place. Of course, they weren't going to press charges. They were businessmen, weren't they? Why would they want to get involved in a huge court fight? Why would they want all that negative publicity? They hadn't lost any money, had they? In fact, hadn't they *made* money?

Tom's more relaxed state of mind was further reinforced by the conversation he and Barry had after the Cal Factor meeting as they drove home in the Boy Wonder's Ferrari.

Barry, almost laughing, had told Tom to forget about it, no one had been hurt. And Tom replied that he knew, and that Barry was right. It was just as he'd told Barry at Allstate when Barry used to visit him as a kid. If everybody makes money and no one gets hurt, what's the problem?

Barry and Tom had hoped to walk out of Cal Factor with a $400,000 check in hand, which they intended to wire immediately to Jay Botchman. Jay, in turn, would send Barry the new $2.1 million loan, momentarily easing the incredible pressure to make good a whole host of loans Barry owed and to keep the Ponzi afloat.

Now, instead of having $400,000, they had nothing and would have to explain away this fact, not only to Jay but to Maurice and to Richie Schulman. For they'd both put their reputations on the line helping Barry to secure the loan from Jay.

To compound the pressure under which Barry and Padgett found themselves, they had to come up with an explanation *immediately*, for a conference call to Jay and Schulman was scheduled for that very afternoon.

As Barry and Tom arrived at Padgett's small Interstate Appraisal office in Van Nuys, they were met by Maurice and Victor, and together they walked back to the "hole in the wall" (as Tom called it), where he did business.

Immediately placing the call, Tom tried to keep his voice down so that Debbie in the front room—his secretary and object of his unrequited love—would not overhear the conversation.

He began to tell Jay that several insurance company checks they'd been counting on had been delayed because people had left early for the weekend, and that therefore they'd be unable to send his payment as planned that day. Barry started to cut in with an excuse, setting off Maurice Rind's always-close-to-the-surface volatility, and he screamed at Barry to shut up and let Tom talk.

Tom could do nothing more than stall, promising that Jay

would have his money by early the following week.

After the call, Maurice was still angry, but what could he do? If the checks had been delayed, they'd been delayed. The real crunch would come next week if they couldn't deliver.

After everybody'd left, Padgett went to the little refrigerator he kept in his office and popped open a beer. "You don't look so good," said Debbie.

Sunday, Barry called Tom and said he'd managed to raise $300,000 of the $400,000. He'd done so by sheer hustle, going to first one and then another of his smaller individual investors: men like Hal Berman who'd invested with Barry before, and were willing to help out because they liked him, the high interest he was promising, or both.

On Monday, Barry wired Botchman the $300,000 and got a message from Jay in return: "You owe me four hundred, not three hundred."

Over the next several days, in what Mark Morze calls "an unbelievable photo finish," Barry rounded up the additional $100,000 and sent it off. And Jay Botchman, true to his word, wired $2.1 million into ZZZZ Best's account at the tiny Bank of Granada Hills.

— 6 —

WHEN BARRY'S $2.1 MILLION reached the Bank of Granada Hills, the management was thrilled. That much money made Barry the largest depositor by far at the small local Valley bank, where the Boy Wonder was already regarded as a celebrity.

Everybody who worked there, it seemed, had seen Barry on TV, either on one of the news shows or on the ZZZZ Best commercials he was then doing.

Now their most famous customer—who'd drive up to the bank, talking into the car phone of his Ferrari and trailed by his right-hand man Mark Morze in his Mercedes—was also their biggest depositor.

Barry's star status at Granada Hills and other local banks was to go a long way in helping to avoid catastrophe, for Barry and Morze had been frantically rotating ZZZZ Best's limited funds among the Bank of Granada Hills, Wells Fargo, Security Pacific, and Charter Pacific Bank to keep up the illusion that ZZZZ Best had substantial deposits while they desperately waited for Jay's big check. If they'd continued to do it just one more day, says Mark Morze, they'd "probably all've been arrested." For the manager of Charter Pacific Bank of Agora and the manager of the Bank of Granada Hills both called Barry and "chewed him out for kiting checks," but they failed to take any punitive action—which they might well have done against a less prominent and less popular depositor.

When Jay's loan came in, Barry immediately pulled out three-quarters of it and made out checks to Kay Rosario and her investors. The money was repayment for their loans, plus profits, Barry told them, from the San Diego job.

Osher Portman, the bank's vice president, was disappointed in how quickly most of his bank's biggest deposit was withdrawn, but was later somewhat appeased when Barry redeposited much of that money as Kay and her investors turned their checks back to Minkow for reinvestment in another restoration job.

Impressed with Barry's Boy Wonder reputation as well as his big deposit, the Bank of Granada Hills agreed to make ZZZZ Best a loan for over $200,000, thus giving Barry the dual distinction of being not only the bank's (momentarily) biggest depositor but its biggest borrower as well.

He was the boy millionaire, and the bankers truly believed in his image and his rap. "They loved it all," says Mark Morze: "'My employees call me Mr. Minkow,' 'I'm in charge; it's my way or the highway,' 'I go to work at six,' 'I never take time off, and I've got a bleeding ulcer to prove it.' They really loved it. Every stockholder at that bank wanted Barry to marry their [sic] daughter."

It wasn't only the stockholders who loved Barry at the Bank of Granada Hills. Everybody there seemed awed and charmed by him.

"Barry *owned* that bank," says Mark Morze. "He was dating several of the women there, using them to get confidential information that he'd use to deal with the managers. These women were high school or junior college grads making four bucks an hour, who saw Barry as their ticket out. If they knew about Joyce, he'd tell them he was breaking up with her but had to do it slowly. It was really kind of pathetic; he'd use them up and wring them out like a sponge.

Morze says Barry also knew the buttons to push with bank managers, men in their late thirties or early forties. The button he pushed with these men, according to Morze, was their desire to make the kind of big money that at their age was clearly out of reach if they continued working at a bank.

"How much are you making here?" Barry would ask. "About $150,000?" (knowing full well they weren't making close to a third of that amount). "Well, pretty soon I'm gonna need somebody just like you to be my executive VP of finance; you think you might be interested?" Barry'd love to see them jump at the bait, says Morze, and would tickle Mark under the table or clandestinely wink at him as "the managers drooled at the thought."

Barry's courting of the bank managers enabled him to get instant credit on deposits, "a little float" on overdrafts, a little looking the other way when he factored his receivables or kited his checks. "They'd be just a little sloppy in their due diligence," says Mark Morze. "They had starlight in their eyes."

— 7 —

COMPARED TO THE GREAT Wall Street Drama in which Barry Minkow was soon to star, the farcical gangster episode he became involved in during the summer of 1986 was certainly nothing more than a colorful sideshow. What was significant, however, was how, at twenty, he just glided through it while simultaneously preparing his most spectacular score.

It all started, Arthur Uhl remembers, right around the time Joey moved into Barry's house in the early summer.

That first week or so, Arthur hadn't noticed what he was later to take for granted: that Joey was carrying a .45 on him at all times. Arthur discovered this fact quite by accident one day when, stopping by Joey's bedroom to drop off some laundry, he saw a gun and holster, along with "one of those straps that goes around the shoulder," atop the nightstand next to the bed on which Joey was lying.

Later that day, Uhl asked Barry what Joey was doing in the

house, and Barry told him that Joey was there "to make sure nothing happens."

Arthur nodded and decided not to inquire further. He had worked for enough wealthy people to know that bodyguards were not uncommon, and if Barry thought he needed one for business or personal reasons, it was not Arthur's place to ask why.

Had he investigated, however, he might have learned that Joey, that is, Joseph Mangiapane, was protecting Barry because of threats and phone calls Minkow had begun receiving from people connected to Jack Catain, and perhaps from Jack himself.

Mangiapane, forty-nine, had gotten the job through Maurice Rind, who had known Joey since they were teenage pals back in Queens. Maurice felt Mangiapane would be just the man for the position of live-in bodyguard, protecting Barry's house and person twenty-four hours a day for the next couple of weeks. For in addition to being a professional limousine driver and a man of quiet and reserve when he had to be, Joseph Mangiapane was also an ex-Army boxing champ who sometimes trained other boxers like Mike "the Bounty" Hunter—a fighter owned by Joey's old friend, the actor James Caan. When they were sixteen, says Maurice Rind, Joey gave Caan, who is also from Queens, a beating. "That's how far back they go." Joey was not a "made guy," according to Maurice, but he could handle himself."

But if Joseph Mangiapane was not "made," he was not strictly legitimate either, being available on at least one occasion for hire as a strong-arm man as well as a bodyguard. In 1987, in Los Angeles, he pleaded guilty to extortion—threatening and roughing up one businessman at the request of another, according to the charge.

Barry's need for a bodyguard began sometime in July 1986, five or six months after his break with Jack Catain and right around the time Barry had been subpoenaed by a federal grand jury looking further into Catain's affairs.

Catain was fearful of Barry and angry at him as well. His fear was that Barry would say something to the grand jury that would be harmful to him; his anger was over the fact that Barry had stopped paying him as per their agreement, and at a time when it looked as if ZZZZ Best might make some very big money on Wall Street.

Through Maurice Rind, Barry had hired Arthur Barens, a smooth, high-profile LA attorney well known in local legal circles for his unsuccessful attempts at defending Marvin Pancoast (the

killer of former Alfred Bloomingdale mistress Vicki Morgan) and
Joe Hunt of the "Billionaire Boys Club."

Before engaging Barens, Barry had already paid Catain about
$500,000 as part of the financial settlement agreed to in December,
and was now refusing to make any further payments. Barens's role
was to block a writ of attachment that had been filed by Catain
against Barry's bank accounts and property.

In subsequent court hearings, Barens was able to have the writ
of attachment denied. More importantly, he made it clear to Catain,
his business associates, and his attorney that if any new complaint
was filed against Barry, Barens on his behalf would "immediately
cross-complain against Catain to recover these unjustified sums
[already] paid to him by Mr. Minkow." "In summary," Barens
wrote to a financial consultant of Catain's, "I believe that any
complaint brought by Catain against Mr. Minkow or ZZZZ Best to
be [sic] groundless and that it is Mr. Minkow who is entitled to
reimbursement of large sums of money from Catain."

When Barry had agreed to the settlement in December, he had
done so in large part to avoid the scrutiny and negative publicity
that might have resulted if he had been sued in open court by a
man of Catain's reputation. At the time, ZZZZ Best was on the
verge of becoming a public company, and bad publicity was the last
thing he wanted.

But now it appeared that the tables had been reversed, with
Catain the target of a grand jury investigation, and Barry being
called in to testify against him. So when Arthur Barens closed his
letter to Jack Catain's financial consultant, he added a meaningful
zinger: "I must also point out that Catain is presently being investigated by a federal grand jury concerning his ties to organized
crime. In that regard, I also represent Mr. Minkow, who has been
called by the grand jury to testify as a witness and Catain's victim."

Barens's legal reputation, as well as his implied threat that
Barry might well tell the grand jury a good deal more than he'd
told the FBI when the bureau had questioned him in December,
were apparently enough to stop Catain from pressuring Minkow
directly, for he was no longer in any position to shake Barry down.
(And once again Barry, in fact, told the grand jury very little.)

What he could do, however, was to get back at Barry indirectly
for beating him out of the money he still felt he was legitimately
owed and for "going with" other mob-connected guys who had

broken the code of the street by "taking" Minkow away from him.

What followed was a complex face-off with "friends" of Catain's (including Carmen DeNunzio, who had apparently patched things up with Catain) telling Rind, Schulman, and Victor not only to stop doing business with Barry but to pay them Catain's share of the money he was owed from the restoration jobs.

Catain's friends decided to pay Robert Victor a visit. They told Victor he owed them $1.5 million, theirs and Jack's share of the restoration jobs. "Victor was scared shitless," says Rind, and so was Barry, who simultaneously began receiving a series of threatening phone calls. It was then that Maurice decided "to bring Joey into the picture." Whether or not he was concerned with Barry and Victor's welfare, one thing was clear: his money was in jeopardy.

Over the weeks of threats, Maurice and Richie became increasingly frustrated. "We were being treated like wise guys, but we were legit," says Rind. "There was never a 'sit-down,' never a claim to anything."

Finally a meeting was arranged between Catain's friends and Joey Mangiapane, and "Joey got our point of view across,' says Maurice. That point of view was: "We're legit. We're not gonna lose the restorations jobs, pay money to you, *and* have to pay [back] Jay Botchman millions of dollars; are you insane?!" The reply was a message to Barry for Richie: "Tell 'em I'm not afraid of that fat Jew" (referring to Schulman).

Catain's friends continued to make calls to Barry and also to Victor, who now refused to go to the office and was conducting business from his car phone. A second meeting, said Rind, was arranged with "Jack's people" and a weightier friend of Rind's "from back East." At this meeting, which took place at the Valley Hilton Hotel, Maurice's friend expressed the group's position more forcefully. Apparently that meeting convinced Catain's associates to back off.

Jack Catain, a sick man, finally died of a heart attack in February 1987, after having been convicted of counterfeiting the preceding November. But long before that, within days of the meeting in fact, the threatening phone calls had ceased, the guys from Palm Springs had relinquished their claim, the bodyguards had been let go, and Barry Minkow, never missing a beat, had moved on to more important things. Later, however, he would find use for the episode.

— 8 —

THE WAY BARRY TOLD IT, Ada Cohen could just see him down on his little knees cleaning that carpet, hoping to be successful, taking care so that that Oriental rug, that very costly and exquisite rug, would be perfectly restored.

And Bernard Pincus, who was listening along with Ada as Barry weaved his tale that summer afternoon, also had a picture conjured up in his mind. His was of Barry laboring over this tremendous Persian rug, valued probably in the millions, cleaning it inch by inch with a toothbrush.

Barry was telling his Persian rug story in the dining room of his new home while sitting at the head of the table, playing host to Cohen, Pincus, and the rest of Kay Rosario's almost exclusively female, middle-aged, and elderly investment group. They had been brought together by Barry and Kay for lunch, one of several such meetings held periodically for Kay's group, in which Barry would advise them on the status of their investments, the progress of ZZZZ Best, and—as always—why he needed additional money.

All afternoon, Barry had been his usual buoyant, confident self, first conducting a tour of his home, which the ladies later described rapturously. They thought the surroundings "lavish," the pool with its iridescent *Z* "exquisite," his new red Ferrari sleek, the yard "well planted," his house "well furnished," and the attentions paid them by the very well-mannered Arthur Uhl "darling." Dressed in a "lovely black suit," Uhl would kiss the ladies' hands by way of greeting.

It was after lunch had been served that Barry launched into his Persian rug story, telling it as an illustration of why he needed their investment help for his next project, the restoration of a large water-damaged building in Sacramento that was going to cost $7.5 or $8 million. The entire building had suffered damage, Barry explained, due to the backing up of its water pipes and the subsequent flooding.

In addition to having to clean this Persian rug and other very expensive rugs "inch by inch" with a new cleaning process he'd developed, a lot of labor was going to be involved in replacing the floor boarding, carpeting, and other materials, as well as in the painting.

As always, Barry's presentation was totally convincing, complete with photocopies of cashier's checks from Travelers made out to ZZZZ Best for work already completed, bogus financial statements signed by a mythical CPA, and copies of the bound ZZZZ Best "bible" Mark Morze had created to simulate the look and feel of a bona fide business prospectus.

These, along with Barry's sincerity, high-energy charm, and high media profile, reinforced the already existing inclination of the ladies to want to help this nice, ambitious young man who was so like what they wanted their children and grandchildren to be.

Oh, there was an occasional misgiving. Like when Ada Cohen had asked to visit a job site "to see all the big things" being done, and was turned down flat. It was simply impossible, Barry told her in front of the entire group. Restoration sites, after all, were hard-hat areas. And when Ada had protested that she didn't at all mind wearing a hard hat, the usually agreeable Barry Minkow was adamant that it simply could not be done. That was a little disappointing.

And then there was the time at Kay's house, more embarrassing than disappointing really, when Ada and Kay were examining the financial projections and architectural plans for that huge Sacramento job and noticed that the word *architectural* at the plan's top was misspelled. She never did bring it to Barry's attention, however. For one, Barry was "very dear" to her, and she didn't want to cause him any embarrassment. Secondly, she "didn't want to endanger [her] position within this wonderful dream that was going to come out."

After all, the regard of Ada and the ladies for Barry and ZZZZ Best wasn't solely altruistic, and their judgment wasn't clouded solely by Barry's charm. Most of them were receiving, on a regular basis, 1 percent per week interest on their investment, or 52 percent a year. This meant that a big investor like Elaine Orlando, who by the end of August 1986 had put up $300,000, was earning $3,000 a week in cash.

And by that time, Barry was starting to mention an extraordinary step he was about to undertake, a laborious process that would allow for a giant public sale of newly issued ZZZZ Best stock underwritten by a large, well-known Wall Street investment banking firm. The ladies, if they wished, could be part of that, too. "We were told, that there would be a [stock] participation," says Elaine Orlando, "[and] that if Barry liked you, and if you were in and supporting him . . . on the bottom rung, that you would participate in any profits later on because he intended to be the General Motors of Carpet Cleaning."

Part III
The General Motors of Carpet Cleaning

— 1 —

ALMOST A YEAR BEFORE Ivan Boesky's transformation from Wall Street's greatest modern messiah to its greatest embarrassment, and more than twenty months before the shock of Black Monday, Barry Minkow was already intent on putting his ZZZZ Best stock to work for him.

Reaganomics was still in high vogue in Washington, and the greedy, self-made men on Wall Street were busily engaged in the wild speculation, unlimited borrowing, gluttonous consumption, and savage corporate takeovers that would define the era.

Money was pouring into the market, and on the Street men like Boesky were using illegal insider information to buy and sell stocks in anticipation of takeovers or mergers. At the same time, a new breed of maniacally driven "creative financiers" like Michael Milken—out of Drexel Burnham Lambert, the same investment banking firm that had closely worked with Boesky—was underwriting billions of dollars' worth of low-rated, high-interest "junk bonds" for companies like ZZZZ Best that, because of their credit history, size, and limited capital, had previously been unable to raise money from traditional lending sources.

In such a setting, with such role models, it should have come as no surprise that Barry Minkow would fit right in and succeed as spectacularly on Wall Street as he apparently had on the cluttered, sun-baked boulevards of the San Fernando Valley.

Initially, the transformation of ZZZZ Best into a publicly owned company had done little to change the life of Barry Minkow. The fact that he now owned the vast majority of shares in his company *had* somewhat enhanced his credibility when he attempted to secure an additional loan or lure in a potential new investor. But in the main, ZZZZ Best's going public had not solved Barry's cash flow problem.

The difficulty was that, while he had all this stock, he couldn't do much with it, being prohibited by SEC regulation from selling it for two years.

Much of the remaining stock—about 20 percent—was jointly

owned by Maurice, Victor, Richie, and Barry, and *could* be traded. But without a market for those shares, they too were currently worth little to Barry.

Since ZZZZ Best had gone public at the beginning of the year, Maurice had been exploring the possibility of getting ZZZZ Best listed on NASDAQ, the automated quotation system of the National Association of Securities Dealers, which would beam ZZZZ Best's latest selling price to 185,000 securities brokers and the stock market pages of America's leading newspapers. Assuming, then, that ZZZZ Best's stock price could be made to rise, either through performance, publicity, manipulation, or perhaps a combination of the three, the chances of selling the stock for a large profit would be greatly enhanced, which was what Maurice had had in mind from the beginning.

But, like going public, being listed on NASDAQ would not solve Barry's immediate debt problems. The process would take too long, and the payoff wouldn't be great enough.

What could solve Barry's problems, however, was the issuance of *new* ZZZZ Best stock. If the public could be persuaded to buy large amounts of ZZZZ Best stock—as investors surely would after that stock had been hyped by a salesman as good as Barry had become—it would provide a new source of cash that *would not have to be paid back*. Minkow would then be able to pay off his debts, finance his expansion dreams, and no longer have to rely on nickel-and-dime loans from small banks or short-term usurious financing from private investors. People would be holding ZZZZ Best stock, not high-interest loan papers, and Barry would be home free.

Before any new stock could be issued, however, ZZZZ Best would have to meet certain SEC and NASD requirements designed to thwart exactly the kind of scam that he, Mark, and Tom were working. These requirements included, among other things, an audit done by a certified public accountant and a detailed prospectus delineating the kind of information and data that potential buyers needed to know in order to make a sound decision about investing.

The danger of submitting to such close scrutiny was extraordinarily high. Barry and his associates would in effect be paying highly trained accountants, corporate lawyers, and stock underwriters to examine a company built, in part, on monumental deception.

But for Barry, Morze, and Tom Padgett, the benefits appeared to outweigh the risks.

Tom was in far too deeply at this stage not to go along with Minkow in what might prove to be the final big score. Nearing forty, he was, like millions of other working-class men of his generation, finding it difficult and humiliating to adjust the high expectations he'd had in the sixties to the more limited opportunities, lower wages, nonunion jobs, and growing conformity of the eighties. Tom Padgett was, in short, fast becoming what single women dismissively refer to as a loser. And, goddamn it, it wasn't *fair*. He'd gone to college, hadn't he? And what had it gotten him when he'd graduated? A job in a factory that paid so little he had to borrow money from his mother to get drunk. Hadn't he done his time in Vietnam? Hadn't he *always* done what he was supposed to do? And for what? So Tom Padgett, whose capacity for self-delusion was exceeded only by his capacity for self-justification, went along with Barry Minkow "like a good little soldier" as soon as the idea for the public stock offering was mentioned to him.

Mark Morze, too, jumped at the idea. Intimately familiar with ZZZZ Best's books, he knew how necessary an infusion of new cash was. He also knew the truly remarkable amounts of money he could make if the offering could be pulled off. With his love of action and the kind of women some *big* money could buy, how could he possibly pass up the chance of a lifetime? A chance to literally make a couple of million dollars did not, after all, frequently present itself, and should not, therefore, be pissed away. Sure, it was a gamble, but Mark Morze *liked* to gamble; that's what he did for fun.

As for Barry, he just couldn't stop. Whatever the demons driving him, they were not to be appeased by moderate success. He wanted nothing less, he was now telling people, than one day to follow his idol Ronald Reagan into the White House. To have his shot, Barry Minkow would take whatever risks necessary and, in the process, seek to satiate his insatiable ego and quell the insecure little boy within.

The first step in the stock-offering process was to hire a CPA to do a full-scale audit of ZZZZ Best—a move filled with potential pitfalls, but one absolutely essential for SEC registration and NASD membership.

So one day in early 1986, Barry called Mark Morze into his

office and told him he had some good news. George Greenspan, a CPA and attorney whom Barry had met when Greenspan was assisting Maurice and Harold Fischman in bringing ZZZZ Best public, had agreed to do the audit.

Eager to take advantage of this good fortune, Barry asked Mark to buy a first-class ticket, fly to New Jersey, and start the process of getting Greenspan "to approve the audit." If Mark could do that, Barry said, there was $200,000 in it for him when the offering was approved.

Over the next several months, Mark Morze flew to the East Coast perhaps half a dozen times, on each trip bringing the additional information Greenspan was demanding. Eventually, Greenspan himself came to Los Angeles to continue the audit. Actually, Greenspan was conducting two audits simultaneously—one for the period through April 30, 1985, and the second for the fiscal year up to and including July 1986.

For the first audit, the "data and numbers" Greenspan received, according to Mark Morze, were "close to the truth." Only the San Diego job and the documents and figures relating to it (a very big chunk of ZZZZ Best's income) were false—fabricated, says Morze, by Barry. The second audit, however, was filled with phony data for multimillion-dollar restoration jobs, "made up ad hoc" by Morze upon demand.

By this time, Barry and Mark were entering into serious negotiations with Rooney, Pace, a Wall Street underwriting firm, over the public stock offering. They were told that the SEC required audited statements for the preceding *three* years—thus, an audit for the 1983–1984 fiscal year also was needed.

At this point, Mark really began to hit his stride and reveal what Tom Padgett would later describe in reverential tones as "Morze's genius."

Having found another accountant, named Larry Baker, to handle the 1983–1984 audit, Barry and Morze were now faced with a dilemma. Much of the documentation for those two years simply did not exist, and the phony paperwork Barry had created was not suitable for their purpose. The solution was simple, Mark Morze decided. He would make up the primary documents "from scratch."

But he did not plunge in impetuously as Barry might have. Instead, he studied the situation and the kind of documents he would need to produce, much as a scientist might analyze a problem.

Take, for example, his approach to cashier's checks—hundreds of which Mark would falsify or manufacture in the next year or so. After buying several cashier's checks for small amounts and examining the series of numbers on them, Mark concluded that there was a kind of code. Through long hours of thought and the examination of scores of canceled cashier's checks from ZZZZ Best and his previous clients, Morze was able to determine the codes and what each meant.

Pasting a genuine cashier's check on a piece of cardboard—because he was "going to be handling it a lot"—he would use it as "an original master," in much the same way a counterfeiter would employ a master counterfeit plate.

Making a clean photocopy from the original, Morze would white out the payee, date, and amount and then type in the required information. Afterward, a final photocopy would be made—adjusted for "better or worse quality," whichever was appropriate for the specific use required.

His modus operandi for the 1983–1984 audit was, if anything, even more cleverly conceived and painstakingly executed.

Invoices and tax returns were photocopied as the bogus checks had been. But the fifteen to twenty bank statements—which needed to match the tax returns and, of course, did not exist—had to be entirely manufactured, and this entailed a far more elaborate ruse.

For those, he would gather a dozen or more bank statements from former clients, cutting and snipping until he had a stockpile of assorted check numbers, dollar amounts, and dates, which he would then reassemble and paste down over a recent ZZZZ Best bank statement and photocopy. The result was a wholly new and convincing document. His object was to produce monthly bank statements that would match the totals of the figures declared on the 1984–1985 tax returns, and such was his skill that he could make the final balance come to any amount required.

It took Mark Morze five to six hours of laborious cutting and pasting to handcraft each bank statement. And, as somewhere around eighteen of them were needed, Morze was forced to pull numerous "all-nighters" to get the job done.

Morze's skills as a forger would probably have been sufficient to fool Larry Baker into signing the 1984–1985 audit in any case, but as it happened, one of the banks Barry used (West Valley Bank) had gone out of business, thereby providing a perfectly plausible reason why Mark was giving Baker copies of everything instead of originals.

Then again, there is no reason to believe that had West Valley still been in business, Larry Baker would have asked for the originals. After all, nobody else did. Not George Greenspan, not the weighty accounting firm of Ernst & Whinney, which Barry would later engage. Nobody. And that was a key factor for Mark Morze, a true innovator in the creative uses of the Xerox machine.

With his "master plates," Mark Morze was subsequently to produce a blizzard of spurious papers—bogus cashier's checks, imaginary invoices, phony work sheets, hundreds of letters falsely describing the status of ZZZZ Best restoration jobs, and dozens of different fake business forms and contracts.

He got so good that Barry developed a standing joke. "Own your home?" he'd ask rhetorically. "No? Well, give Mark an hour, and he'll come back with a deed and the check you used to pay for it."

At the time George Greenspan was preparing his audit of ZZZZ Best, he was a veteran accountant in practice for over forty years, who tried, according to Morze, "to do everything legit."

He checked out the two restoration jobs supposedly completed in San Diego and Arroyo Grande, but never, unfortunately, visited the sites. Instead, he "communicated with the individual of the firm that gave out the contract," that is, with Tom Padgett.

Never demanding to meet with Padgett or to see his books, however, Greenspan settled for simply talking with Tom over the phone. Or at least that's what he thought. In reality, he spoke to Mark Morze, who pretended to be Padgett while Tom himself, distraught over his recent loss of the coveted Debbie to another man, lay on the floor of his Interstate office in a drunken stupor.

Morze was pretending to be Padgett not only because Tom was in too pitiful a state to be relied on for such a delicate task but also because Mark and Barry were the ones who had been dealing with Greenspan. Tom knew little about what Greenspan had been shown, and there was no room for a slipup. Interstate, after all, was ZZZZ Best's only source of restoration jobs and, as such, would be responsible in the months ahead for 86 percent of ZZZZ Best's entire business.

Curled up on the carpet with his twelve-pack, Padgett listened as Morze, pretending to be him, told Greenspan how well Interstate

was doing, expanding now into Texas and planning shortly to go
nationwide. With the expansion, continued Morze, Interstate's 100-
employee staff would also be greatly increased. "He told him," says
Padgett of Morse, "what all the accountants [who would follow]
wanted to hear."

Later, Greenspan was to say in his defense that not only had he
spoken to Tom Padgett, "the customer of ZZZZ Best," but that he
had "received documentary proof from ZZZZ Best that those [res-
toration] contracts existed as far as the paperwork was concerned."

But George Greenspan never questioned why just a one- or two-
page contract was used on a large restoration job. By his own
admission, he was familiar with the construction industry. Why did
he—like the big-time auditing firm of Ernst & Whinney, which was
to replace him—fail to ask where the *rest* of the contract was?

"I used to do books for small construction companies, and a
simple job, say, for a garage, had a folder *this* thick," says Mark
Morze, indicating with his thumb and forefinger a space of about
six inches. "How could jobs for millions of dollars have contracts of
just one page?"

Greenspan also claimed, like Maurice, to have received assur-
ances from Robert Victor that the restoration jobs were sound and
he (Victor) was watching over the ones with which he was involved
(a statement that Victor later denied making).

In addition, Greenspan said, he'd had his staff "trace . . . that
all the payments were made for this [restoration] contract [and]
that ZZZZ Best [had] received payment on its receivables, which
amounted to a couple of million dollars."

He had also "audited expenses that were incurred in regard to
this contract, as far as materials [and] labor [were] concerned," as
well as "the percentage of profit earned," and the profits "seemed
very much in line in [that] competitive kind of business to us." (The
bogus receipts for carpeting and materials were from Carpet
Corner, and were obtained from a friend of Barry's who worked
there. The receipts for equipment were from Dan Krowpman;
those for labor were made up by Mark.) But as Mark Morze later
commented about Ernst & Whinney, "What can you say about an
accounting firm that doesn't question a 39 percent profit margin on
a business that's not risky like motion pictures?"

Greenspan said he had also spot-checked purchases as well as
ZZZZ Best checks. "Every time we asked him [Barry] about a
check, he came back with an invoice for the exact amount or around

the same amount" or with "bills that backed up these purchases"—created, of course, by Mark.

And when Greenspan asked why so many of ZZZZ Best's payments were made in cash or by cashier's check, Barry had a ready explanation: "When he [Barry] started in business, nobody would take his checks because they were bouncing all the time, so he had to use cashier's checks because suppliers and people he would do business with, [for] substantial payments—over $5,000, $10,000—they wanted certified checks or cashier's checks," Greenspan said. "There was [always] a satisfactory explanation on his part and on the part of Mark Morze, who was the accountant previously."

"Basically the books would be tight," says Mark Morze, "with a good audit trail for everything. It is just that actual work wasn't being done."

And, of course, Barry swore to Greenspan in writing that everything was fine. In a "management representation letter" to Greenspan & Company, dated August 21, 1986—a time when Barry was engaged in the delicate initial stages of preparing a prospectus for ZZZZ Best's public offering—he wrote, "There have been no . . . violations or possible violations of laws or regulations whose effects should be considered for disclosure in the financial statement or as a basis for recording a loss contingency."

Greenspan, however, did feel that ZZZZ Best, a "growth company," had an accounting system that was totally inadequate for its needs and a controller, Mark Morze, who was "incompetent."

ZZZZ Best would have to replace Morze, Greenspan told Barry. And before he left LA, Greenspan himself was "instrumental" in hiring a new controller for the company.

The new controller, Bruce Andersen, was set to work to straighten out the chaotic state of ZZZZ Best's books. He would deal strictly with the carpet-cleaning side of the business, however. Barry and Mark Morze would manage the restoration jobs and supply him with the figures necessary for his financial statements. Bruce Andersen, in turn, would put the restoration data he received into his computer and pass it on first to Greenspan and then to Ernst & Whinney, which later verified four or five restoration jobs, all of which were false. As a law enforcement official later said of the accountants, "They approached their work not like a police investigator. They didn't have the suspicious mind. So what they did was look at various documents and [just] make sure that all the figures added up."

About the time that George Greenspan was completing his audit, in the spring or early summer of 1986, Tom Padgett met Maurice Rind at a local restaurant.

Maurice had been wanting to meet with Tom for some time without Barry who, much to Maurice's annoyance, would invariably answer every question that Maurice put to Tom before Padgett even had a chance to open his mouth.

As there was no new business taking place between Padgett's Interstate and Rind, Barry and Tom decided to make Maurice happy and lift the usual prohibition against Tom Padgett meeting alone with a would-be investor or anyone already being scammed. Their instincts proved sound. Rind was in—for him—a relaxed mood, and the meeting proved to be of the "how's everything going" variety. That day, in fact, it was Rind who was hyping something— electrical generators, twenty-two of them, eleven of which were the big 200-kilowatt Murphys that Maurice claimed Barry could use on his restoration sites.

Maurice had just purchased $2 million worth of the generators for $600,000 through the Cayman Islands, thereby avoiding bur- densome U.S. regulations and taxes. (The LAPD has since said that Rind, in reality, paid about $200,000 for them.)

He'd bought them as an investment, he told Tom, but Barry was going to use them as a way for ZZZZ Best to meet the SEC and NASD qualifications requiring a company to have at least $2 million in hard assets before being listed with NASDAQ (or having a stock offering). And, said Maurice, he also intended to rent them out to be used on remote movie locations and as backup at events such as the Super Bowl.

While Barry was going to buy the generators from him for $300,000 to $400,000 and shares of ZZZZ Best's stock, Maurice would continue leasing them out through a new corporation known as 4 Z Equipment Company. Chip Arrington was again selected to be a beard—this time 4 Z's phantom president. Was Tom interested in investing, Maurice wondered, or did he know anyone who might be? Padgett told Rind he'd think about it and ask around, and then quickly put it out of his mind.

But the purchase of the generators was an important event for Barry and Mark. Buying the generators and completing the audits had accomplished two of the important preliminary steps that were to enable them to transform ZZZZ Best from a marginal, second- rate company to one of Wall Street's hottest tickets.

— 2 —

IN THOSE EARLY MONTHS OF 1986, Barry Minkow and Mark Morze were busy indeed.

In addition to the progress they had made in meeting two big NASD-SEC requirements, they were also working with a loan broker who was putting together an improved version of the ZZZZ Best "bible" of tax returns, newspaper clips, and financial projections that Barry and Mark had been using in lieu of a prospectus as they tried to attract new investors.

The loan broker functioned as a sort of middleman between those, like Barry, seeking loans and banks or private investors, receiving in return a "finder's fee."

He, in turn, introduced Minkow to another loan broker, named Richard Charbit. A short, stubby man in his early forties who, says Mark, "had the sizzle," Charbit also had a French accent, a questionable background, a Rolls-Royce, and a house, not just in Beverly Hills but on Rodeo Drive.

At that time, Morze says, "Barry was playing the game with five, six, or seven different people—borrowing money and joint venturing, but Richard Charbit would soon prove to be an extraordinarily valuable connection—providing Minkow and Mark with far more than investment capital. One day in late May, while Barry, Morze, and Charbit were in Minkow's office trying to put together a bank loan package, Richard Charbit spoke the words that must have sounded to Minkow and Morze like the Hallelujah chorus.

"Why are you always trying to borrow money," Charbit asked, "when you can raise it through a public stock offering?" Charbit explained that he had an association with Rooney, Pace, an investment banking firm and securities underwriter, and thought it possible that the firm might be able to raise as much as $6 million for ZZZZ Best. In return, Charbit would, of course, receive a hefty finder's fee.

In the following weeks, Barry discussed Charbit's suggestion with Morze, who encouraged him to take Charbit up on his offer—which would, if brought to fruition, bring Mark the $200,000 Barry had already promised, plus a great deal more. Barry asked Maurice Rind and Harold Fischman for their advice and was told that he would be a fool to invite that kind of scrutiny. But his own inner voice—and Mark Morze—told him to go for it.

By this time, Mark had become Barry Minkow's indispensable man, supplanting Tom Padgett's more ordinary intellect and good but not great con man capabilities with talent of a totally different magnitude. And by then, Barry had also told Morze what Mark had already long suspected—that not just a couple but every last one of the restoration jobs was false, that Interstate Appraisal was as bogus as the jobs, that Barry "owned Padgett," and that "Padgett wouldn't know a restoration job if it bit him." Minkow's main man was now Mark Morze.

Only he had that rare combination of bookkeeping experience, razor-sharp intellect, and a mature con man's utter believability. Ruthless, driven, he had the courage and imagination to do what needed to be done when Padgett's intellect and Barry's creativity were tapped out. Only he could get ZZZZ Best's books right so that they'd survive any audit. Only he could juggle the details of ten or fifteen phony restoration jobs and come up with the details for each—payment schedules, costs for materials, false documentation—on demand. Only he could build the illusion of a thriving business by taking massive amounts of money from loans and funneling it into ZZZZ Best accounts so it looked like income. And only he had the answer to any question and the solution to every problem—even when Barry himself was at a loss and had nothing to say. In short, only Mark Morze had the talent to make everybody, including the pros, believe in the months to come that the 86 percent of ZZZZ Best's business that didn't exist, did.

In return for all this talent, and for the multiplicity of services to be rendered, Barry Minkow upped his promised payment to Mark Morze from $200,000 to $1 million—if and when the underwriting went down.

While Barry Minkow and Mark Morze were savoring the possibilities and discounting the risks of Richard Charbit's proposal for a public stock offering, they were also busy—as they had to be—acquiring loans. Massive amounts of new money were necessary in order to make their outstanding loan payments to banks and investors, to maintain the appearance of a prosperous multi-million-dollar company, and to provide cash for the check-kiting loop flowing from Interstate to Morze's own bookkeeping firm,

Marbil Management—which supposedly supplied labor and materials for the restoration jobs—then on to ZZZZ Best and back
through the loop again, so that the same money looked like new
money over and over again. Using Marbil Management as the labor
supplier for the restoration jobs also enabled Morze to avoid the
laborious task of fabricating a weekly payroll supposedly involving
hundreds of workers and tens of thousands of dollars.

So, using the newly purchased generators as collateral and
their relationship with Charbit as their entrée, they began negotiations for a one-million-dollar line of credit with Bank Hapoalim, an
Israeli bank with an office in Encino.

Once again Charbit came through with a key contact: Paul
Schiff, a Hollywood producer and financier with national and
international connections, who would prove to be one of their biggest investors. A cool, self-made man in his midforties, Schiff (a
pseudonym used at his request) had a veneer of sophistication about
him. He dressed tastefully and spoke French, and he never called
men "babe" or spoke of "taking lunch." Nonetheless, it was impossible to sit in his sleek, exquisitely decorated office more than five
minutes without becoming aware that, despite the absence of any
obvious trace of the Bronx or Vegas, one was in the presence of a
classic Hollywood hustler, a tough, sharp deal maker not easily
fooled or outmaneuvered. And, like Maurice Rind and Richie Schulman before him, Paul Schiff was also a man always on the lookout
for a good investment opportunity.

Therefore, when Schiff was approached about a loan to ZZZZ
Best, he was ready to listen. First Lazare Tannenbaum, the vice
president and manager of Bank Hapoalim, spoke with him. Then
Richard Charbit (who, while helping ZZZZ Best with its stock
offering, was simultaneously working on getting a $1 million loan
from Bank Hapoalim for ZZZZ Best) also talked to him.

At a meeting at Schiff's plush Beverly Hills home, Charbit
showed him "a whole series of documents—bank statements indicating a huge volume of deposits, fax, and telex transfers from
Chubb, Hartford, and Travelers showing that insurance companies
were directly paying ZZZZ Best—things of that nature that gave
credibility to the operation." Schiff was favorably impressed and
felt that a deal might be struck.

First, there was the manner in which the deal was structured,
which was Barry's standard you-put-up-the-money-we-split-the-
profits-fifty-fifty. "Anyone in the movie business was a sucker for

that approach," says Schiff, "because that's how we do business in film—cost off the top, then fifty-fifty. Money gets fifty, talent gets fifty." And the figures Barry and Morze showed Schiff indicated a consistent 30 to 40 percent profit—spectacular for a low-risk industry like restoration or construction, where the profit margin is typically 9 or 10 percent.

In addition, apparent safeguards were promised to Schiff as part of the agreement. As collateral for the loan, Barry was offering his twelve million shares of ZZZZ Best stock, which Schiff immediately took upon the signing of the loan agreement and put into his account at First Interstate Bank.

At the end of June, Schiff met Charbit and Barry for lunch at Prego's in Beverly Hills. A joint venture agreement had been drawn up for a sixty-day, $750,000 loan to ZZZZ Best from First Interstate Bank—with Schiff, a big First Interstate customer, guaranteeing the repayment. But Schiff first wanted to check Barry out before cosigning the note.

Schiff's initial impression of Barry was mixed. On the one hand, it was clear the kid was a super salesman, a good promoter, sincere and hardworking, and very knowledgeable about the business of carpet cleaning.

On the other hand, Barry's age and basic inexperience with construction projects diminished his credibility. "When I asked Barry a number of questions about carpet cleaning," says Schiff, "I was impressed with his answers, but when I asked about restoration, he made it evident he didn't know much and that Mark Morze was the guy. I heard later," continues Schiff, "that with other people, he'd hold himself out to be an expert, but with me it was always, 'Mark may be the employee, but he runs that particular show.'"

Schiff met Morze not long after his luncheon with Barry, and he was much impressed not just by Mark's expertise in building restoration but also by the way Morze handled himself. And while Schiff and Barry would soon be meeting regularly on Saturdays for breakfast and conferring almost daily on the phone, it was to Mark that Paul Schiff would turn if he had any questions. For Barry had told him early on, when "you're speaking to Morze, you're speaking to me—he has specific responsibility for the restoration jobs—call him directly."

On July 7, the contract was signed, and three checks of about equal worth totaling $750,000 were issued. One went to ZZZZ Best, one to Cornwell Quality Tools and Equipment, and one to Mandy's California Woodworking, where another of Barry's friends was allegedly providing flooring supplies for the restoration jobs.

"After that," says Paul Schiff, "Barry began to perform, and performed all the way. Every single payment—six or eight of them—was made on time, to the penny. So that well before the due date on his first loan, he had paid it off from [what appeared to be] his accounts receivable. He now had a very credible track record [with me]."

Then, in late August, when Barry got his underwriting commitment from Rooney, Pace, he became even more legitimized in Paul Schiff's eyes. Minkow was now dealing in the big time, with big-time lawyers and accountants like Hughes Hubbard & Reed and Ernst & Whinney. And on the strength of those participants, Schiff renewed the loan and raised its limit to $1.5 million.

— 3 —

JUST AS THE LATE SPRING and early summer of 1986 began to turn into a season of hope for Barry Minkow and Mark Morze—one in which they might, just might, get out from under and make the *big score*—Tom Padgett started falling apart over Debbie.

In the first few months of the year, the situation had been quite different for Tom Padgett. Then he was living the life of the modestly successful entrepreneur on the verge of big things and courting the girl of his dreams.

Every morning he'd get up early and work out, then drive to Woodland Hills, pick up Debbie, and head to the office. There they'd meet her cousin Sandra and go out for a long lunch. Debbie and Sandra were still on Tom's payroll, of course, courtesy of Barry.

Tom had met and befriended Sandra in early 1984, when she brought her car into Allstate for an appraisal. Through her, he subsequently met Debbie. Seventeen at the time of their introduction, she had long, dark hair, a slender 5'8" figure, and a "low-key sweetness about her" that immediately attracted Tom Padgett, who thereafter was "unable to look at another woman."

Now twenty and "working" for Padgett, however, Debbie

wasn't all that keen to look at Tom—at least not romantically. But ever the existential hero in his own movie, Tom Padgett *knew* that if he could just keep Debbie around him, *things could happen.*

And in the spring, things did.

Debbie got a boyfriend. A very jealous, violent boyfriend. And that turn of events sent Tom into a severe depression that was further exacerbated when Debbie's new beau forced her to quit the employment of Tom Padgett.

It was then that Tom—who'd been planning to buy Debbie a car, who'd been "building a business for her" and wanted "to marry her and have a family"—became completely unglued.

On the day Debbie quit, Tom called Barry and, sobbing into the phone, threatened to kill Debbie's boyfriend, alternately slugging down a beer and caressing his .44 automatic.

His breakfast became a six-pack, his day a drunken walk along Hollywood Boulevard, often armed with his .44 and spoiling for a fight. The fact that this other guy was "going to bed" with Debbie was driving Tom Padgett crazy.

Barry, meanwhile, was flipping out over Tom's behavior. "How could anyone fuck up a business over a *woman?*" Barry would ask incredulously.

"I was drunk around the clock," says Padgett, "lying on the floor with beer bottles all around, not available for meetings, not wanting to go on. Can you see the worry Barry had? How unstable it all was? What if I shot this guy?"

It was clear to Tom that "Barry really felt bad" and was trying to do everything he could to help Tom get himself together.

It wasn't Barry, however, who pulled Tom Padgett out of his deep funk. It was, instead, a phone call that Tom received from a 300-pound albino named Mark Roddy.

Tom had met Roddy through Sandra, and although he'd always thought of Roddy as "a sharp, money-making guy—a presence," they'd never been close friends.

But when Sandra told Mark Roddy about Tom's depression, he was thoughtful enough to call not just once, but daily, to offer comfort and advice.

In addition to rescuing Padgett from his despair, Roddy also become his alter ego in the scams to come in much the same way that Mark Morze was becoming Barry's.

Although not *really* a 300-pound albino, as he was later invariably described, he was, to be sure, an albino, with his baby soft hair so pale white and his face and body so truly pink they had earned him his street name: "the Ultimate White Man," or "UWM" for short. At about 5'10", Roddy weighed closer to 280 than 300 pounds. But he carried his weight well. And with a perfectly trimmed white moustache, black aviator sunglasses, well-cut suits, and an easy Irish charm, Roddy, in his midthirties, was more a dapper Jackie Gleason figure out of *The Hustler* than a slovenly fat man.

It was Roddy, in fact, who refined both Padgett's end of the hustle and Tom himself. Tom Padgett was fond of wearing cutoff jeans and T-shirts with inscriptions such as "How can I tell you I love you when you're sitting on my face?" So his wardrobe and his understanding of "power dressing" were much improved by his contact with Mark Roddy.

Roddy told Tom to get some black or dark blue suits for those occasions when Barry would introduce him to potential investors as the man awarding insurance contracts to ZZZZ Best. Black, Roddy explained, was the power color. Since Tom was the one giving the business to ZZZZ Best and those potential investors, he should appear powerful, not conciliatory.

Roddy also advised Tom on the proper automobile—a Lincoln Town Car—black, of course—and just the right watch—a Rolex, naturally. It could even be the somewhat gauche, diamond-studded model, since, as the "giver of business," he didn't have to worry about whether the diamonds might seem offensively nouveau riche.

With the Ultimate White Man in constant attendance, Tom began shopping for Brioni power suits at Battaglia in Beverly Hills and getting his hair cut at Eddie Carroll's.

In the months to come, Mark Roddy would become Tom Padgett's adviser and confidant, urging him to forget Debbie and to try to make some *real* money with Barry Minkow. As Barry himself had said, that was the only way he'd ever get Debbie back. Then, with the money, he could obtain his other dream—a beach house in Newport Beach, that Orange County enclave of the rich and powerful to which only those who had *truly* made it could aspire.

Roddy knew about those things. He may have been broke then, but he'd made money before and tasted all it could buy: coke-whores, a beach house, a yacht, a rented Lear jet to take his "harem of women back East"—he'd had it all.

To Tom Padgett, Mark Roddy was a true "high roller." The

first time they talked, he had told Tom, "If you're afraid to fall, you can't move forward."

"He had that energy," says Tom Padgett of Mark Roddy, "that high-charged, hustler energy. Somehow I wanted to get the guy involved in the business. 'This guy's done it,' I thought, 'and he's gonna help *me* get there.'"

— 4 —

ALTHOUGH TOM PADGETT'S FAILURE to manage his personal life was worrisome to his partners, it was his peculiar politics that threatened to jeopardize the entire scam. As Barry and Mark Morze went about finessing the audit by George Greenspan, negotiating loans for serious money, and courting Rooney, Pace, they lived in fear. For at any moment, the devastating fact that Tom Padgett was a Nazi might be discovered.

More precisely, Tom Padgett was a follower of the God Odin and a member of the White Aryan Resistance. His involvement began back in 1980 when he first noticed an ad in the classified section of *Soldier of Fortune* magazine. The ad read, "Odin and Thor live: We have no masters." Tom Padgett looked at that ad, and "it rang a bell" that resonated deep in his belly, for Odin and Thor were the gods of the religion of his ancestors—passed down genetically to his Irish forebears by the Vikings who settled in Ireland.

The macho mythology of Odinism attracted Tom Padgett as much as did the Northern European white supremacist tenets on which the modern version of the "religion" was based. The Gordon Liddy within him responded to the appeal of Odinism as a "warrior's religion" that promised those who died in battle a trip to Valhalla—the home of the slain, where heaven is fighting all day, drinking all night, and getting ready for the ultimate battle against the forces of darkness.

At a 1983 meeting of the Odin Fellowship, Tom Padgett met and became friends with Tom Metzger. A former Grand Dragon of the Ku Klux Klan, Metzger ran for the California State Senate in 1980 as an open Klansman, winning the Democratic primary before losing in an election in which he received an astounding 35,107 votes.

After leaving the Klan "because he was no longer a Christian," Metzger became the head of the White Aryan Resistance, or WAR. ("You've reached WAR . . ." begins the message on the organization's answering machine, continuing with various slurs against "kikes," "niggers," "greasers," and "wetbacks" before ending with the admonition, "On any issue, before you choose, look for the influence of the Jews.")

At the same time, Metzger also began a public access cable television show called "Race and Reason," and Tom Padgett, who had recently also joined WAR, was "honored" to be the very first guest on the show's premiere in 1984, when he enlightened the viewers on the virtues of Odinism. (Later, Metzger's son would be one of those who sparked the melee in which TV talk show host Geraldo Rivera had his nose broken.)

Then in August of 1986, when Barry and Mark Morze were starting to negotiate with Rooney, Pace on the public stock offering, Tom Padgett became the cohost of "Race and Reason."

An odd type of anti-Semite, Padgett excluded almost all of his Jewish friends and associates—especially Barry—from that amorphous group called "the Jews" for which he had so much class resentment. And he seemed to have no idea of the possible repercussions of appearing on such a show—particularly to a man involved as he was in a high-profile fraud with a publicity-conscious rising media star like Barry Minkow.

It was as if, for Tom Padgett, the Holocaust and 2,000 years of Jewish persecution had never occurred and millions of Jewish-Americans were not now traumatized and acutely sensitive to anti-Semitism. As cohost of "Race and Reason," he appeared with guests like Radio Werewolf, a band into Gothic death rock, who took their name from the Nazi underground; associates of the late George Lincoln Rockwell; and an assortment of Holocaust revisionists, British soccer thugs, and skinheads.

That the show might *piss off* people in a position to deal him, Barry, and their entire scam a fatal blow apparently never occurred to Padgett. He proudly wore a large gold Odinist ring prominently featuring the lightning bolt insignia of the SS, and he seemed genuinely hurt and amazed when a young Jewish-American associate producer for "60 Minutes" told a local reporter how disgusted and unsettled she'd felt while interviewing him for a "60 Minutes" segment on ZZZZ Best. "Why would she feel that way?"

Padgett asked. He'd been polite and helpful to her, hadn't he?

It wasn't his appearances on "Race and Reason," nor the Odin SS ring that first brought Tom Padgett's political activities to people's attention, however. Rather, it was an incident that had taken place several months before.

In May, Metzger had been arraigned—along with eight other neo-Nazi codefendants—at the Municipal Court House in downtown LA on misdemeanor charges stemming from a 1983 cross-burning incident. Tom Padgett, the Reverend Butler of the Aryan Nation, and other white supremacists decided to go along to court with him.

Also present in the courthouse hallway and on the steps outside on that May day were Irv Rubin, head of the thuggish Jewish Defense League, and some of *his* followers. All told, there were somewhere between twenty-five and forty men in the combined groups.

As they'd done during earlier court appearances in the case, the JDL members taunted the defendants and their supporters outside the courtroom. Then, after the hearing, they followed the neo-Nazis to nearby Union Station, where some of them had parked their cars, and where Metzger and his entourage planned on having a few beers.

When Rubin and the JDL followed them in, a ten-minute confrontation ensued in which chairs and fists were flung. Leaping into the heart of the melee amidst shouts from the white suprema-cists of "Odin!" "Hitler!" and "Yahweh!" was none other than Tom Padgett.

The next day, on the front page of the *Daily News*—the local San Fernando Valley newspaper—and *above* the fold, was a large color photo of the brawl, with Metzger in the upper center exchang-ing punches with an obese JDL member; a WAR and a JDL mem-ber on the floor choking each other; and Tom Padgett, right hand clenched in a fist, about to leap on Metzger's burly foe at the exact moment the photographer snapped the picture. "It couldn't have been more perfect!" Tom Padgett said later.

The next morning, Chip Arrington walked into Barry's office with a copy of the paper. Barry immediately called Padgett and warned him to keep a low profile. "Just give money to the cause," said Barry. "You don't need to go out and fight like that. What if the investors see this?"

Apparently no investors saw the picture, or at least none made the connection between the unnamed wild man in the photo and the respectable head of Interstate Appraisal Services who was giving ZZZZ Best such a startlingly high percentage of its business.

But Irv Rubin and the JDL had made the connection.

And sometime in the weeks to follow, Rubin let his knowledge be known, first to Maurice Rind, an old acquaintance and JDL supporter, and then to Barry himself.

According to Rind, he had run into Rubin by chance in the parking lot of Brent's Deli in Northridge. In the course of their conversation, Barry's and Padgett's names came up. A tall, balding, limp-eyed man fond of strutting about with his followers in tow, Rubin said he was outraged that Barry was doing business with Padgett, and was going to call Barry and let him know it.

"Slow down," Rind replied. "I know the kid. Let me give him a call and find out what the story is."

The next day Rind called Barry and asked him, as he said he would, "What the fuck is the story with this guy Padgett?" He then told Barry, "The JDL was looking to give Padgett a beating," and that Rubin was *pissed*.

"Barry begged me to get the JDL off his ass," says Rind, who set up a meeting with Rubin in Minkow's office.

At that meeting, Rubin asked Barry some not unreasonable questions. "How can you do business with a Nazi?" he demanded. "What kind of a Jew are you?"

Barry replied truthfully that he had no control over Padgett's politics, that Padgett was an important part of his business, that he was running a public company, and that he had a fiduciary obligation to the stockholders not to let his personal feelings interfere with his business. Rubin was not satisfied, so Rind came up with a solution:

"I told Barry, 'Barry, you're not neutral in this situation. Padgett's supporting his situation [the neo-Nazis], so you support the JDL and neutralize it out.'" Rind suggested that Barry sponsor the JDL's radio show and "calm down the situation."

So in the months to come, Barry Minkow gave, by Irv Rubin's account, $13,000 to $14,000 to the Jewish Defense League to sponsor a half-hour local radio show that later ran every Saturday night from January to April 1987. "It wasn't a shakedown," says Maurice Rind, "it was a *deal*. I made the deal. Barry and Rubin didn't like it, but they both agreed."

After Rubin left, Barry told Morze how much trouble the JDL leader could have made for them. "I sure bought him off real cheap," he said.

— 5 —

THE MEETING AT BANK HAPOALIM should have been a piece of cake. Charbit the loan broker, working with Barry and Mark to put the loan package together, had also been running interference for them at the bank, where his friendship with the manager had proved helpful as well.

Moreover, Bank Hapoalim—at least on the face of it—wasn't being asked to guarantee an unsecured million-dollar line of credit, the amount for which ZZZZ Best was asking. The credit line (which was eventually scaled back to $800,000) would be secured with the promised payments from the restoration jobs, the gigantic generators that Barry had just bought from Maurice Rind, and other ZZZZ Best assets.

So when Tom Padgett and Mark Morze showed up on a Tuesday afternoon in late August for a final meeting prior to the loan's closing (Barry was out of town working on the stock offering), they were, according to Padgett, "relaxed and ready for anything they'd throw at us."

Even the matter of Tom's signature.

Barry, it seems, had been forging Tom's signature on many of the restoration job invoices, and had then used them in his usual unplanned fashion to substantiate the pending loan. The problem, however, was that Barry had never bothered to accurately imitate Padgett's handwriting, so that when the banking officials looked at the forged signatures, "there were," says Tom, "real discrepancies."

The issue had already been raised by Lazare Tannenbaum, the polite but sharp bank manager. To get around the problem of the signatures, the boys had mulled over the possibility of having Padgett walk in with his right hand taped up due to a "recurring tennis injury." Then no one would ask him to sign his name as a base signature to compare to the others, for it would obviously be impossible. The idea was rejected, however, as just a bit *too* obvious. It was decided instead that Tom would simply agree to sign but point out while doing so how sore his hand was, and how it had been that way for the past several months. In fact, Tom would say, that was the reason for the discrepancy in his signature. For as he was constantly reinjuring his hand, he'd been forced to have his secretary sign almost everything for him.

Sure enough, everything went as expected. When Tom was asked to sign, he did so, adding the explanation about his secretary.

Tannenbaum's reaction to the story—as well as that of Howard Nissenoff, a husky red-haired VP and loan officer—was to follow up with a series of tough, shrewd questions that Morze and Padgett had not anticipated, ending with a request they'd not planned for either: They'd like to go over, said Nissenoff, to Padgett's Interstate office and have a look around.

"When?" asked Tom.

"Now," replied the banker.

"Now?"

"*Now!*"

"Now" was impossible, thought Padgett. "Now" meant the distinct possibility of finding Sandra in jeans reading a magazine in a tiny, almost barren office. Or worse, they might find *no one* at the office, the telephone answering machine on, and Sandra at the beach.

So "now" was clearly out of the question, Tom Padgett said. He was literally on his way out of town, he explained, flying off to a restoration site in Kansas. Yes, that was right, said Mark, coming quickly to Tom's aid. The Humana Hospital job. He was taking Tom to the airport, in fact, right after this meeting, so now really *would* be impossible. "But you'll be back Friday, won't you?" Mark asked, turning to Tom. "Why don't we do it then?"

Tom said Friday would be fine, as did Tannenbaum, his assistant, and Charbit. "And that was when the real story began," says Tom Padgett.

The next day, after speaking with Padgett and Morze, Barry sent several ZZZZ Best trucks to Interstate's office with filing cabinets, chairs, and desks, a computer, and a blackboard to list the status of restoration jobs currently in progress. On Tom's desk was placed a big, fat dummy file marked "San Diego."

On Friday morning, before the scheduled inspection, Padgett and Morze, Sandra, and Morze's sister Minta met at Bob's Big Boy restaurant across the street from the Interstate office.

Minta Morze was instructed to sit behind the computer and look busy, as much a prop in the tableau being laid out as the computer itself. Sandra had been told the day before what was expected of *her*: wear a dress, be on time, and once Tannenbaum

On a fast track: Minkow was voted Most Likely to Succeed and Class Clown by fellow students in his 1984 high school yearbook. (The female counterpart has no affiliation with Minkow.)

Dan Krowpman, Barry's weight-lifting buddy, who loaned Minkow $1,500 to start his own carpet-cleaning business at sixteen.
(KNBC News)

The building in downtown LA that Barry named as the site of his first phony restoration job. Claiming he had a contract for $60,000, he obtained a $15,000 bank loan for "up-front expenses."

Guarded entrance to Westchester Estates, the private community of million-dollar homes where Barry Minkow, nineteen, bought his luxury private residence.

Priced at $700,000, Minkow's home in Westchester Estates was one of the more modest houses in the area.

Barry's pool, complete with two cascading waterfalls and a blue Z on the bottom, was the center of attention at the Boy Wonder's 1985 Christmas party.

Jeri Carr, whose public relations firm promoted Barry Minkow and ZZZZ Best to national fame on television. (Courtesy of Jeri Carr)

The selling of Barry: The cover of Minkow's self-published *Making It in America*, a combination Reverend Ike–"Dare to Be Great" testimonial to himself and to the glories of entrepreneurship.

MAKING IT
IN AMERICA

BY BARRY MINKOW

18 Years Old and a Million Dollars

City of Los Angeles

COMMENDATION

WHEREAS,

Barry Minkow

of Los Angeles, has set a fine entrepreneurial example of obtaining the status of a millionaire at the age of eighteen years old, and

WHEREAS, BARRY MINKOW, at the age of nine years old began cleaning carpets and it was a trade he fully mastered by the age of fifteen, when he ventured into his own entity, and

WHEREAS, ZZZZ BEST CARPET CLEANING, INC. began as a small home-garage business run by Barry with one employee and $6,200.00 in the bank, and has grown to become one of the most reputable and reliable carpet cleaning services throughout Southern California, and

WHEREAS, ZZZZ BEST now encompasses three locations servicing areas between Ventura and San Diego, 64 employees, and a list of clientele including many large corporate and entertainment businesses, as well as residential homes, plus an added variety of services and

WHEREAS, BARRY MINKOW, had a tremendous struggle being accepted as a knowing businessman until he reached the age of 18, because no one believed the word of a youth Today Barry stands confident on top of his empire; and

WHEREAS, BARRY MINKOW, successfully graduated high school with honors in June, 1984 and in eighteen short years, he has perhaps experienced a lifetime, and feels he has gone through enough to make his statement of encouragement to young entrepreneurs He is overflowing with enthusiasm to see others his age do the same . . . "To do what you want to do . . . and make it." DREAMS CAN BECOME REALITY

NOW, THEREFORE, I, TOM BRADLEY, Mayor of the City of Los Angeles, on behalf of its citizens, do hereby commend BARRY MINKOW on your outstanding achievements and your tremendous success, and

FURTHER, extend best wishes for continued success in all your future endeavors. _____

March, 1985

Tom Bradley
MAYOR

In May 1985, Mayor Bradley presented Barry with this official commendation from the City of Los Angeles. Noting that Barry "stands confident on top of his empire," the mayor congratulated the Boy Wonder for his "outstanding achievement [and] enthusiasm to see others his age do the same." The certificate is now something of a rarity.

Robert Victor (aka Robert Viggiano). A heavy investor in ZZZZ Best, Victor had a long arrest record and alleged ties to the Colombo crime family.

Maurice Rind, a former stockbroker twice convicted of stock fraud, helped Barry Minkow turn ZZZZ Best into a public company. (KNBC News)

Told to find and photograph an eight-story building in Arroyo Grande, California, as the site of an alleged multimillion-dollar ZZZZ Best restoration, Mark Morze, Barry's associate, shot this building from the ground. The photo passed inspection with the lender bank.

Tom Padgett drinking his beloved Corona and wearing one of his
dark "power suits." He also had his "power" car—a black Lincoln
Town Car. (Joe Domanick)

Barry J. Minkow, founder, majority shareholder, president, and chairman of the board of ZZZZ Best Co., Inc.
(Courtesy Jeri Carr Public Relations, Inc.)

Following President Reagan's "War on Drugs" speech, Barry launched his own crusade with a book and heavy PR on the theme "My Act Is Clean. How's Yours?" (KNBC News)

The fruits of chutzpah: Barry Minkow's $130,000 red Ferrari Testarosa, a present to himself at age twenty-one.

The fictitious $7 million restoration job in Sacramento. "Find a site we can show the lenders," Barry told Padgett, "or there will be no stock offering . . . no tomorrow."

Padgett displays his "Odin" ring. A member of the White Aryan Resistance and a confirmed anti-Semite, Padgett made an exception in the case of Jewish-born Barry Minkow.
(Joe Domanick)

Mark Morze in Las Vegas, with friends. In 1986–1987, when the money was rolling in, Morze spent at least forty-seven weekends in Vegas, usually at the Imperial Palace in the penthouse suite.
(Courtesy Mark Morze)

Barry Minkow on TV commercials for ZZZZ Best. Looking
mature and handsome in a suit and sensible haircut, he assured
viewers that ZZZZ Best was a substantial company and
guaranteed "the work and price in writing."
(Courtesy Jeri Carr Public Relations, Inc.)

To convince accountants at Ernst and Whinney that the bogus
San Diego job was real, Barry authorized Padgett to rent the
building and complete three months' construction in eleven days.
Padgett pulled it off, but it cost ZZZZ Best $1 million.

At Barry's twenty-first birthday party, Mark Morze gave him a three-foot working kite made from an enlarged check. Most of the guests did not catch the meaning of this inside joke.

Mark Morze after questioning by the FBI. Always quick to make the right moves, Morze hired a high-powered lawyer and started singing like an opera star.

On the run after the collapse of ZZZZ Best, Padgett contacted FBI agents Orr and Sadler at a deserted UCLA baseball field and "spilled his guts."

Brian Morze, Mark's highly educated older brother, joined the scam in its later stages as a troubleshooter and is now serving a three-year jail sentence.

U.S. Attorney Jim Asperger outside Federal Court House in Los Angeles. Despite his youthful appearance and nice-guy manners, Asperger was better prepared to prosecute ZZZZ Best's intricate paper crimes than many a more grizzled career prosecutor. (Joe Domanick)

U.S. Attorney Gordon Greenberg. A former Chicago gang prosecutor, Greenberg has a self-effacing humor that conceals his competitiveness and strong ego. (Joe Domanick)

David Kenner, Barry Minkow's defense attroney. At forty-six, Kenner was well known in Los Angeles for his defense of drug dealers, suspected organized crime figures, and white-collar criminals.
(Courtesy David Kenner)

Barry Minkow after fingerprinting and questioning by the FBI. Indicted on fifty-seven counts of stock fraud and other charges, Minkow was unable to make the $1.5 million bail and remained in jail until he was tried in 1988.

and Charbit were sitting in Tom's small inner office, buzz Padgett on his phone announcing a series of bogus calls designed to make Tom look insanely busy.

When Charbit and Tannenbaum joined Mark and Tom in the office, the performance began.

"We'd like to take you to a job site," said Tom Padgett, launching into this standard spiel, but . . ." and, promptly on cue, there was a buzz on his phone from Sandra: "Tony calling." "Yeah, Tony," said Padgett to the phantom Tony, "get that job going. They won't do it? Then do it yourself—that's what I pay you for!"

He hung up, and almost immediately there came another buzz: "Sam." "Sam, how's the weather in Ventura? What?! Don't tell me the drywall guys haven't shown up. Get *another* crew out there!"

As he hung up, Padgett turned apologetically to Tannenbaum and Charbit. "You can see what a madhouse this place is." His words were interrupted by yet another call: "Jim, yeah, this is Tom. No. Sacramento is looking good. We're about 75 percent into it. Yeah, yeah, don't worry, I'll get it."

"Sorry," said Tom, again hanging up. Then he buzzed Sandra. "Sandra," said Padgett in his best wound-up-and-slightly-harassed-executive voice, "no more calls unless it's really important."

About this time, Barry showed up. He and Tom immediately began to play their scene, Tom chiding Barry once again for "overloading" himself and falling behind in the San Diego job, and threatening to make Barry himself drive down to oversee it.

"Sorry to have to get on him even in front of you," said Padgett, turning to the bank manager, much as a proud father might do when speaking about a cherished but overexuberant son.

And Lazare Tannenbaum not only understood but was "eating it up," according to Tom Padgett. True, it must have seemed odd that a tiny office was giving ZZZZ Best over $20 million worth of work. "But, hey, he was just doing due diligence—checking it out," says Padgett. "He wasn't a professional investigator trying to destroy the deal. Everything looked OK. For this to have been a fraud, we would have had to do what we did."

— 6 —

"The thing about zzzz best that people never realize," a stock market analyst later said in explaining why Wall Street would be interested in the company, "was that it *looked* so good. Carpet cleaning is something anybody can relate to, and Barry already had great revenues, lots of customers, a company that was growing all over the place and that was all over the papers. It's easy to understand why Rooney, Pace would want to get involved."

Indeed, ZZZZ Best's revenues as well as its profits *were* looking extremely good. For the fiscal year ending April 30, 1986, ZZZZ Best reported profits of almost $950,000, up nearly 300 percent from the year before, while its sales came close to quadrupling. This amazing surge of business was immensely aided by the fact that close to half the revenues being reported were from a huge imaginary restoration project.

For the following three months, ending in July, the figures were truly spectacular. The additional restoration jobs reported totaled over $5 million in revenues, more than the entire previous *year* (with about 86 percent of those revenues coming from bogus insurance restoration work), resulting in a three-month profit of more than $900,000. General Motors, whose size and status Barry cited as he promoted his company, was earning about five cents on every dollar in sales, but ZZZZ Best, according to its figures, was earning *seventeen* cents on the dollar.

With that kind of growth and profit, it was only natural that Rooney, Pace, a firm known for its ambition and hustle, would be attracted. After all, that firm had also experienced spectacular growth.

Founded in 1978 by Pat Rooney and Randolph Pace, Rooney, Pace was a prime example of the quick-buck mentality prevailing on Wall Street during the great bull market of the eighties. In 1981–1982, Rooney, Pace began building a reputation on Wall Street by underwriting small, heavily financed companies like ZZZZ Best that had been in business a relatively short period of time. By the first quarter of 1983, the company's growth had become explosive, resulting in pretax profits of $23.4 million for the fiscal year ending in May 1983—a remarkable gain of better than 40 percent.

By the end of fiscal 1985, however, due to go-for-broke mismanagement, the company had pretax losses of more than $43 million, and the SEC, the New York Stock Exchange, and the NASD were accusing the firm of numerous systemic violations.

By the end of 1986, Rooney, Pace—the firm that would be responsible for underwriting ZZZZ Best's stock; the firm overseeing the veracity of Barry Minkow, Mark Morze, and Tom Padgett; the firm that was once the talk of Wall Street—had dwindled from twenty-three offices to just five, and from 600 to 200 employees, with its stock down to about $1 a share on the American Stock Exchange. Within a month, the company had shut down and was in the process of liquidating its assets. By the end of 1987, Randolph Pace had been suspended from the securities business for nine months for breaking federal underwriting laws. And by mid-1988, Pat Rooney had been convicted of conspiracy and filing false income tax returns for 1983, and sentenced to four months in jail.

No one has ever suggested that Rooney, Pace was in any way connected with the massive fraud that would underlie ZZZZ Best's stock offering. But it couldn't have hurt to have had as an underwriting firm a company famous both for encouraging small, risky companies and for wanting to make the deal.

— 7 —

IT WAS ALL SUCH INCREDIBLE BULLSHIT; that was what angered Mark Morze. All these bill-padding lawyers and accountants smugly waving their LLDs and CPAs around and endlessly arguing about *bullshit*.

It wasn't as if the dreary hours he'd just endured while the "professionals" debated ZZZZ Best's prospectus had been spent on anything substantive, like how to explain why Barry had to pay Jack Catain hundreds of thousands of dollars just months earlier. Instead, they were arguing over language in mind-boggling detail, like whether it was better to use the adjective *significant* as opposed to, say, *large*. They'd spend an hour—an *hour*—just discussing that. "It was like someone had written a suicide note," Morze said later, "and the next time I saw him, all I talked about was how bad his syntax was—how he'd dangled his participles."

It was already November 1986, almost three months into the public offering process, and Morze was sitting at his second—and, pray God, last—meeting, in the office of Hughes Hubbard & Reed, the prestigious New York and Century City law firm Barry had hired to represent ZZZZ Best in drafting the prospectus that was shortly to be sent to the SEC.

Between choking back a mad desire to bolt out the door and trying valiantly to conceal his contempt, all Morze could think about was the monumental inefficiency of it all, about how these *professionals* had been having almost weekly meetings like this since at least early September, and how he could have handled the whole fucking thing in a three-minute conference call.

Present at the meeting that day, in addition to Mark, were twelve to fifteen others. They included Chip Arrington and ZZZZ Best's controller, Bruce Andersen; the underwriters and attorneys for Rooney, Pace; Mark Moskowitz, Barry's attorney from Hughes Hubbard & Reed; representatives of the Big Eight accounting firm of Ernst & Whinney; Charbit, the broker; and Schiff, the investor. Barry was away on one of his increasingly frequent motivational speaking tours but was scheduled to call through later that evening.

Like Mark, everyone had been sitting in the same room since seven that morning without even getting to leave for lunch, instead eating the Chinese food that had been sent out for. And God, how Mark hated that: having to talk business to someone who had a goddamned egg roll sticking out of his mouth.

But once they got through this meeting, Morze reminded himself, they'd be almost there, just a month or less away from the public offering and twelve or fifteen million bucks.

He'd been right, he thought, when he'd told Barry to ignore Maurice's warnings that the public offering couldn't be done and that Charbit was full of shit. Who you gonna trust, he'd asked Barry then, a guy like Charbit who drives a white Rolls-Royce, has a mansion on Rodeo Drive, and a gorgeous wife twenty years younger than him, or some jackoff from Brooklyn who lives in a little apartment in the Valley and smokes little cigars? In a comparative analysis of "the sizzle factor," Morze had pointed out, "Charbit comes up a ten, and Maurice is a minus one."

Barry had listened to him, and Charbit had come through. First with the loan from Bank Hapoalim, then, when Charbit had promised Randy Pace would call, Randy Pace had in fact called. Now with the stock offering almost complete, Charbit was coming through again.

True, Richard Charbit had scored $220,000 as part of a three-year consulting agreement, and 150,000 shares of common stock, but he'd been worth every penny of it.

Without him and the money that the stock offering was going to generate, there was no way they could have kept the Ponzi going another three months. Indeed, it was a wonder they'd made it through the *past* three months—which had been, Mark recalled, "hand-to-mouth, eating-Campbell's-soup time." For in spite of Barry's high-living lifestyle and even Mark's own glitzy front, most of the hundreds of thousands of dollars they'd been getting from banks and investors had been used to pay back previous loans and meet other related expenses, to stall an investor here, or to gain a two- or three-day respite there. Floating about $500,000 endlessly, circulating it from bank to bank, Barry writing a check to Mark's Marbil Management, and Mark writing one back to Barry, waiting until a new loan came through.

Padgett, who'd taken the small bonuses he received periodically from Barry and much of his $1,000-a-week salary and blown it all on the commodities market, was in even worse shape than Mark. Still living in his roach-infested North Hollywood apartment, he had to hit Barry up for a couple of hundred dollars just to get by. That's how bad things were.

Even ZZZZ Best's carpet-cleaning division was now losing large sums of money. Turnover was bad, expenses were high, and the division was in desperate need of cash simply to meet the payroll, rent, and operating expenses. When Barry and Chip had been able to devote their energies to it, the division had done far better. But with Chip now busy running around opening new carpet-cleaning locations to make the business look as if it were profitably expanding, and Barry devoting about a half hour a day to carpet cleaning and all the rest of his time to keeping the scam going, this legitimate end of the business had become just another hole through which ZZZZ Best funds were pouring.

And there were other expenses that had to be met. For example, the fees to Rooney, Pace, to Hughes Hubbard & Reed, to Ernst

& Whinney, and to others connected with the stock offering. A bounced check or missed payment to *those* people could ice the whole deal.

Plus, *plus*, there were all the other problems they'd had to deal with. Like the time around October when Rooney, Pace had told Barry it needed a letter from the bank where Padgett's Interstate Appraisal Services did business, stating Interstate's average monthly cash flow. Since Interstate's average cash flow was in the neighborhood of a couple of hundred dollars instead of the million or so it should have been to look right, the demand presented a serious problem.

But, as with so many others, the difficulty had been resolved by a combination of Barry's charm and Mark's ingenuity. Barry quickly got on his car phone, called the operations officer at Valley National Bank where Interstate as well as ZZZZ Best had an account, and "schmoozing" the bank official "real good," managed by the end of the conversation to get the woman to write a vague letter saying essentially that Interstate Appraisal Services was a good company to do business with.

Since Barry had asked for the letter, it was sent directly to him, and he turned it over to Mark, who added a sentence at the bottom that completely changed its intent from the purposely vague to the specific. Interstate's account, wrote Mark, was an "upper 6 or lower 7"—financial terminology indicating that Interstate's average cash flow was near $1 million—an amount that would be consistent with its purported activity with ZZZZ Best.

But that sort of problem was nothing special to worry about. *Every* day was like that. Every day was crisis management day at ZZZZ Best. In fact, Barry kept a special calendar showing who had to be paid each day and also keeping track of the check kiting. Mark would walk into Barry's office, and Barry would give him six or eight things that *had* to be done *today*. By noon, "he'd come up with twelve more." And those were just the emergency tasks. There was also the daily routine: first, go to at least four to six banks, withdraw cash from the "float money," and deposit it into Morze's Marbil account so he could write checks, making it look as if they were paying out payroll and other restoration expenses. At the same time, stall and lie when the bankers called to ask where the new locations were, or why Tom Padgett couldn't be reached, or why a particular check was once again not covered.

Then, like Barry, Mark would see at least one major investor such as Schiff daily. (Barry never let more than a couple of days go by without meeting with his main investors, each of whom thought he or she was Barry's *special* financier.) Sometimes the visits were to schmooze, but often they had to be made. For each investor had a payment schedule, and every thirty or sixty days he or she would be expecting a large amount of money as a return on investment. In the case of someone like Schiff, who had invested in twelve or fifteen jobs, payments would be due almost every week.

To buy time, Mark or Barry would meet and invariably persuade the investor—Kay Rosario or Schiff—to roll the money over, that is, to reinvest the loan in some new, bogus restoration job.

To make the scam convincing, Mark would withdraw some of the float money and purchase a cashier's check for the amount due—say $300,000 to Paul Schiff. He'd show Schiff the check, then tell him they were about to start another restoration project and suggest he just go ahead and roll over the check for the new job. "They'd always say yes," Mark recalled, "because they were making so much money." Then Morze would have Schiff sign the cashier's check over to ZZZZ Best, whereupon he'd bring it back to the bank, redeposit it, buy another cashier's check made out to a different investor, and repeat the entire procedure. By late October, the squeeze was really on. "If any one [of those investors] had said, 'I've *got* to have my money,' we'd have been dead," Morze recalled.

And it was all because of *these* people and their petty quibbling, he though disgustedly, looking around the room, that the finely calibrated payment and loan schedule he and Barry had worked out had been so completely thrown off and the public offering delayed from October to December.

As a result, not only did they have to scramble around like madmen trying to get new loans, the amount of money owed investors for restoration jobs almost tripled during the three-month period between early September and December. This was because Barry and Mark had been expecting to pay off numerous loans due in late October with the proceeds from the stock offering. When it was delayed, they had to get the investors to roll over their money, thus buying time but also vastly increasing what they owned without any new infusion of capital.

To keep up with the daily crises, Mark Morze had bought a cellular phone for his car, a phone he says, "you could not see me without." Fifty times a day he'd be cooling out some potential troublemaker. "Hello," he would say, "this is Mark Morze. I'm running late." Or it would be Barry constantly calling through with new instructions: "Go to the bank, get $10,000 in green [cash], and go to . . ." The phone, in time, seemed to become an extension of Mark's ear.

Near the end of the business day, Mark would head back to the bank, take the float money out of his Marbil account, and deposit it back into the account of ZZZZ Best. On the check he'd deposit, he'd write as the remitter Interstate Appraisal, so it would look as though new money had been paid to ZZZZ Best by one of Tom Padgett's insurance companies for recently completed restoration work.

Then Mark Morze would go home and spend two or three hours making up false documentation. The following day, the whole routine would begin again.

For example, not long after Mark had changed the credit-rating letter for Interstate Appraisal, Tom's company was booted out of Valley National Bank for bouncing three big checks in a row, checks he and Barry had expected to cover with the millions coming in from the stock offering in October.

A similar indignity took place when Interstate, searching for a new banker, opened an account at TransWorld Bank. "We fucked up real fast," Mark remembered, "writing checks and trying to get money to cover them." Five checks totaling nearly $1 million had quickly been written to investors and banks, and just as quickly they'd all bounced.

Consequently, Tom's company was *again* kicked out of its bank—an acutely embarrassing situation for an allegedly multi-million-dollar business, and just at a time when Rooney, Pace and Ernst & Whinney were "looking at them real close."

But once again Barry came up with a solution.

"Go to Turnbow," Barry told Morze and Padgett, referring to the paternal, kindly former manager of West Valley Bank, who now held a similar position at Sterling Bank—adding as always the words of contempt that would invariably spring to his lips at the mere mention of Turnbow's name: "I own the guy; he's in my pocket." Whether or not that was the case, Turnbow not only helped Interstate open an account but saw to it that Tom's company got instant credit as well—an essential element for check kiting. "If the banks had only let us write on what we had in our account, we'd have been fucked," thought Morze. "ZZZZ Best, Marbil, Interstate, we all needed instant credit. It was the only way we could convince everybody that $500,000 was really $5 million."

— 8 —

BARRY, MORZE, AND PADGETT weren't only kiting checks and rolling over old loans; they were desperately seeking out new loans as well. In late September—thanks once again to the backing of partner Paul Schiff—they were able to obtain two loans, totaling $1.5 million, from First Interstate Bank. These were among the first of several "gap loans" that would tide them over until the public offering.

Although the officials of First Interstate felt comfortable with the new funding because of Schiff's guarantee, ZZZZ Best's performance in paying back two previous loans (also totaling $1.5 million), and Barry's "charismatic dynamism," Richard Motika, the loan manager at First Interstate's Beverly Hills office, wanted to take a closer look—and "get [his] arms around the flow" of contracts, receivables, and financial reports so as to understand the business a bit better.

Moreover, Motika—an energetic man of about forty-five who resembles Gerald Ford at a similar age—wanted to eliminate Schiff as the guarantor of loans, to "take him out of the loop" and rely strictly on ZZZZ Best's cash flow when negotiating future deals. A business's cash flow was, after all, one of the important criteria on which the decision to grant a loan was usually based, and Motika felt he would be even more comfortable if that was the way the bank handled ZZZZ Best.

Besides, Barry had already mentioned to Steve Monchamp— the First Interstate loan officer in charge of ZZZZ Best's account— that after the $1.5 million in loans currently outstanding had been paid off, he was interested in another loan, this one for $3 million, guaranteed by the money from the stock offering. So Motika also wanted to check out Barry Minkow, the dynamic entrepreneur he'd heard so much about but had never met.

The boys, for their part, were also keen for the meeting, wanting to lay the groundwork for the new $3 million loan and to mention in passing that they'd like an extension of about a month or so (from November to December) on the repayment of the two loans recently granted. So in early October, a meeting was held at First

Interstate's Beverly Hills office. Present were Motika, another bank official named Mike Farmer, and Barry, Mark, and Padgett.

Richard Motika was immediately taken by Barry Minkow, who struck him as a "hands-on" leader, "clearly in control—an entrepreneur who could build a company . . . had a vision . . . and could reach that vision."

"Force of personality," Motika later explained, "has a lot to do with the success of a young company . . . [and] Barry had the kind of charisma that really made a difference."

As the meeting progressed, Barry did well in explaining why ZZZZ Best was able to generate such an extraordinary profit margin. He simply gave them his old good-shopper routine, describing for the zillionth time his ability to personally find "seconds" or closeouts on wholesale carpeting and then immediately cut a deal, whipping out his personal checkbook and writing $100,000 checks "on the spot" from his own account, in the process often saving as much as 30 percent. This astute shopping and instantaneous buying gave ZZZZ Best a tremendous advantage, Barry explained, over other companies that had to buck such a large cash decision up the chain of command, thus losing the cash-on-the-barrelhead opportunities Barry was so good at finding and quickly exploiting.

Barry's good-shopper rap also helped explain why his name popped up so often on First Interstate's report of check-kiting suspects and its list of check overdrafts.

Each time Barry wrote an overdraft on his or ZZZZ Best's accounts, First Interstate honored it and then politely notified him. And each time, Barry would make good the check, getting money however he could. So Motika largely ignored the frequent appearance of Barry's name on the overdraft list—or at least he did not take it as cause for alarm. For whenever he saw Barry's name, he'd remember that early October meeting and Barry describing how he had to write checks on the spot without knowing at that moment if he had enough money to cover them. The ability *not* to have to worry about that was after all one of the key ingredients in Barry's success, and Richard Motika, good banker that he was, understood.

What Motika was finding more difficult to understand as the meeting progressed, however, was the obvious uneasiness Barry and Tom Padgett displayed each time questions were raised concerning insurance company names or visits to restoration sites. Padgett seemed "reluctant to give any names at all," thought

Motika. In fact, Motika found him unusually silent and "not very forthcoming, expansive, or open—unlike most entrepreneurs."

From their actions and pained response, Motika got the impression that it was the confidentiality imposed on them "that was creating the barrier," and not Barry or Tom.

Finally, Barry told the bankers that while he understood their concerns, the jobs were all extremely safe investments. In fact, he said, in many cases they were even bonded.

This was a wildly audacious statement on Barry's part. Just as there were no jobs, there were as yet no bonds—not even forgeries.

But the mention of bonds—which were essentially guarantees that an investor was insured in the event that ZZZZ Best went bankrupt and failed to complete a job—broke the impasse and appeared to put the bankers at ease. Padgett recalls their attitude as being, "That's great; if we can't talk to the insurance companies, we'll talk to the bonding people."

Sensing a compromise they could live with, Barry looked at Mark, and Mark turned to Tom and said, "Well, as long as there's no negative exposure, do you think we can work it out?" Tom replied that the confidentiality agreement he'd signed applied to the bonding company as well as the insurers, but that he thought he might be able to work something out. He'd need, however, a couple of days to arrange it.

With that, the meeting adjourned. As Barry, Mark, and Tom were leaving, Mark told the bankers he'd get back to them.

The following day, Mark called a Wilshire Boulevard answering service, opened an account in the name of Liberty Western Bonding, and received a phone number. Then he called the phone company and had his "new company" and its number listed with the information operator. A day later, he phoned information, asked for Liberty Western, and got his line at the answering service. He then called two additional times, just to make sure the number was locked into Pacific Bell's information system. It was.

Next, he dialed First Interstate's loan department and spoke with Tim Morphy, an expansive, straw-haired loan officer in his midthirties. Mark told Morphy he'd been able to arrange for him to call Liberty Western and speak with an official named Mark Stewart. Morphy, however, would have to call between three and four o'clock on the specific day he was now giving him because, as Morphy knew, the guy was breaking the confidentiality agreement by even talking with him.

"OK," said Morphy. Then, as Morze had known he would, Tim Morphy asked for Liberty Western's number. "Just a minute," said Mark, pausing for a moment before coming back on the line. "Goddamn it, I had it right here, but I can't find it. Why don't you put me on hold and call information?" A moment later, Morphy was back on the line, giving Liberty Western's number to Mark. "Well, *that* worked like a charm," thought Morze as he hung up.

Then Mark called the answering service and arranged the last exquisite detail. He requested that Morphy's call (the only one, after all, that would be coming through) be placed on call forwarding and diverted to the house of a friend of Mark's. At the designated time, Mark Morze was at that friend's house, as the service operator answered "Liberty Western?" and transferred Morphy's call.

With "people in the next room doing their best to stifle their giggles," Morze identified himself as Mark Stewart, breaking into his best fey, high-nasal, Newport Beach accent. This further cracked up the gigglers in the bedroom, who were by now beside themselves.

Yes, he told Tim Morphy, Liberty Western *had* bonded dozens of jobs for Interstate Appraisal Services. And no, he "really couldn't give the exact numbers," but "suffice it to say, they're all six- or seven-figure jobs." Then, as a final gesture of cooperation, Mark Morze told Tim Morphy that, yes, he would indeed send him a letter confirming the call.

True to his word, he did.

It was right around this time, perhaps the very same day as the October meeting, that Barry offered a job to Steve Monchamp, First Interstate's officer in charge of ZZZZ Best's loans. Monchamp had been asking to visit a restoration site since July, when the initial $750,000 First Interstate loan had been made, and now he was pressing Barry really hard.

Barry had been playing his usual why-don't-you-come-to-work-for-me-and-make-some-real-money game with Monchamp, who had been most useful as a liaison between ZZZZ Best and Motika and Schiff.

Now, perhaps as a reward for his service or perhaps because he was getting just a bit *too* demanding in his site visitation requests, Barry made Steve Monchamp a serious job offer: operating the proposed corporate offices in Northern California. It was to be "sort of a public relations" position, although Monchamp had had no experience in PR.

But the pay was good—$47,500, a hefty raise over his $35,000-a-year salary at First Interstate Bank. And a $500 monthly car allowance would raise Monchamp's total pay and benefits to $53,500—an increase of more than $18,000. That kind of money, Barry knew, would be too difficult for a midlevel executive in his thirties to turn down. And it was.

In mid-November, Steve Monchamp left First Interstate Bank, and the following month he began his vaguely defined executive position with ZZZZ Best—never exactly sure of what it was that he was supposed to be doing. He'd thought he'd be working in restoration, but whatever he was asked to do seemed always to have to do with carpet cleaning. When he complained to Barry, he was told not to worry, that he would, in time, get to work on the restoration side of the business.

But to Mark Morze, Barry said something quite different. "What," he asked Mark, "am I gonna do with the guy?"

— 9 —

AS THE UNDERWRITING MEETING droned on, Mark Morze tuned out, focusing instead on the kaleidoscopic events of the past several months. It seemed only days since Barry had hired Steve Monchamp away from First Interstate, and Mark was still not totally certain if he'd done so because he liked Monchamp or because he'd seen in his hiring another mini-cure for another of ZZZZ Best's endless problems.

There had been so many mini-cures over the past year and a half, thought Mark. The credit card float. The loans—through Jack Catain—from Kay Rosario and her group of investors. The fake equipment leases through Danny Krowpman. The first Cal Factor loan. The $2 million credit line from Jay Botchman—$800,000 of which went to Kay's investors and right back to Barry. Schiff and the first two $750,000 loans from First Interstate; Charbit and the $800,000 line of credit from Bank Hapoalim. Schiff again and the second series of loans from First Interstate, totaling $1.5 million, plus the three- or four-week extension on their repayment. The $1.5

million "bridge loan" that had recently come in from Rooney, Pace. And, finally, the $500,000 loan Barry had just gotten from Neal Dem, a prosperous Chatsworth businessman and member of ZZZZ Best's board of directors, who'd come through with a last-ditch, last-moment loan in return for the promise of quick repayment at the time of the stock offering and an option to buy Barry's restricted stock at a dirt-cheap price once it became available in 1988.

They were all mini-cures, thought Mark as he drifted in and out of the meeting, but then Barry's entire life was a series of mini-cures, just as Mark's had now become.

But the stock offering, the stock offering, now *that* was going to be the *maxi*-cure.

And there was no question that it would go through.

Quick study that he was, Barry had figured out right from the beginning that the "professionals"—all of whom were either working for him or stood to benefit from a successful stock offering—weren't going to ask questions any more probing or knowledgeable than those he, Mark, or Tom had already been asked hundreds of times in the past.

And sure enough, that was indeed the case. But it wasn't just what the pros *asked* that filled Mark Morze with such contempt. No, it was more the questions they didn't ask—questions any lay person would have put.

To believe, for example, that a $7 million restoration contract like the Sacramento job—a contract with millions of dollars' worth of purchases and *no* specifications—could fit on one piece of paper, well, it was hard to believe that anybody could be that stupid. Every time he'd gotten a dent in his fender, for Christ's sake, they'd hand him a twenty-five-page invoice to sign.

And the profit margins! Alarms should have *rung* in the heads of all these Wall Street people when they were told that ZZZZ Best was doing $50 million worth of business with one company at profit margins of close to 40 percent. Why hadn't any of them picked up a phone and asked another restoration company about profit margins in the industry? And $7 million restoration jobs: if they had mentioned numbers like that to other restoration firms, the laughs would have broken their eardrums.

Nor had anyone ever asked about construction licenses, traffic abatement permits, payroll records for the hundreds of people who should have been working on the projects, OSHA reports, or local and state permits and inspections.

This last, thought Morze, was truly unbelievable. How do you seal off streets to do a mammoth restoration job without permits? How do you build or reconstruct *anything* without permits and inspections?

The few times someone did ask about inspections, Morze remembered, Barry would make up something stupid like, "The only inspections we have to pass are the insurance companies'—and Padgett takes care of those." Or he would tell them that the requirements ZZZZ Best had to meet "were the same ones as interior decorators," because everything they did "was cosmetic."

And what about *me*? Mark thought. Here I am, a history major in college and then a bookkeeper, but all of a sudden I'm writing up cost estimates on multimillion-dollar restoration jobs in one day, and nobody even asks, "Who *is* this guy?" It probably took Blackmon, Mooring Steamatic with all their people *four days* to estimate the $2.1 million MGM Grand job—the biggest contract in their forty-year existence. It really *was* unbelievable.

But thank God for Larry Gray, the Ernst & Whinney accountant handling the audit for the prospectus. If he had demanded original documentation, Mark reflected, that would have been it, the ball game, the end of the line. But the guy had settled for the same creative copies they'd given Greenspan. And once they saw that Gray was satisfied with copies, well, anything was possible. Nor did Gray ever ask to see Interstate's books—at a time when Interstate was giving ZZZZ Best almost all of its restoration business.

And *this* guy, thought Morze, looking down the table at Mark Moskowitz, the Hughes Hubbard & Reed attorney, he sure isn't any rocket scientist either, even if he did go to Harvard. He'd bought Barry's stupid story about flying up to the Sacramento job when there was labor unrest, grabbing a cab to the site, hopping up on a girder, and giving an inspirational speech to the workers and calming everything down. Imagine it. Moskowitz seemed like a nice guy, but Barry really had him sandbagged. He treated Barry like he was a younger brother. Barry would go over and baby-sit Moskowitz's children, and give them gifts on occasions like their Bar Mitzvah. There was even talk that Barry had put the kids into his will, and that he and Moskowitz were going to build huge houses together—side by side high atop a peak that separates the San Fernando and Simi valleys.

Of course, the fact that Moskowitz's law firm was making about $400,000 from the offering and was working for Barry hadn't hurt anything. Ernst & Whinney, too, had a reverse incentive: Barry was paying their fees, not Rooney, Pace or the SEC. Moreover, a public offering of the size of ZZZZ Best's was undoubtedly one of the biggest jobs the relatively tiny Reseda branch of Ernst & Whinney was likely to see.

Like Rooney, Pace and the law firm of Hughes Hubbard & Reed, Ernst & Whinney was under tremendous self-imposed pressure to make the offering work. The competition in stock underwriting, like that in big-time law and accounting, was fierce, and Barry was the golden goose nobody wanted to kill.

It was nine o'clock at night, and everybody in the conference room was exhausted when Barry finally called through after his speaking engagement. Placed on the speaker phone, he wanted to go over the entire seventy pages of the prospectus. When he was told that it was nine at night and that would be impossible, he picked a few things to focus on. Primarily, he was concerned about his biography. It was too short, he said, and not flattering enough. It seemed to take forever to convince him that it was a prospectus, not a press release, and everything in it was *supposed* to be short.

Then, as the meeting was about to break up, Faith Griffin, an official from Rooney, Pace, simultaneously shattered Mark's reverie and belied his contempt—at least for the moment—for the underwriting investigation.

"This underwriting can't go forward," Griffin announced, "until we see a couple of these restoration jobs. You have over $20 million in restoration work," she told Chip, Andersen, and Morze, "of which $7 million is for the Sacramento job. We have to see three jobs. You can pick two, but one of the three *has* to be Sacramento, it's so big."

Despite Mark Morze's caustic impressions, Griffin was genuinely concerned about proceeding with the offering without first verifying the restoration work. ZZZZ Best had come from nowhere, and her brokerage house was now about to underwrite $15 million in new stock for a fledgling company run by a twenty-year-old kid. The jobs—particularly Sacramento—*needed* to be checked out.

Larry Gray, the Ernst & Whinney accountant, also was concerned about seeing the Sacramento site and joined Griffin in insisting they be permitted to do so. Over the past weeks, he had told Barry on several occasions that he wanted to visit a job site, but the Boy Wonder had always managed to put him off. Now Gray was no longer willing to wait. It wasn't that he was particularly suspicious, but he felt he should compare the bills he'd seen with the work actually completed.

So when Mark responded with the usual can't-be-done-because-of-confidentiality routine, Griffin and Gray were adamant that it *would* be done. "I don't care about that," Griffin told Mark. "You figure it out. I'm instructed to tell you that there is no deal without a visit to Sacramento."

The next day, Tom Padgett got a call from Barry. "Get over here," Barry said. "We've got trouble."

When Padgett arrived at ZZZZ Best's headquarters, Barry told him what had gone down at the prospectus meeting, and how Griffin and Gray would not be turned around.

"We have no choice," said Barry. "They've got to see something. I'll try to stall them, and you take Roddy, get up to Sacramento, and find a building that will substantiate that much damage [$7 million]. Then we'll get Morze to walk them through."

Within a day or so, Tom Padgett and Mark Roddy were on a PSA flight to Sacramento.

Earlier, Tom had convinced Barry to put Roddy on Interstate's payroll after the albino had gotten busted in New Mexico in August for a coke deal gone bad. Tom had even managed to talk Minkow into engaging Arthur Barens to defend Roddy, and to give the attorney $15,000 toward his defense. Roddy was charged with interstate transportation as well as dealing and was looking at some *serious* time. With a prior bust for an earlier coke deal, the albino's future was not looking auspicious. But he'd been there for Padgett when he was going through his Debbie blues, and Tom was determined to be there when his friend needed help.

Now Tom was glad he'd helped the albino out and that he was going along with him to Sacramento. Roddy was full of laughs and energy, and in spite of his girth, really had a way with women.

Besides, Padgett was nervous, and having Roddy along was comforting. Flying up to Sacramento, he thought about how everything depended on *him* finding a building and passing it off as the Sacramento job. If he struck out, there would be "no stock offering, no payback of investors, no tomorrow! It would all come tumbling down."

He'd never thought the offering process was going to be easy, but compared with dealing with the banks, investors, and loan due dates, it hadn't caused him much anxiety. Every time someone at Ernst & Whinney had wanted something, he or she would ask Barry, and *Mark* would come up with it. The firm had only contacted him twice, each time by mail. One letter asked him to verify about fifteen restoration jobs he'd given to ZZZZ Best. ("Jesus Christ," the albino had said as he'd watched Tom initial each of the jobs listed on the letter. "Do you know the felonies you've just committed?") The second was a letter promising *him* they wouldn't contact the insurance companies.

But now all of a sudden, Ernst & Whinney was insisting on this inspection stuff. Well, he'd just have to remember what he'd been taught in Vietnam: "Fear is a natural emotion. Use it to focus."

— 10 —

AFTER ABOUT HALF A DAY of driving around Sacramento with its "older, kind of back-East buildings, neighborhoods, and mom-and-pop stores," Tom and Roddy came to the conclusion that there was only one building in town that could even remotely substantiate $7 million worth of damage: the Capitol Bank Building, a new, modern, eighteen-story tower on the Sacramento Capitol Mall. It had actually been the first building they'd looked at as well. One of Ernst & Whinney's accountants had mentioned to Barry that he "bet the 'Sacramento job' was the Capitol Bank Building." So before Tom left, Barry had told him "to make sure and check the Capitol Bank Building."

And the accountant was right, thought Tom, this has to be it.

The next morning, Tom and Roddy got up, put on "nice suits," and drove to the Capitol Bank Building to talk with the manager.

Tom was thankful that things so far seemed to be going well. Their first hurdle had been to rent a car. Such a relatively simple task was usually a problem, for neither he nor the albino had any credit cards, and car rental firms were not keen to let a car out of their sight without "seeing some plastic."

But they'd gotten one with ease, and now they also had an early appointment with the building manager.

As they drove to the Capitol Mall, Tom and the albino went over their game plan once again: They had a large, expanding telemarketing business, and they wanted to lease some space. Actually, not just *some* space, but *considerable* space—three or four thousand square feet. The larger, the better, in fact, for that would mean a bigger commission for the building manager, whose cooperation was essential.

Tom felt really confident as they walked in to meet the manager. Thanks to the real estate courses he'd been taking, he now knew "all the negotiating terms" and "had a feel for" what he was about to do.

Sure enough, everything went smoothly. There was plenty of space still left to rent in the newly completed building. In fact, several floors were not yet quite finished, which made Tom Padgett *really* start feeling good—good enough so that he didn't panic and jump on what was available, but told the manager instead that he'd have to think it over, and would stop back in a day or so and let him know.

Next, they put into effect the second phase of the game plan—finding an office for Assured Property Management.

Assured Property Management was, like Tom's Interstate Appraisal Services, a totally bogus company dreamed up by Mark Morze. ("Morze's genius again!" Tom was to say later in awed admiration.) Its sole purpose was to add yet another layer of credibility to the scam.

While Tom's company gave ZZZZ Best the restoration jobs, Assured Property Management—which was to be "run" by Roddy—was theoretically to *manage* the building, serving, during the restoration, as a liaison between the building's tenants and the insurance companies and making sure everybody was happy.

That very day, they found and rented the perfect little furnished office for Assured in a building that specialized in small suites and provided a receptionist who served all the corporations in the building.

Pleased with themselves, they decided to celebrate that night. They had arrived in Sacramento on Monday night and less than twenty-four hours later had set up the first leg in making the Capitol Bank Building *theirs*, and had found an office for Assured.

So Roddy started belting back White Russians, and Tom started hitting the beers until Roddy got so drunk he called an escort service for a call girl. Unfortunately, by the time she arrived, the Ultimate White Man had passed out.

The next morning, they picked up Morze at the airport. They needed his blessing before proceeding.

First, they made a dry run, showing Mark the Capitol Bank Building and Assured's new office, and familiarizing him with the routes to and from each.

Then the three of them, dressed in suits and looking the part of entrepreneurs expanding their telemarketing business into the Sacramento area, walked into the Capitol Bank Building.

Padgett felt excited, "like a soldier on a tense mission that is now about to be accomplished."

Seeing the new building with its several empty, partially completed floors, Mark, too, became excited. "This is *great*," he told Tom.

Feeling loose and with few people around, they began to look for the sprinkler system, because Barry had told several members of the underwriting team that there had been a fire, and the sprinkler system had malfunctioned—spilling forth far too much water and damaging everything. They wanted, therefore, to be able to point out the sprinkler system to Gray and Moskowitz and whoever else was to fly up for the inspection. (Another version had it that a vandal had emptied the rooftop water tanks, thus causing the water damage.)

Finding the sprinklers, they then addressed their next concern, getting the keys for the building so that they could conduct the inspection tour on Sunday. It *had* to be on a Sunday when nobody would be around to foul things up. Supposing, for example, that during the tour, Gray or Moskowitz "has to take a leak," Tom explained later, "and while he's pissin', he says to the guy next to him, 'Man, they really did some job fixing that water damage,' and the guy looks at him and says, 'The fuck you talkin' about water damage? This building's only a year old.'"

So it had to be on a Sunday. And it had to be set up. Tom, therefore, went back to the building manager, told him he was 99 percent sure he was going to lease the space, but that he "needed approval of a couple of major investors," who were coming in on Sunday from out of town. Would there be any problem getting the keys then? No problem, the manager said, just tell the guard.

That accomplished, the boys prepared to leave, but decided to take a final look around—without the manager—at the still incompleted floors.

What they were looking for were the notices they'd spotted

earlier, stating the name of the building contractor, the contract number, and the expected completion date. A few of these were taken down, the names whited out, and ZZZZ Best's name inserted instead. The altered notices were to be replaced in strategic, hard-to-miss spots on the day of the inspection tour.

They also came across an unexpected find: blueprints of what appeared to be the entire building. Talk about enhancing credibility. Padgett looked around, saw no one, grabbed the prints, stashed them in his briefcase, and the boys took off.

Leaving Roddy to hold down the fort in Sacramento, Mark and Tom flew back to LA and reported to Barry that all was ready. It was now left up to him to tell the underwriting people that the inspection tour was on, but that it had to be done on Sunday.

Originally four members of the underwriting team were to go, but when Barry told them the site could be visited only on Sunday ("the only time we won't disturb the workmen"), two were forced to drop out, and it was agreed that just Moskowitz and Gray would make the trip.

After the meeting with Barry, Tom turned around and headed straight back to Sacramento. It was now Friday. The inspection was on Sunday. He had things to do.

Most of Saturday morning was spent giving the Assured office "a lived-in look." First, he and Roddy scattered writing pads, pens, pencils, and other office materials around. Then they put up a map of Sacramento, and with crayons drew official-looking circles around "job sites."

Leaving the office, they stopped by a poker parlor, where Roddy played and Tom drank until it was time to pick up Mark at the airport.

After leading Mark through another dry run to the Capitol Bank Building and Assured Property's office, they returned to the hotel, where, already "well oiled," Tom introduced Morze to his new love: Moosehead, a Canadian beer that Mark had never tried. About four six-packs later, Morze called Barry to give him a status report and, for Tom's benefit, started bitching about having to spend the evening with Padgett and a fat albino in a room cluttered with dozens of beer bottles. Even though it was the night before the big day, Tom later recalled, it turned out to be a pretty good time.

At five o'clock Sunday morning, still pretty hung over, the boys got up, and Tom drove Mark back to the airport, where he caught a flight to LA.

Arriving in Los Angeles, Mark got into his car—which he'd left at the airport the night before—drove to Mark Moskowitz's house, picked him up, and then drove on to Larry Gray's and back to the LA airport.

After the short hop back up to Sacramento, the three men deplaned, Morze rented a car, and they headed to the office of Assured Property Management. Mark was apprehensive, but not overly so. These two guys, he thought, were definitely not "deal busters." Just days before, they had signed confidentiality letters that said, among other things, "We will not disclose the location of such building, or any other information with respect to the project or the building, to any third parties or to any other members or employees of our firm [nor will we] make any follow-up telephone calls to any contractors, insurance companies, the building owner, or other individuals involved in the restoration project."

After Tom had dropped Morze at the airport, he went back to their hotel, picked up Roddy, and drove to the Capitol Mall.

They still had work to do.

At the Capitol Bank Building, they approached the guard. "Say," said Tom, "you could really do us a favor. My friend here," Padgett continued, pointing at the unforgettable albino, "is going to be back here in a couple of hours with my partner, a guy named Morze," whereupon Tom proceeded to describe Mark. "Now, he's going to be with some investors, and we want it to seem like we're known around here, so if you could say something like, 'Mr. Morze, you're back again,' I'd really appreciate it," said Tom, as he handed the guard fifty bucks.

Nodding, the guard repeated "Mr. Morze," and pocketed the money.

Then Tom went into the building, put the bogus signs now reading "ZZZZ Best" back on the wall, and scattered three or four ZZZZ Best T-shirts on one of the uncompleted floors. This last was so Morze, feigning anger, could spot them and curse out his "workers" for leaving them lying around like that. Hadn't he warned them before that it was a fire hazard? ("Morze was a genius—a genius—at this improvisational stuff," Tom said later.)

Having completed his mission, Tom Padgett, who wasn't even supposed to know about the inspection (a violation of the confidentiality agreement between Interstate and its insurance clients) and *certainly* shouldn't have been in Sacramento, went back to his hotel to watch football on television, and in between try to study his insurance books.

Barry, meanwhile, was pacing back and forth in LA, constantly calling Tom for reassurance. Tom was apprehensive, but Barry seemed even more so. There he was, in LA, having to rely on *them*, when he knew nobody could do something like this as well as he could. He was, after all, the superstar.

All Tom could do was to keep reassuring him: "We've laid the groundwork, Barry, just stop worrying."

Roddy acted cranky when Morze pulled up to Assured's office. As planned, after he'd been introduced as an old college buddy of Tom's, he grumbled good-naturedly about how his Sunday had been ruined and how there were "always problems when lawyers and accountants are involved." Then he got into Mark's rented car, and the four of them took off to the "restoration site." It was a beautiful, crisp fall day, November 23, 1986, little more than two weeks before the public offering.

Tom's fifty bucks turned out to be a good investment. Wearing the plastic ID Morze had given him on the way in, Larry Gray noted "the pleasantries and greetings" exchanged between Morze and the security guard in the lobby as Mark signed the visitors' book.

Moskowitz, too, was impressed by the VIP treatment the guard extended to Mark during the signing and as they waited for the elevator to take them to the twelfth floor, where the tour was to start.

Arriving on that floor, Mark explained to them how water from the roof storage tanks and sprinklers had been released during "an act of vandalism" that had "caused extensive damage" and was still under investigation.

As they worked their way randomly down to the third or fourth floor, Mark explained what the "water extraction" restoration work entailed: pulling up carpets and flooring to dry them out, treating subflooring for water damage, and restoring fixtures, moldings, and wood paneling.

Mark also mentioned how particularly proud he was of the thirty or so bathrooms ZZZZ Best had restored, putting in new wiring, plumbing, and toilets and completely retiling them.

After looking at the stolen blueprints and some photos of the projects, they began making their way out of the building. As they did so, Larry Gray looked at Morze and said, "Gee, it doesn't even look like anything went wrong here."

When Roddy returned to the hotel, he was visibly elated. Everything had gone perfectly, he told Tom. And when he called Barry to tell him the good news, Barry said that, yeah, he knew. He'd already spoken with Mark, who'd told him the same thing. Tom felt good, not just for himself but for Barry.

Barry had seemed so relieved.

On December 4, 1986, five days before the public sale of ZZZZ Best stock, Barry Minkow took Mark Moskowitz to view two other restoration sites, as Faith Griffin had demanded. Moskowitz had told Barry that he hoped he had two jobs close by because he didn't feel like traveling. This suited Barry perfectly, because perhaps the only two *real* restoration jobs ZZZZ Best had—tiny and insignificant though they were—just happened to be located in metropolitan LA. Of course, Barry didn't mention to Mark Moskowitz that even these two tiny jobs had been subcontracted out to small firms, since Mark Morze was the sole ZZZZ Best employee in any way involved in the restoration work.

— 11 —

FOR JOEL HOCHBERG, the food at the swank Malibu seaside restaurant called Splash was "the best in town." Johnny Carson dined there, he'd been told, and, as he ate, Joel could understand why. The Cajun roast beef, charred just so on the outside, had been mouth watering, and as he relaxed over a drink after dinner Joel was more than pleased with his entrée choice. For it was the first time at any of Barry's official functions that Barry had permitted everyone to order directly off the menu.

It was August or September of 1986, and about fifty ZZZZ Best employees, mostly upper managers, were sitting around two long banquet tables, listening to Barry's startling announcement of why he'd called them together.

He intended, said Barry Minkow as he stood before his employees, to immediately institute a stringent drug-testing policy for all ZZZZ Best personnel.

Then, perhaps in response to the stunned looks on the faces of the relatively young managerial staff—many of whom, it might be assumed, were fond of getting it on in their free time—Barry "pointed at several people and asked, 'What's your feeling about this?'" One of those at whom he pointed was Joel Hochberg. Joel, newly hired and a self-described "company man like George Bush," knew Barry well enough to know that Barry wasn't really asking. So Joel did what he had to: "I'm for it," he said.

Others were not so compliant, but Barry was adamant, and by the time the meeting adjourned, he had made it clear to everybody that the policy was now in effect and that those who didn't like it were free to leave.

Afterward, as they were making their way out of the restaurant, Barry slid up to Joel, winked, and out of the side of his mouth, said, "Hochberg, let me know when you've got five days clean [for testing]."

Since Joel had stopped his suicidal alcohol addiction through AA about three years earlier, he'd been totally dry and had, in fact, become the kind of reformed alcoholic who could—and *would* without prompting—look at his watch and tell you down to the day and hour the last time he'd had a drink, literally knocking on wood as he did so.

He still, however, liked his occasional line of blow or a joint after a day's work, as Barry well knew, and that, he figured, was the reason for the warning.

But, Jesus Christ, it wasn't as if Barry himself were any Nancy Reagan. True, at parties or anyplace else, Barry always had a diet soda and never a drink in his hand. Everybody knew how much he hated alcohol.

But what about the times at Barry's house when he'd spend an entire evening in the *bathroom* with the guy snorting coke? And what about afterward, when they and a bunch of the other people at the party had gone through all they had, and Barry started screaming for Joel to get more? "How much is it, Hochberg?" Barry had asked.

"Two hundred and fifty dollars."

"Two hundred and fifty?" said Barry. "Here's three hundred. Get something better."

Then there was Easter break, just a couple of months before

Barry announced his testing policy. Barry was driving a new red convertible and was tooling around with the top down, just like Magnum.

"Come on, Hochberg, let's go to Palm Springs," he'd said, and off they'd gone. And with that car, remembered Joel, they "didn't need a rod or reel; the girls just jumped in." Of course, the $350-a-night room hadn't hurt either. Nor had the five grams of coke Barry'd brought along.

But Barry was certainly no druggie, and around the office at ZZZZ Best, he was always super cool. Once, Joel remembered, Barry called him into his office, where he was having a good-natured but serious argument with one of his secretaries about whether or not he'd used drugs. "Hochberg," he said, "don't bullshit, you get high, but tell this woman, have *I* ever done drugs?"

"No," said Joel, who shortly thereafter was rewarded for the right answer with a $500 bonus.

"Five hundred dollars?" Hochberg thought later. "I wonder what the picture I've got of him sitting around a plate of cocaine is worth?"

If Joel had been a blackmailer instead of Barry's friend, it might have been worth a good deal. For once Barry had declared his drug-testing policy, he made it a very high profile endeavor indeed.

In the ensuring months, without warning, ZZZZ Best employees would be told that at five o'clock it was their turn to urinate into a bottle. Once when Joel tested "dirty" due to a mix-up in urine samples, Barry told him, "Give it up, or I'll accept your resignation. We're a public company now, and getting bigger."

— 12 —

BARRY MINKOW HAD BEEN MOVED not just to test his employees for drugs, but to launch an entire antidrug crusade, after watching President Reagan's now famous "War on Drugs" speech.

Like many of his generation, Barry idolized Ronald Reagan. So after Reagan's speech, Barry called his PR team at Jeri Carr's and told them he wanted ZZZZ Best to get behind the President's "war."

They responded with an intense media blitz worthy of the Great Communicator's own PR handlers.

A check for $10,000 was given to Narcanon, an antidrug-abuse program. Another $20,000 was given jointly to the Simi Valley Unified School District and the area's police department. (Hal Lipman, the father of Barry's girlfriend, Joyce, was an associate school superintendent for the Simi Valley School District as well as a member of ZZZZ Best's board of directors.)

Accompanying the $20,000 donation were several flattering articles in the local newspaper, the *Simi Valley Enterprise*. Under the headline "Millionaire Pledges War on Drugs," a huge photo depicted Barry holding the handle of a large professional-looking steam cleaner—a determined look in his eye—as he is about to descend on a carpet littered with pills, joints, baggies, and drug paraphernalia. The caption headed "Clean Sweep" announced that "Barry Minkow, Chairman and Chief Executive Officer and President of ZZZZ Best, Inc.—the fourth largest carpet-cleaning and restoring business in the United States—has embarked on a national anti-drug abuse effort, 'My Act Is Clean, How's Yours?'"

The photo, as well as the "My Act Is Clean, How's Yours?" logo, became an integral part of ZZZZ Best's press kit, and was distributed all over town by Carr and her staff.

From the kit, local reporters learned not just about the drug campaign and the donations connected with it, but about other acts of generosity by Barry as well. There was mention, for example, of the money he gave to Mothers Against Drunk Driving to fund a Charlton Heston commercial and the award he received in return from MADD. The press kit also pointed out that he had given $20,000 to the West Valley YMCA, where he'd worked out as a youngster, and more than $30,000 to a local girls' softball league.

Nobody who knew Barry Minkow could doubt the generosity of spirit in which he made all these contributions nor forget the scores of times he helped friends and acquaintances in need. But if the donations were helpful, so was the press coverage.

— 13 —

CHIP WAS EXHAUSTED. In addition to his regular duties that October, he'd been putting in fourteen-hour days for weeks on end, going over the prospectus with the underwriting team.

As the preliminary prospectus—a sort of rough draft or working document distributed to potential investors prior to the SEC's approval of the offering—neared completion, Chip also began to prepare with Barry for the time when they would take their "dog and pony show" on the road. The purpose of such "shows"—in which top corporate managers travel around the country hyping their business—is to solicit would-be investors and convince them to buy the company's stock when it is offered for sale.

Chip, as the theoretical number two man in ZZZZ Best's hierarchy, was chosen—along with controller Bruce Andersen—to accompany Barry on what was essentially a traveling stock sale.

Before embarking on their trip, however, the three ZZZZ Best executives were carefully rehearsed by the Rooney, Pace underwriters.

Among those doing the coaching was Faith Griffin, a Rooney, Pace investment banker. An attractive, smartly dressed woman with shoulder-length, dark blond hair who looks like a cross between Jane Curtin and Lauren Bacall, Griffin had started in the underwriting business in 1971, bringing between 50 and 100 companies public since then. It was she who would be responsible for preparation of the ZZZZ Best prospectus as well as helping to market the stock and set up meetings with brokers and investors.

Initially, Griffin had been wary of Barry's age and had recommended that Hughes Hubbard & Reed be brought in as Barry's law firm. She insisted too on a Big Eight accounting firm. After all, betting $8 million on a twenty-year-old kid was not something one approached lightly. But after getting to know Barry, she found him to be "extremely bright" and "very dynamic"—someone who "came across like one of those extraordinary personalities . . . convinced that he was going to conquer the world." And other people had also been young when they started business, she noted, like Steven Jobs at Apple Computer, whom Barry claimed he knew.

In her fifteen years on Wall Street, Griffin had often observed that "people that are successful have a sense of drive, they give their all to a business," and that was certainly the case with Barry Minkow.

There was, in addition, Barry's "impressive grasp of the financial aspects of ZZZZ Best. He seemed very knowledgeable about his business and the potential of ZZZZ Best to generate great revenues ... [and seemed] very astute about the numbers of his business."

But Barry was not only familiar with ZZZZ Best's finances; equally important to Faith Griffin was Barry's knowledge of his business. "He'd walk into an office," says Griffin, "get onto his hands and knees, and tell you the grade of carpet and the square footage. He really seemed to know what he was talking about." And when he described the restoration business, he could do so in great detail, telling her how ZZZZ Best specialized in water or smoke damage and how his company's emergency services helped minimize the damage.

Barry also left no question about what a shrewd businessman he was. He told Griffin the big-profits-because-of-buying-carpet-cheaply story and his dramatic anecdote about halting a strike in Sacramento with a motivational speech.

So when it came time to coach Barry and the others for the road show, Faith Griffin was more than happy to do so. Barry, Chip, and Bruce Andersen were shown how to talk, what to say, when to speed up, when to slow down, and how to articulate better the points they wanted to make. A slide show was also developed that detailed ZZZZ Best's management, product, earnings, and growth potential, and Barry and the others practiced how to key their presentation to it.

But the hard part was teaching Barry the social graces. There was, for example, the time he was idly playing with a red plastic coffee stirrer during an underwriters' meeting and, as Chip sat across from him watching in horrified fascination, began using it to pick lint out of his navel. "You can't imagine the faces of the people there," said Chip. But Barry seemed totally unaware that his behavior might be offensive or inappropriate. It was the same when he would flirt with Sharon Brodwin, a young Hughes Hubbard & Reed attorney and a member of the underwriting team, by taking his shoes off and slyly tossing them at her under the table.

Sometimes Barry *needed* to be twenty.

Although the upcoming road shows were to prove wearying, Chip was being well rewarded. In addition to his $42,000 salary for 1986, he would receive a $50,000 bonus when the money from the stock offering came through. (Bruce Andersen had been promised a bonus of the same amount.) The bonus was a reward for the underwriting meetings they'd attended and the ten "performances" they were to give on the "dog and pony" road show.

Putting up with Barry's ego and eccentricities and submitting to occasional humiliations weren't always easy, but Chip—who really did like Barry in spite of everything—couldn't complain. In just three years with ZZZZ Best, he'd managed to purchase a house he was proud of and was driving, in car-conscious LA, both a Chevy Corvette and a 300 ZX leased by the company. And now he was to receive a bonus of $50,000. Not bad for someone who, left on his own, might well have still been cleaning carpets.

On the road show, however, Chip began to feel he was earning every penny he made. First he had to join the others in convincing Barry that he couldn't walk into an expensive hotel conference room full of potential investors and present himself as the head of a major new dynamic corporation while dressed like a teenager going out to shoot some hoops.

Finally they persuaded Barry to let Rick Pollock, the "famous tailor," come to his office and fit him for several suits.

Then they had to get him on the plane, a major undertaking, since Barry had a terrible fear of flying.

First, Chip had to be sure to bring Barry's Walkman, which meant buying a new one before almost every flight because Barry kept losing them. This happened five or six times.

And with the Walkman would have to be just the right New Wave tapes. "Don't come back until you get the ones I want," Barry would tell Chip.

But the worst was getting him settled down on the plane. On every takeoff and landing, Barry would bury his face in a pillow and hold on tightly to Chip's hand or knee. Chip had never seen a grown man so scared. It was embarrassing.

It wasn't any fun when they got to their destination either. They'd be met at the airport by a limo, which was nice. And so were the places in which they stayed or where the presentations were given: the Parker House in Boston, the Metropolitan Club in Chicago, the St. Francis in San Francisco. But Barry would always insist on going directly to their hotel, which he would never leave unless the presentations happened to be scheduled elsewhere.

In fact, except for the sales presentation, Barry would rarely even leave his room. Chip liked to go out to see the sights or take in a ball game, but he could never get Barry to go.

Once after a show in Chicago at the Sears Tower, they had three and a half hours to kill before their flight home, and Chip wanted to go up to the top floor and see the view. Barry not only refused to go, but he wouldn't let Chip go either. Instead, they drove directly to the airport and caught an earlier flight back to LA, where the business day was still in progress.

New York was a similar experience. It was Chip's first visit. They were staying by the World Trade Center, and he was very excited and wanted to have dinner at Windows on the World, the building's famous restaurant on the 102nd floor, with its spectacular views of the city. But Barry said no, so Chip had dinner in his room as always and went directly to bed. But, of course, Chip Arrington had no way of knowing the tremendous pressure Barry Minkow was under.

Together with Paul Schiff, who was present for about 50 percent of the shows, and Robert Grossmann of Rooney, Pace's West Coast division, who attended all of them, Barry, Chip, and Bruce Andersen made several whirlwind trips to Beverly Hills, LA, San Francisco, Dallas, Chicago, Minneapolis, Atlanta, and New York— cities with big-money stock people.

Chip soon grew proud of the presentations they put on. Along with the slide show, Barry would talk about restoration, Chip would run down the carpet-cleaning business, and Andersen would represent ZZZZ Best's financial history and present condition. Would-be investors, Chip Arrington recalls, were impressed by Barry and the company's "great looking" growth plans and "extremely strong profit-loss statements."

"It just didn't look like there were any holes in it," Chip would say retrospectively. The presence of Paul Schiff, an older, mature, heavy-duty investor, was also reassuring to future investors, as was the introductory speech by Robert Grossmann, representing a well-known Wall Street underwriting firm.

But undoubtedly the greatest reason for the phenomenal sale of ZZZZ Best stock was Barry Minkow himself. Paul Schiff, who never spoke at the shows but merely lent his weighty presence, began to note how "astute" Barry was in selling his company and what an "exceedingly fast learner" he was. "He'd make a mistake," remembers Schiff, "and Grossmann or Griffin would point it out, and he'd never make that mistake again. They'd tell him to say something a different way or leave it out, and he'd immediately understand."

And while Barry Minkow was always "a kid" to Paul Schiff, he was a remarkably cool one. "I never saw signs of change in Barry," says Schiff. "The kid who was trying to get a $750,000 loan was the same kid when he was dealing in millions. He was his own greatest fan—cocksure of his ability to overcome any problem—but he was also a guy who, it appeared, had done it and could back it up."

— 14 —

THE REACTION OF THE Rooney, Pace underwriters to Barry's road show was ecstatic. "Do you know what you've got here with this kid?" one asked Mark Morze. "He opens his mouth, we leave fully subscribed. He's made ZZZZ Best the hottest issue we've ever seen. He's the teenage Ray Kroc."

But the problem was right there for anybody to see—right there in the prospectus. One didn't even need to be suspicious, as Alan Abelson, the editor of *Barron's* and author of its "Up and Down Wall Street" column, certainly was not.

His comments on ZZZZ Best—published exactly one day before the SEC approved the stock offering—had, in fact, a rather friendly tone toward Barry and his company. In the breezy style that characterizes his column, Abelson noted, "ZZZZ Best came within our ken thanks to a prospectus issued in connection with a proposed offering. What ZZZZ Best proposes to offer, aided and abetted by Rooney, Pace, are one million units . . . and, word is, if the sky doesn't fall or Western Civilization come to an end, the offering will be made this very week."

Adding that he was "happy to say [that ZZZZ Best wasn't] one of your pathetic little start-ups," Abelson went on to describe "ZZZZ Best's humble but honorable trade," to approve of its "wonderful name" ("how easily those Z's roll off our typewriter"), and to point out that "its founder and president is only 20 years old."

Having thus dispensed with the standard ZZZZ Best promotional pitch in his opening paragraphs, Abelson then shifted gears and pointed out what hundreds—perhaps thousands—of ZZZZ Best investors would either fail to comprehend or choose to ignore:

"One of the things we discovered right off the bat," wrote Abelson, "is that the prospectus reports that a fantastic proportion of the business—86% of revenues and 85% of gross profit . . . came from one customer. That customer is described in the prospectus only as Interstate Appraisal Services. . . . Interstate itself, as it turns out, has been in business *only a year and a half. Which means that ZZZZ Best is extremely dependent on a relatively new operation.* [Italics added.]" (Not mentioned by Abelson but included in the prospectus was a further cautionary note: "The company has no written or oral agreement with Interstate with respect to future restoration work and there can be no assurance that it will continue to direct business to ZZZZ Best.")

So there it was, right *there* in the prospectus, a glaring red flag that Abelson in a cursory reading of the ZZZZ Best prospectus had picked up on, but that less savvy investors would miss or give little weight to.

Abelson's observation was a caution, not a suspicion of any wrongdoing. But after complimenting ZZZZ Best for "unwaveringly and . . . forthrightly owning up to the abundance of competition it faces . . . in the restoration work performed for insurance companies," Abelson sounded another wary note: "Revenues per [carpet-cleaning] location . . . fell in the latest quarter to $38,900 on average, from $45,600 in the like 1985 period."

In addition to Abelson's cautionary comments, there were other red flags in the prospectus. In a section dealing with Barry's financial and business relationship with Jack Catain—included at the insistence of Mark Moskowitz—it was noted Barry had paid $500,000 to Catain as part of the "agreement" between the two parties, and that Catain claimed $270,000 was still owed to him, a claim described by Arthur Barens as "entirely spurious and without merit." The prospectus also revealed that Catain was under investigation by a federal grand jury for certain "business activities"—including some related to ZZZZ Best—and that he had recently been convicted on federal charges of conspiring to sell and selling counterfeit money. (According to Faith Griffin, Moskowitz learned of Catain's criminal record only after some of ZZZZ Best's files had been subpoenaed by the Catain grand jury. When Griffin asked Barry why he'd not told Moskowitz earlier, he said he had been embarrassed about it.)

There were other signs that might have alerted a sharp-eyed, skeptical investor. An astounding quarterly revenue increase for the three months ending July 31, for example. In 1985, revenues for the period had been just under $64,000. For the same three months of 1986, they had skyrocketed to almost five *million*, four hundred thousand dollars, exceeding revenues for the entire previous fiscal year that had ended April 30, 1986.

But if the prospectus contained red flags, there were many signs of reassurance as well. Many of the lies that Barry and Morze told to the underwriters were simply repeated in the prospectus; for instance:

> The profitability of a restoration contract depends on the company's ability to control its expenses. The principal expense, in all cases, is the cost of replacement flooring materials which can vary substantially. Although the company has benefited from quantity discounts as its insurance restoration business has grown, the profitability of such business remains, and is expected to remain, largely dependent on the expertise of Barry J. Minkow in purchasing flooring materials at favorable prices.

The purchase of the electric generators was also mentioned. They had been acquired, according to the prospectus, because "extensive water or fire damage to a commercial facility frequently affects a building's electrical system, [and] generators are often necessary for such restoration work to provide an external power source at the job site." The generators would also "enhance [ZZZZ Best's] opportunities for additional insurance work."

The statements that Dan Krowpman and Cornwell Quality Tools and Equipment were supplying over $1 million in equipment and material, although totally fraudulent, also sounded a reassuring note in the prospectus, as did the "13 insurance restoration projects in progress, aggregating $24,362,000."

But above all, it was the names Ernst & Whinney and Hughes Hubbard & Reed, and to a lesser extent Rooney, Pace, that added weight and credibility to ZZZZ Best's prospectus.

True, the reputation of Rooney, Pace was no longer impressive. But the firm had done nothing as yet so notorious that a knowledgeable investor might have been warned off. Indeed, the company was a member of the New York Stock Exchange and had recently helped bring out a number of new stock issues.

Moreover, underwriters like Rooney, Pace are subject to heavy civil liabilities imposed on them by Congress in the event that a misstatement or omission due to their negligence results in a fraudulent offering. Underwriters are, therefore, in effect putting their companies on the line when they vouch for a new stock, and many investors, knowing this, regard the underwriters' participation in an offering as an important safeguard.

Hughes Hubbard & Reed's involvement and approving signature on the prospectus were also a reassuring sign to a broker or investor. On Wall Street and in the investment community, Hughes Hubbard & Reed is known as a Great Old Law Firm—venerable, but also exceptionally competent.

But "what really made the stock offering go," according to one veteran Wall Street lawyer, "was Ernst & Whinney lending their name to the prospectus. . . . [When looking at a stock deal], I look for a Big Eight or high-quality firm I'm familiar with. A Big Eight firm has tremendous resources and their name is on the line, so you assume the auditing process is thoroughly done. Otherwise, they wouldn't stick their neck out. A lot of accounting firms will turn down accounts if they have any reason to be suspicious. So it was a big benefit for Minkow to have gotten Ernst & Whinney. To an average reader, with that kind of backing [and the high revenue growth], it looked like an interesting deal. Who knew it would be a gigantic fraud?"

On December 9, the SEC, after reviewing the prospectus, approved it, and ZZZZ Best's stock was placed on sale. SEC approval appeared to add yet another layer of safety and credibility to ZZZZ Best's offering.

Perhaps not generally understood, however, was that the SEC does *not* review a prospectus for accuracy or potential fraud. The commission doesn't, in other words, *investigate* a company and check to see that if a company reports it has 500 employees, for example, it indeed *does* have 500 employees. Instead, the SEC takes the word of a company and its underwriting team.

The December Saturday when the *Barron's* article appeared, Tom Padgett, still living in "Roach Haven," got a call from Barry Minkow. Barry was very excited. "Have you seen *Barron's*?" Barry kept repeating. "Go get it, we're in it, we're in it."

Sure enough, when Tom went out and bought *Barron's*, "the weekend *Wall Street Journal*," there he and Interstate were. From Barry's point of view, it was a little shaky—what with stuff like "all that business coming from one source," but as for Tom Padgett, he was proud. So proud that he got on the line and called his parents. There was, after all, "a hell of a lot of prestige in being in *Barron's*."

— 15 —

IT WAS EARLY DECEMBER, and the float money was up to over a million when Barry, Bruce Andersen, Mark Moskowitz, and Chip met with officials from Union Bank to try to set up yet another gap loan.

Barry had been attempting without success to get any kind of loan from Union since 1985, when—through a Jack Catain connection—he'd met Susan Russell, and with Catain sitting at his elbow, had asked the Union Bank vice president for a working capital loan of $200,000.

But Russell, a plump woman with a Dorothy Hamill haircut who'd been in banking about nine years, turned Barry down cold. Her instincts and experience warned her off. The financial condition of ZZZZ Best, she felt, was "weak," and the company was too dependent on one individual—Barry.

In June 1986, Barry again requested a loan and was again denied, primarily due to Russell's unease over the fact that Interstate Appraisal was ZZZZ Best's sole source of restoration work.

Sometime in October, however, Susan Russell's assessment of ZZZZ Best began to change. Barry had sent her a copy of the preliminary prospectus, outlining the company's rapid growth in sales and profitability. Russell was impressed and called Barry to tell him so.

During the course of the conversation, a meeting was arranged for early November.

The gap loan Barry was seeking was ostensibly needed to keep the restoration jobs going until payment from the stock offering came through, but in reality its purpose was to help maintain the float.

Russell, for her part, wanted to get Barry to deposit those big public offering bucks into Union Bank.

As it turned out, accomplishing *"that* didn't require much of a sales job," according to Vanessa England, a Union Bank associate who accompanied Russell to the meeting. Barry Minkow was not shy in letting Russell and England know that he was seeking a bank other than First Interstate in which to deposit his funds, and that he would be happy to make Union Bank that institution. So Russell got what she wanted, and Barry, who would soon have almost $12 million to deposit *somewhere*, got a short-term forty-five-day loan for $600,000 until the money from the public offering came through. (Due to Barry's spectacular sales job on the road shows, the size of the offering had been raised from $8 to $13 million, with about $1.5 million of that going to Rooney, Pace for the underwriting.)

Russell's wariness had been eased not just by the prospect of all that interest-bearing money coming to her bank but also by the fact that Barry and Bruce Andersen had told her that Ernst & Whinney and Hughes Hubbard & Reed were involved in the audit of ZZZZ Best for the stock offering. Russell then interviewed Mark Moskowitz, Larry Gray of Ernst & Whinney, and George Greenspan, who had done ZZZZ Best's original audit.

In addition, Russell called Faith Griffin at Rooney, Pace, who told her, according to Russell, that they'd checked out all the carpet-cleaning satellite offices *and* the completed insurance restoration projects. (As the conversation took place *before* the visit to the Sacramento site, either Russell's recollection of this last point is in error, or Griffin, for whatever reason, relayed inaccurate information to her.)

In any case, thus assured, Russell approved the loan, and Barry received his $600,000 on November 7.

Then, in late November, with the stock offering stalled but only days away, Russell received another call from Barry Minkow. He needed an additional $300,000, Barry told her, to meet his restoration job obligations prior to the imminent stock sale.

So following a meeting at ZZZZ Best, another was held at Union Bank. It included Mark Moskowitz, Barry, Chip, Bruce Andersen, and the bankers.

The matter of the $300,000 was quickly disposed of in Barry's favor, but then he and Mark Moskowitz made a second, far grander proposal: an additional $1.3 million loan to be funded immediately after the stock offering for the purchase of supplies for upcoming restoration projects *and* a $7 million line of credit for up-front financing of future restoration projects.

Compared to the Union Bank's previous dealings with ZZZZ Best, these sums constituted an entirely different magnitude of business, but the request was approved in a relatively short time. After all, Barry Minkow was about to bank almost $12 *million* with them. This perhaps was why nobody at Union Bank bothered to ask the obvious questions: If Barry was going to get close to $12 million within a week, why did he need a new $1.3 million loan now? And why would he then need a $7 million line of credit beyond that?

Barry had done such a good job on the road show that the stock offering, when it was finally approved by the SEC, sold out swiftly through brokers across the nation.

Actually, it took just about a week—from the initial day of the sale on December 9 to its closing on the sixteenth—for the phenomenon of a complete stock sellout to occur.

Over $13.6 million was raised in that week, and another $1.5 million was raised in one week in January when additional stock was placed on sale. All told, about $15 million of stock was sold.

With ZZZZ Best's stock selling out, Barry encountered no problems in getting his $1.3 million loan from Union Bank on December 11, with the promise of the $7 million line of credit to come after the money from the offering was actually in hand.

By way of thanks, the day before he was to receive his multi-millions from the offering, Barry gave one of the motivational lectures of which he was so proud for the employees and officers of Union Bank.

Entitled "Rejection and Telemarketing," the Boy Wonder's presentation centered around developing business via the telephone. As might be surmised from the presentation's theme, Barry "shared insights with the people at the bank on how he handled rejection."

"He was very flamboyant," Vanessa England recalls. "He stood in front of about twenty-five of the bank's personnel with a marking board and gave his lecture in an aggressive manner."

"Face the fear," Barry told them, "and the fear will disappear."

The following day, December 16, 1986, Barry J. Minkow—along with Mark Morze, Bruce Anderson, Mark Moskowitz, and a few others, stood in the offices of Freshman and Marantz—the attorneys for the underwriters—and received a check for $11,549,224.

"Lo and behold," Mark Morze remembers thinking, "we got the cure."

Mark Morze's euphoria lasted about an hour—the time it took to get to Union Bank, deposit the $11,549,224, and start, at last, to write checks to all the people and all the banks with hooks into Barry. It was then that Barry Minkow—ever the optimist—turned to Mark Morze and shattered his state of bliss: "Jesus Christ, Mark," said Barry, "this *still* isn't enough."

Incredibly, the $11,549,224 was simply not enough to pay off *all* they owed and still maintain the appearance of a dynamic, growing company.

As they wrote the checks, Barry would say, "OK, we owe Schiff a million and a half, give him a million. Charbit two [million], pay him one. Rosario *x* number of dollars, we'll give her half." They also paid Dan Krowpman $250,000, Neal Dem $505,000, Richman Financial (Rind and Schulman) $500,000, Fiduciary Leasing another million, and so on. By the time they'd finished writing checks against what they owed, even at the rate of about eighty cents on the dollar, they'd gone through $8 million. If they had paid it all back, they would literally have had nothing left.

And money *had* to be held back, not just to maintain the illusion of prosperity but to meet the bank loan payments coming due in the next several weeks. Those payments had to be made, or the multimillion-dollar lines of credit they were about to get from Union and First Interstate Bank would not be approved.

There was, moreover, an additional problem. The actual destination of the $8 million they'd just paid out had to be hidden from ZZZZ Best's auditors and accountants.

Ernst & Whinney; Rooney, Pace; and Hughes Hubbard & Reed—none of them had any idea Barry owed that much money. Most of the debts had been concealed in the prospectus as the liabilities of joint ventures (or had simply never been mentioned to anyone by Barry and Mark). And the joint ventures, of course, were to be paid off from the proceeds from the particular job when it was completed, not from the public offering money.

Even the investors being repaid thought the money was coming from the restoration jobs then being completed. In fact, it was stated in the prospectus that only $1.5 million of the money from the offering was to be used to pay off debts.

So the problem became how to explain to controller Bruce Andersen and the others where the $8 million had gone.

But as he had so often done, Barry came up with the solution, and Mark Morze summoned up his creativity and craftsmanship, played the Xerox machine like Horowitz the piano, and produced altered copies of checks that looked as if they had gone to purchase materials and supplies for *new* restoration jobs instead of to pay off investors.

But if the $8 million outlay was explained as expenditures for new restoration jobs, new jobs literally had to be made up. And dozens were, all over the Southwest: Tempe, Arizona; Tucson; Concord, California; Fremont, California; Dallas; and Houston. These last two Mark didn't like; they were too big, too easy to check out. But Barry said no, they'd have to go with them. He'd already told people that he had jobs there.

But Barry did take care to avoid cities and towns where either Hughes Hubbard & Reed or Ernst & Whinney had regional offices. *That* would be playing a bit too close to home.

As materials were supposed to account for about 40 percent of the cost of a restoration job—and they'd supposedly paid out $8 million—about $20 million in new contracts were made up.

To delay paying investors like Schiff, Rosario, and Charbit all they were owed, Barry and Mark once again convinced them to roll over their money. This, however, created the old snowballing effect of accumulating new debt without new investment while further depleting ZZZZ Best's capital, for sometimes an investor refused to be stalled, and payments had to be made.

New jobs, therefore, had to be made up not just to fool the auditors but to get the new loans and lines of credit to keep the Ponzi going. And to keep up appearances and comply with the terms of the prospectus, new money had to be spent on new carpet-cleaning locations (already a losing proposition), the opening of unneeded warehouses, and a blizzard of television commercials.

Mark Morze had been wrong. The money from the public offering had not been the maxi-cure. It was just another delaying action.

Although Barry, Mark, and Tom were still struggling to push their Ponzi boulder up the hill, there was now a difference. As First Interstate's Richard Motika points out, the market had given ZZZZ Best a vote of confidence, and had oversubscribed its shares. And if *that* was the market's reaction to ZZZZ Best, well, that was good enough for Richard Motika and his fellow bankers at First Interstate. Indeed, it seemed good enough for Susan Russell and Vanessa England at Union Bank as well.

So if Barry needed a $7 million line of credit to prepay suppliers for insurance restoration materials just one day after receiving $11.5 million, Union Bank was willing to give it to him. On December 17, $4.8 million of the $7 million line of credit was placed in ZZZZ Best's account. (The remainder of the $7 million had already been used in earlier gap loans.)

And if Barry needed $3 million from First Interstate for restoration expenses just *two* days after getting his $11.5 million, that was fine with them, too. He had all that underwriting money to back up the loan and was, in addition, signing over as collateral the receivables (the amount due to ZZZZ Best) on the six restoration jobs he was borrowing money for. Plus, Barry was *personally* guaranteeing the loan, and Richard Motika had gotten to know Barry, a very "vibrant" guy, who "commanded a great presence," and in whom he had a lot of confidence.

But if the officers of Union Bank knew that Barry had drawn $8 million out of his account there—as they surely had to know— they don't appear to have asked where the money was going, nor to have questioned the soundness of ZZZZ Best, which remained in business almost solely because of the line of credit they had just extended to it.

The big rewards were yet to come, but Barry almost immediately gave a few mini-rewards to Mark, Tom, Chip, and Bruce Andersen. As was his way of promising big and delivering medium, Barry gave Mark Morze $200,000 instead of the $1 million he'd promised. But $200,000 was still $200,000, and Mark was skimming hundreds of thousands more off the top in expenses. He also paid Chip and Andersen the $50,000 bonuses he'd promised them and took the first steps in arranging the down payment on the Newport Beach home that Tom Padgett had always dreamed of.

Although generally well pleased with the way things were

working out, Tom was just the slightest bit pained by the offering. Taking from the banks was one thing, but ripping off mom-and-pop stock investors, well, that just "went against our Robin Hood image."

He *was* consoled, however, every time he picked up the *Wall Street Journal* and saw ZZZZ Best listed right there on NASDAQ. It was annoying, of course, that because of its name, the company was always listed at the end—and friends were always calling to complain they couldn't find it. But Tom would just tell them it was there, all they had to do was look.

— 16 —

WHEN BARRY MINKOW FIRST CALLED Jeri Carr in late November and announced he wanted to have a black-tie Christmas sit-down dinner party for 800 to 1,000 people, she just laughed at him. Not only were the logistics of arranging such an affair staggering, but finding a hotel banquet hall in the Christmas season that could hold that many people seemed impossible. Downtown hotel rooms of that size had to be booked six months to a year in advance.

But Barry merely repeated what he always said, that he "didn't pay her to say 'no.'" She was "the best," and therefore she could arrange it.

And so she did. For December 20, in the Grand Ballroom of the futuristic glass and chrome Bonaventure Hotel in downtown LA.

The party was to be a combination ZZZZ Best pep rally and homage to Barry, a celebration of the successful stock offering, and an awards ceremony for everyone who'd helped Barry along the way.

And when Barry said everyone, he meant *everyone*: the entire ZZZZ Best staff; the entire underwriting team; the ZZZZ Best board of directors; the bankers from First Interstate, Union Bank, and Bank Hapoalim; *all* the investors; and scores of Barry's family and friends.

Like Truman Capote planning his famous masked ball, Barry further decreed that all the men were to wear black suits or tuxedos. He alone would be dressed in white.

As if to underscore his seriousness, Barry asked Joel Hochberg, who was being fitted for his tux at the same shop where Barry had his measurements on record, to bring him back a white tuxedo.

When Joel arrived at the shop and told the manager about the white tux, the guy started goofing on Barry. "Where is this guy goin'?" asked the manager, "the prom or what?" Joel dutifully called Barry and reported that the manager had actually laughed out loud when asked to supply a white tux. Instead of being dissuaded, Barry simply said, "Fuck him, I want white!" and slammed down the phone.

Barry was not the only one determined to take care with his wardrobe on that night. With a $5,000 Christmas bonus Barry had given them, Tom and Roddy descended on Battaglia in Beverly Hills, where they spent $2,500 preparing for the big night. In addition to a new suit, Tom got a white tuxedo shirt at $250, $400 Italian shoes, a gray silk checkered tie, and a $50 black belt. Roddy unfortunately had to make do with just purchasing accessories. He was too fat to buy a suit off the rack, and there was no time to have one custom-made. When Barry heard about how much Tom and Roddy had spent, he said, "God, you guys are worse than my JAP."

Great care was also given to the seating arrangements. Mark Morze actually got out a ruler and, using a seating chart of the Grand Ballroom, drew the largest rectangle possible. The four farthest corners of that rectangle were the spots where Barry's major investors would be seated. Barry had told each of them that he or she was making a far higher profit than the others, and he didn't want them comparing notes.

Since Barry didn't really approve of drinking, on the night of the party there was no open bar. The guests milled around, buying their own drinks and schmoozing until dinner. After that, Barry J. Minkow, dressed in white, took over.

Portable mike in hand, he stepped center stage and riveted the assembled guests. He worked the stage like Jimmy Swaggart, spoke with the glibness of the youthful Bert Parks, jived like the Reverend Ike, and radiated the warmth of Ed McMahon. He was powerful. He was mesmerizing. He was the favored child basking in the glow of the adoring; he was the patroon—big daddy dispensing largess to the worthy; he was the twenty-year-old Boy Wonder, living out the ultimate I'll-show-you fantasy.

It was Barry Minkow's night, and, oh, how heady it must have been: Thirteen hundred employees spread out in California, Arizona, and Nevada. Sales of over $5 million in the last three months of the year alone, and projected sales in 1987 of over $50 million.

"I'm gonna recognize," he announced, "all the people who've helped make ZZZZ Best zee best."

And the litany began. Each person whose name was called received a handshake and/or a hug, a smile of gratitude, a moment to bask in the glow of Barry Minkow, and, of course, an award—for some a large bronze eagle atop a wooden base more than a foot high, for others a copy of a ZZZZ Best stock certificate encased in hard clear plastic or a trophy made of crystal.

"Vera Hojecki, who's been with me since . . . get this, ladies and gentlemen, since I started in a garage . . .

"My second father . . . Mr. George Greenspan . . .

"One of my advisers . . . the man who got me my first line of credit . . . who introduced me to Rooney, Pace . . . Richard Charbit . . .

"When nobody else was there . . . there was a man named Paul Schiff . . .

"One of the people I've come to know and enjoy . . . Tim Morphy of First Interstate . . ."

And on and on, smiling and pressing the flesh as he honored all the worthy and remembered old friends.

As Barry continued, there began to arise in the Grand Ballroom of the Bonaventure Hotel the chant of "Barrrry . . . Barrrry . . . Barrrry . . . ," and the hundreds of employees he'd flown into LA from all over the Southwest, seated together at their own tables, began to vie with each other for the loudest chant.

"Barrrry! Barrrry! Barrrry! . . ."

Eventually it became so loud that Barry Minkow, like a presidential candidate at a nomination convention, had to step back, smile, and let it subside.

And as it did, Barry would pick up his mike swinging loose at his side and say, "Thanks for coming, Santa Barbara! Thanks for coming, Anaheim!" Once again the tables would vie to outdo each other in chanting and cheering. And the awards would continue . . .

"Susan Russell and Vanessa England from Union Bank . . .

"Ken Pavia . . . he has a different way of doing business . . . today he's one of my dearest friends . . .

"Ernst & Whinney . . . the best auditing team in the Western hemisphere . . . Larry Gray . . .

"The man responsible for giving me $50 million worth of business . . . Tom Padgett . . ."

("$50 million!" thought Tom Padgett on his way up to the podium, "$50 million!")

"Mr. Mark Moskowitz . . . who took me and guided me . . . we wouldn't have $15 million in the bank without him . . .

"Bob Grossmann . . . five months ago I met him . . . the rest is history . . . $15 million . . .

"Mark Morze . . . I would not be here today if it was not for his outstanding ability, ingenuity, . . . and financial ability . . .

"When I obtained this person, I obtained a winner . . . he gets tired of hearing how wonderful he is, but ladies and gentlemen . . . Mr. Charles Arrington!"

Everyone, *everyone*, seemed to receive an award that night, except for Jeri Carr, who was genuinely hurt by Barry's omission. "Mind you," she was to say later, "the person who put him where he was did not get an award."

Barry, however, got an award. His was from the ZZZZ Best managers and was inscribed "To ZZZZ boss from ZZZZ Team."

Then Christmas carols were sung, people started dancing, and a professional video production company went around interviewing the party goers:

"I know ZZZZ Best's going straight up, and I'm going with it," said one ZZZZ Best employee.

"It's a family instead of a company," said another.

"You've had the rest, now try ZZZZ Best," said a third.

And from Barry's loyal, gentle father, an unintentionally ironic, well-meaning, comment: "The secret of ZZZZ Best's success is Barry himself. He's so dynamic . . . he's contagious—sort of like a disease."

And in the background of the video, played under and in between interviews, could be heard the chorus of a then-popular rock song by Robert Pepper: "There's no easy way out . . . ," went the song. "There is no shortcut home. . . ."

— 17 —

IT WAS WHILE DRIVING AROUND LA in his new white BMW in the closing days of 1986 that Barry Minkow began to live out his *Playboy* fantasies. With him were Lisa Driscoll and Monica Ordman, two "eighteen- or nineteen-year-old knockouts," who, says Mark Morze, had that *look*. That dining-at-Chasen's-in-lace-body-stocking look; that young, ripe look that made a man say, "*That's* definitely worth the chance of breaking up my marriage over." And they had that attitude, too: adventuresome enough to enroll in the Nick Harris school for private eyes but not bright enough to see the humor in it, and ingenuous enough to tell you with a straight face that at the school they were known as "Charlie's Angels."

Barry had met Lisa at the New Time Clothing Store in the Panorama Mall. His girlfriend, Joyce, had just gotten a job there, and Lisa, who was managing the store, was working in the back room when Barry walked in. After introducing himself, he took off his jacket and started to lend a hand. Lisa thought him funny and nice.

A couple of days later, Joyce was over at Lisa and Monica's, giving Monica a facial, when in walked Barry with his high school best friend and now main man, Tony Scamardo.

After Joyce had left for another engagement, Barry started giving Lisa his full attention and standard I-won't-be-going-out-with-Joyce-much-longer line. Shortly thereafter, Barry and Lisa started dating. Lisa knew that Joyce was living with Barry, but she didn't really care. Joyce was *dingy*, and Lisa, well, associated with her but was certainly *not* what you would call a friend.

It was about a month or two later, driving around in his BMW with the two foxy roommates, that Barry pulled his *Playboy* fantasy move. Lisa and Monica had been complaining about Monica's boyfriend, a total wild man, who would not leave her alone, breaking down doors and everything. "We've got to find a new place to live," said Monica. Simultaneously turning to the girls and reaching for the car phone, Barry told them he had a place in mind.

The following Sunday, a crew of ZZZZ Best employees were cleaning up their old apartment while the girls and their posses-

sions were being moved into a townhouse in Encino owned by
Maurice Rind and Richie Schulman. The townhouse normally
rented for about $2,000 a month, but for the new tenants it was
rent-free, courtesy of Barry Minkow.

The gesture was not Barry's first act of generosity toward
Lisa. After visiting her, Barry would often leave two $100 bills
neatly placed under the blender in the kitchen, calling Lisa on his
car phone as he left to remind her of the fact. And it was Barry, too,
who paid the several-thousand-dollar tuition for Lisa and Monica to
go to the Nick Harris Private Detective School.

Later, in perhaps the ultimate young man's fantasy, Barry
began dating Monica too.

And there were others. On one occasion, he had Joyce flown off
to Hawaii and arranged for a catered dinner costing almost $850 to
be delivered to his home in order to romance a young woman he'd
become infatuated with. He then asked a neighbor named Jack
Polevoi and Jack's brother, Jerry, to serve it, requesting they dress
in tuxedos because he wished it to be "classy and gourmet to
impress the young lady." Although the dinner failed to produce the
desired result—things not working out between Barry and the
woman—it was not for lack of trying. Jack's wife, Jan, went to
Barry's house beforehand to set the table because Jack didn't know
where to put the forks and spoons, and Jack called home between
servings for further instructions.

Polevoi's favor to Barry was later rewarded with a $1,500-a-
week job with ZZZZ Best and a position as designated keeper and
dispenser of Barry's $10,000 household petty cash fund, a task for
which Jack would earn the name "Bucks," while his twin brother
and helper Jerry would be called "Mini-Bucks."

In spite of the considerable number of young women attracted
to Barry by his wealth and charm, however, it was to Joyce Lipman
that he remained committed, if not true. Joyce provided something—perhaps a sense of stability in the madness swirling around
him—that Barry Minkow must have valued, for it was clear that he
didn't want to lose her. Once she came home early on a Sunday
morning and caught Barry in bed with either one or two women;
the story varies. Distraught, Minkow rushed over to the home of
Ron Byers, another neighbor with whom he'd become friendly, and
asked for his wife's Mercedes.

"Sure," said Byers, "go ahead, take it."

"No, no, you don't understand," Barry told him. "I need to *buy* it." He explained what had happened and how he needed to give the Mercedes to Joyce immediately to calm her down.

After Byers agreed to sell the car, Barry was apparently forgiven, and Joyce got her $40,000 Mercedes 380 SL. The next day, Jan Polevoi saw Joyce driving it down the street. "She seemed *very* satisfied," Polevoi says.

But Barry was always good to Joyce, at least materially. For her birthday, he bought her a beautiful diamond ring valued at over $7,000, and he freely dispensed cash and credit cards for her frequent, and expensive, shopping sprees. And when she tired of the Mercedes, he gave it to Jack Polevoi and bought her a Porsche.

Polevoi reacted to such generosity with total devotion to Barry, soon earning him his second nickname, "Gofer One," his twin becoming "Gofer Two." A semiretired businessman old enough to be Barry's father, Polevoi, for example, had to be sure to be at home every Sunday night to tape "60 Minutes," one of Barry's favorite shows. Minkow didn't know how to use his VCR.

If Barry indulged Joyce Lipman and Jack Polevoi with cars, he also indulged himself. Early in 1987, he'd traded up on his old $50,000 Ferrari for a top-of-the-line $100,000-plus Testarosa model. For business use, he had his company-leased BMW. Once when he was having trouble with his new Testarosa, he borrowed Ron Byers's Cadillac while his car was being repaired. After a couple of weeks, Byers asked for it back, and Barry had to tell him that there was a slight problem: he'd wrecked the transmission playing around with his friend Tony Scamardo, trying to see how fast that big Fleetwood would go in reverse. It was no problem, though, Barry told his neighbor, he'd buy the car, and he wrote a check to Byers for $19,000.

Initially, Ron Byers had liked Barry, who would always take the time to sit around with Ron's kids preaching the dangers of drugs. But after a while, his opinion changed, and it wasn't because of the car. It was because of Barry's ego, which after one or two encounters quickly lost its appeal. If they went out for dinner and 90 percent of the conversation was about Barry, he still wouldn't be satisfied. No, it had to be 100 percent. And on the way home, the guy would actually ask, "How did I do tonight?" What percentage [of the conversation was about me]?" It was insufferable; so bad, in fact, that Ron and his wife had to stop socializing with him.

Barry seemed unable to tolerate anybody or anything else being the center of attraction. There was, Byers remembers, the time they were watching the Sugar Ray Leonard–Marvin Hagler fight and someone mentioned that Hagler was getting $14 million for the fight. "Fourteen million? So what's the big deal?" Barry asked contemptuously. "*I* earned that this morning. My stock went up two and a half points."

But it was always that way with Barry. He owned six million shares of stock. He was going to head the next General Motors. He was going to buy the Seattle Mariners. He was worth $200 million. He was just too much.

Just how unbalanced Barry had become by this time, how egomaniacal, how pitifully insecure, was displayed most obviously during his happy-fans period.

In the late spring, Barry had become the manager of a local girls' softball team, quickly becoming obsessed with ensuring the success of his eleven- to fifteen-year-old players. Recognizing the advantage of having a hometown crowd cheering you on, Barry decided to buy some cheers, offering as much as $100 a head for "fans" to come to his games and scream for his team ($15 for children).

One week when Barry was particularly concerned about winning, he stopped by Jack Polevoi's and told the keeper of the petty cash and his wife to get busy hiring fans for the event. "I want fanfare, I want pom-poms, I want placards, I want bullhorns," Barry told the Polevois. It cost over $4,000, but he got them.

By the end of the softball season, Barry had spent about $26,000 hiring spectators to cheer his team, and boasted of spending another $30,000 to renovate the field on which the girls played. With money like that to urge them on, the fans became so boisterous that on occasion they would scream themselves hoarse.

— 18 —

TONY SCAMARDO TRIED TO calm Barry down, to warn him about the vultures out there looking for ways to rip him off. But Barry would just ignore it, and it finally dawned on Tony that he didn't have to warn Barry, that Barry *knew*. If people liked him because he had money, that was fine with Barry, Tony finally understood. "He accepts that, and he gets what he needs off of that same idea."

Close friends with Barry since they were sixteen, Tony Scamardo (the designated senior class "sex symbol" in his high school yearbook) was a classic tall, dark, and handsome Italian stallion, but with that special Southern California twist: a veneer of studied Valley cool that said it was *uncool* to say two words when one would do, to wear anything but the latest casual clothes in the most mannered fashion, or to extend oneself to make a ninety-degree gesture when forty-five degrees would clearly suffice. Asked a date or time frame for a particular incident, he would reply with just a hint of irony that he didn't know, that it didn't really matter to him, and that he hadn't "marked his calendar when that was."

Although Tony Scamardo was bent on protecting Barry from those constantly trying to put the touch on him, Tony himself was not averse to letting Barry help him out. Their trips to Vegas and Tahoe were, of course, always on Barry, as were the presidential suites they stayed in and the $120 bottles of Dom Perignon they drank. So too were nights out on the town, two or three times a week, when Barry would peel some bills from the grand or two he always carried and without question pay for everything.

So it wasn't a bit out of character for either when Barry gave Scamardo $13,000 to move away from his parents and get his own apartment. Tony returned about half of the money three or four months later when he gave up his new apartment and moved into Barry's house following a temporary falling-out Barry had had with Joyce. That apartment hadn't been just for him, however, Barry's main man was always quick to point out. It was also a getaway for Barry from Joyce, a place where he could take his girlfriends and not have to worry about any hassles from his JAP.

Scamardo, who on occasion did carpentry, was also hired by Barry to work on his house, although, as Tony was later to say, the house, being brand-new, really didn't need any work. But still Barry was willing to pay him between $10,000 and $15,000 in cash for the work, knowing Tony was in no kind of position to turn it down.

So Scamardo put up crown molding and built wall units, wall coverings, and entertainment centers. And perhaps to show his appreciation, he even built a house for Louie, Barry's aging dog, in the backyard on a hill between two palm trees. The doghouse had a window on each side, a vaulted ceiling, carpeting, baseboard, and paneling. It looked, in fact, just like Barry's house in miniature, and was painted the same colors. It even had a sign outside that read

"Louie's Place." It had everything, Tony would point out with pride, "but air-conditioning and a wet bar."

Tony also remodeled Barry's entire Reseda office building, which, unlike his house, certainly needed it. Barry's personal office was done entirely in oak: the paneling, the hard molding, the baseboard. Drop ceilings were also put in, as were air-conditioning units, heating, and a functional wet bar. No expense was spared, says Tony, everything was "ZZZZ best." The cost was between $20,000 and $30,000.

All told, for the remodeling of his home and office, for his cars, his girls, his gambling, his entertaining, furniture for his house, his house payments, paintings he would distribute as gifts, the softball team, and various investments, Barry J. Minkow would, over a ten-month period in 1987, spend more than $2 million.

Meanwhile, Mark Morze, while also enjoying the fruits of his labor, wasn't sailing quite as blithely through this period of prosperity as was Barry. *His* ear, at least, was occasionally to the ground, listening for the nightmarish sound of the other shoe dropping. The sound of an accountant from Ernst & Whinney saying sometime in March or April, "We've just audited your books and discovered you spent $8 million in *two* days right after the stock offering. What could you have spent it on? Something's wrong here."

Or for Union Bank to say, "You just got $11 million; why do you need *our* seven million? We know you didn't spend $8 million for new locations, because there's no way you could spend that much if you opened *100* new locations, and you can't open more than one or two a month. So what happened to the eight? You must still have it somewhere, so why don't you use *that* money for your restoration jobs?"

But the sound of that second shoe dropping didn't come. Not from Ernst & Whinney; not from Union Bank—to whom by mid-February they once again owed $7 million; not from First Interstate Bank, to whom they owed $3 million; and not from Schiff or Rosario, to whom they now also owed millions and who blessedly kept rolling over their money.

Of course, as surely as the money kept pouring in, it went pouring out. Loans had to be repaid, and Mark and Barry were spending money like it was going out of style. And there was, of course, *no* income. Moreover, the carpet-cleaning locations—particularly the new ones—were without properly trained management and personnel, and they were leaking money like a sieve.

True, Barry had taken the first steps in what could prove to be the biggest of deals with the biggest of Wall Street's investment houses, the mighty Drexel Burnham Lambert. And if that deal happened, Mark knew the money they owed would be peanuts, to be paid off in days.

But that wasn't going to occur overnight, and meanwhile millions in loan payments were coming due.

So Barry and Mark worked up a new scheme. Barry would tell Rosario and Schiff that he planned on buying a large, nationally known real insurance appraisal service. ZZZZ Best was not, however, supposed to own such a service because that would raise obvious questions about a conflict of interest. So, he told them they'd have to buy it on the QT. Then, the story went, ZZZZ Best would make bids that would automatically be accepted by their clandestinely owned appraisal service, thus eliminating the competition and setting their own price.

Rosario and Schiff loved the idea, and Kay, according to Morze, put up $2 million (a half-ownership), and Schiff $1 million. (Padgett was supposed to put up the other $1 million for the second half.) In this way, Mark and Barry raised $3 million and added to what they would call the "'87 Hit Parade."

From January to June, the '87 Hit Parade included, in addition to that $3 million, the millions from the banks; $4 to $5 million more from Schiff, who got his investment money from First Interstate Bank, a Swiss bank, and a $1 million mortgage against his house; $600,000 to $1 million from Richard Charbit; and another $600,000 to $1 million from an investor named Ken Pavia.

Mark Morze, however, certainly wasn't spending all his time worrying about business. Far from it. If Barry was squandering over $2 million, Mark was going through about a million and a half himself. There were all those high-rolling weekends in Vegas with all those foxy cocktail waitresses ("I never had multiple partners in bed until I went to Vegas!") and the checks he would write to his main squeeze, Candy Apple, a tall, blond LA cocktail waitress who was, says Mark, "the love of my life." To her he would write checks with endearments in the memo section: "Great Night in a Hot Tub"—$18,000, "Great Legs"—$10,000, "Extra Great Legs"— $15,000. In all, it's estimated Mark gave Candy about $400,000 in furs, jewelry, cars, and a house. The house wasn't much, your basic

$100,000 Valley home, but like a discreet drug dealer, he'd put about another $200,000 in renovations and add-ons into it. Candy Apple hit the Lotto when she met Mark Morze.

On his mother and sister, who lived together, Mark spent around $600,000, buying them a house and a Rolls-Royce.

Meanwhile, Tom Padgett, who had been discussing the possibility of obtaining the Newport Beach home of ZZZZ Best investor Pavia since before the public offering, now began to negotiate with him in earnest.

At Barry's mammoth Christmas party, with the stock money already banked, Tom had told Pavia that he'd like to move in by Valentine's Day, there being a special girl (Debbie) he wanted to spend that special day with ("in my dreams," he would later say, "in my dreams").

In February he'd driven down to Newport, and Ken Pavia had actually given him a prepurchase tour of the house, one that made the boy from landlocked Akron, Ohio, an hour's drive from the turgid, muddy shores of foul-smelling Lake Erie, want to pinch himself: 4,500 square feet, two levels, five bedrooms, $675,000, and so close to the glistening Pacific Ocean that when the tide was up, you needed flippers to walk around the front yard.

Tom couldn't wait to move in, and in April, Barry gave Ken Pavia a $200,000 down payment in Padgett's name just as he'd promised back in 1986 when Tom was coming apart over Debbie. What a difference a year had made in the lives of Barry Minkow, Mark Morze, and Tom Padgett.

— 19 —

BY THE SPRING OF 1987, Barry Minkow—clad most untypically in a conservative navy blue business suit—was becoming a familiar figure to millions of Southern California's television viewers. ZZZZ Best had launched a $2 million advertising campaign focusing— with unintended irony—on ZZZZ Best's honesty and integrity.

The ads featured a variety of absurd-looking carpet cleaners— fat, rude, cigar-chomping men one just knew were trouble, or grotesque twins introducing themselves as Bait and Switch. At the commercial's end, Barry, who had insisted on being in the ads, would appear looking quite mature and handsome in his suit and sensible haircut, assuring the viewers how substantial ZZZZ Best was, and offering to guarantee "the work and price in writing." The advertisements ran not just in LA but in eight-week cycles in San Jose, San Francisco, Sacramento, Santa Barbara, and Las Vegas.

Barry shot three commercials, each in a single take, which left the advertising pros in awe. "They were astounded," says Joel Hochberg, "but it didn't astound me. Six months before, he'd said we'd have commercials, and here they were. By that time, I thought he could do anything."

And indeed it did seem during those months that anything Barry Minkow touched would turn to gold. Four months after the public offering, the value of ZZZZ Best stock had more than quadrupled, going from $4 to $18 a share, due in part to the ZZZZ Best commercials, in part to rumors of a pending deal with Drexel, and in part to a laudatory report written by the same Robert Grossmann who had worked for Rooney, Pace and ZZZZ Best during the stock offering. Grossmann was now with the New York stock brokerage firm of Ladenburg, Thalmann & Co., which was serving as a ZZZZ Best market maker. Calling Barry a "master entrepreneur," the report he'd written noted that ZZZZ Best had "the same potentially explosive sales and earnings characteristics and market opportunities that permitted McDonald's and 7-Eleven to reach the success each has achieved—sales over $1 billion in a relatively short time." Then, in bold type, it went on to "strongly recommend accumulation of ZZZZ Best Common Stock for Growth Oriented Accounts."

In fact, ZZZZ Best was growing (although losing money while doing so) and was soon to have twenty-one offices in three states with over a thousand employees.

Then on March 2, the "Money" section of USA Today reported that Barry had been named one of America's 100 top young entrepreneurs by the Association of Collegiate Entrepreneurs.

A month later, Barry was again mentioned in USA Today's "Money," this time in an article titled "Special Report: 1st Quarter Winners, Losers." The story read, "Happy Birthday, Barry Minkow. Stock in Minkow's company . . . rocketed 332% . . . in the first quarter, its first as a public company. And Minkow turned 21 last month." The article put Barry's worth at $80 million. Elsewhere, however, it was being placed at well over $100 million.

— 20 —

IT WAS MID-MARCH, and Jeri Carr wanted to do something really special for Barry Minkow's twenty-first birthday party, which was coming up at the end of the month. But what does one get a $100 million man?

Idly flipping through the back pages of *Los Angeles* magazine, Carr found the answer in an ad that read "Meshuga-Gram—Hire a hilarious yenta for any occasion." That was it. Jeri immediately called the yenta-for-hire and struck a deal, subsequently spending several hours filling in the professional busybody/actress on the small, mainly inconsequential details of Barry's life: his designation in high school as Class Clown and Most Likely to Succeed; the "Barry Minkow Day" the school had recently declared in his honor; his love of "The Rockford Files"; how much he enjoyed Ding Dongs, Twinkies, and making his own steak sauce; his award from Mayor Bradley; and details of the Minkow Myth of Success.

Meanwhile, Barry's older sisters, Mark Morze, and Elenora and Ana Madrinan were also wrestling with the question of what to get the man who could buy and sell the local mall.

Each would come up with a truly unique answer.

The dress was casual on the night of the party, perhaps because Joyce had planned it as a surprise, and only friends and trusted employees would be present, somewhere between 100 and 300 people. Held at Barry's home, the party proved a grand success.

The yenta showed up and, as planned, regaled Barry and his guests with the minutiae of Barry's life, first perplexing and later amusing him.

Then his sisters' gift arrived: a tall, blond stripper who peeled down to black bra, garter belt, and red panties. Jeri, Elenora, and Ana thought Barry was embarrassed by the stripper, he being a teetotaling antidruggie and all. But if the pictures of the Minkow court photographer on hand to record the event are any indication, Barry seemed to *love* it. He danced with her, she sat on his lap, and he clasped his hands firmly around her waist, all the time grinning a grin that did not *seem* embarrassed.

Mark Morze's gag gift was less obvious. So much so, in fact, that very few people at the party got the gag. But Barry loved it, roaring with laughter when Mark gave it to him.

It was a check, a real check of Barry's from Charter Pacific Bank, that Mark had taken to a special Xerox center and had blown up and then made into a real, life-sized, functional kite. It was a giant inside joke that most of the guests, being unfamiliar with check kiting, failed to see the humor in. But Barry thought it "the dearest gift" he got that night.

The biggest hit of the party, however, turned out to be the rap video put together about a week earlier by Elenora and Ana, featuring Minkow's family, friends, and employees. There were about twenty-five people on the tape, all of whom seemed genuinely fond of Barry and were obviously enjoying themselves. Backed by a professional beat worthy of the Fat Boys, the video started with all twenty-five rapping:

> Happy Birthday, Mr. Minkow.
> Now you're 21.
> We're the ZZZZ Best people,
> And we're having fun.
> Settle back, take a break,
> And listen to us
> While we wish you happy birthday
> And make you a fuss.
> *ZZZZ Best!*

Then after a few employees had danced to the forefront, giving their individual raps, a rotund, balding Mark Moskowitz shuffled forward and, embarrassed and a bit out of place, presented his:

> Happy birthday, Mr. Minkow.
> I'm your legal arm.
> With advice from me,
> You'll come to no harm.
> My fees may be high,
> But I'm not here from greed.
> Happy Birthday, Mr. Minkow,
> From Hughes Hubbard & Reed.

And then came the video's touching highlight as Robert Min-kow, cute and awkward in his movements to the beat, rapped out what would prove to be the video's most inaccurate verse:

I'm your pop,
Better known as Bob R. M.
Now I know
I've raised me a gem.
Happy birthday, son.
You're twenty-one,
And all the fun
Has just begun.
ZZZZ Best!

— 21 —

THE MEETING WAS AT BARRY'S OFFICE, and Mark had the chalk-board out. Drawing a line down its center, he wrote "Interstate" on one side, "Assured" on the other, and below each the word *Function* with some additional notations.

The boys were all there that day to listen to Mark: Barry, Tom, Roddy, and Morze's older brother, Brian, who'd recently been recruited to assist in a new critical phase of the scam with the potential to propel it to dizzying new heights.

"Let's go over it one more time, OK?" said Mark, pointing at the board and looking—as Tom Padgett said to general laughter—like a "professor of scamology." But the purpose of the gathering that day was deadly serious: a review and rehearsal before what might be the biggest meeting of the entire con was to take place.

Barry and Tom, of course, didn't really have to listen as Mark ran down how it was Roddy's job as the head of Assured Property Management to deal directly with the customers of a damaged building, how Interstate awarded the insurance restoration con-tracts, and how the two companies were related. They had it all down cold, being, along with Mark, the story's authors. But the boys wanted to be sure that the albino, whose eyes tended to glaze over when he was hit with too many details, and Brian Morze, who was new to it all, were really getting it.

They were too close now for a slipup.

So Mark once again told his bald, heavy-set, well-spoken brother that his name was no longer Brian Morze but Brian Logan, and that he was to be a second voice speaking for Interstate—Interstate presumably being so important to ZZZZ Best, and there being so much to know in such a large insurance appraisal service that Tom needed a second in command to accompany him to meetings and help in answering the many questions that might arise. Brian's title, as the business cards he'd been given indicated, was chief operating officer of Interstate. But his chief operating function in reality, said Mark—falling into helpless laughter despite himself—would be to decide where they should go for lunch. (It was like that sometimes; the absurdity of it all would just overwhelm them and they'd crack up. Mark couldn't count the times when, full of tension, he'd be sitting in Barry's office listening to him earnestly talking some banker into a desperately needed loan, and while doing so, look up at Mark, point at the phone, grin, and give the guy the jack-off sign.) This, however, *was* serious business, and Mark quickly collected himself and proceeded.

Tom was again cautioned that, yes, the men they were to be meeting were big—the biggest—but they'd been told that *he* was big too, and therefore Tom shouldn't take any shit from them, that is, not allow them to ask any questions that were too probing. If that happened, his attitude, said Mark, should be, "Wait a minute, back off. I've come as a favor to ZZZZ Best and Barry, not because I have to be here. ZZZZ Best's already got 20 percent of my business. That's 20 percent a lot of companies out there would like to have. I'm willing to work with you, but not, you must understand, at the cost of losing my insurance companies."

Moving on into other areas, Mark continued his if-they-ask-this-we'll-say-that lecture, over the course of a couple of hours trying to touch every conceivable base.

For the "they" with whom the boys were to meet were more than just formidable; they were the all-star, big-league representatives of Drexel Burnham Lambert, the powerful Wall Street brokerage house that had almost single-handedly transformed the face of financing in America.

Barry had contacted Drexel in early 1987, when he'd heard that Flagship Cleaning Services Inc., also known as KeyServ, was for sale. Owned by a London-based conglomerate, KeyServ held the upholstery-, carpet-, and drape-cleaning concession from Sears. Such a concession, which is relatively common among department stores, means that a carpet-cleaning company can solicit and do business in the name of that well-known store and have, along with the store's name, its implied endorsement. As a matter of fact, for most customers who look in the phone book or are contacted by a telemarketer, the carpet cleaner with whom they are contracting *is* Sears, or the Broadway, or whatever large store with which the cleaner is affiliated.

KeyServ was among the largest of these home and commercial carpet cleaners, with forty-five locations in thirty-four states, 2,300 employees, and annual revenues of $80 million. If combined with ZZZZ Best's twenty-one locations, 1,000 employees, and reported revenues of $35 million, the result would be one of the largest national carpet-cleaning chains in the United States. It would be like something created by T. Boone Pickens, Barry and Mark told each other. The David, headed by the West Coast Boy Wonder, swallowing up the twice-as-large national Goliath. The publicity alone would make the acquisition worthwhile.

It was with this David-and-Goliath scenario as a rationale that Barry first approached Drexel to finance KeyServ's $25 million price tag and to provide the additional money needed to merge the two companies.

But Barry Minkow and Mark Morze had an additional agenda as well. That agenda, as always, was startlingly audacious: Get the money from Drexel, buy KeyServ, run it profitably, and use those profits to pay off some of their debts. Simultaneously, take the additional $15 million or so they would be given to merge and run the two companies, and use that as well for debt reduction, to keep the Ponzi afloat and keep appearances up. Then hold on until 1988, when Barry would be permitted to gradually sell off his stocks, and they could finally pay the remaining debt. After that, they'd be home free: the owners of a huge, growing national corporation ripe to be franchised into a one-on-every-corner McDonald's, offering not just private and commercial carpet cleaning but also an interlocking series of related goods and services, such as the distribution and sale of carpet-cleaning equipment, chemicals, and accessories, and the branching out into related businesses, such as the standardized cleaning of restrooms in gas stations, hotels, office buildings, and restaurants.

Moreover, Barry would tell Drexel, if KeyServ, using the Sears name, could do $80 million by placing silly goddamned coupons in *TV Guide*, could they just imagine what *he* could do with an aggressive advertising campaign and the telemarketing techniques he'd been using in Southern California?

And Interstate was growing, too, fully willing and capable of giving an expanding ZZZZ Best—one with some *real* capital to lay out for labor and materials—all the work it could handle. All he needed, Barry Minkow told them, was the money to carry out his ideas.

— 22 —

IT WAS NO COINCIDENCE THAT the people at Drexel Burnham Lambert loved Barry Minkow and ZZZZ Best. He and his company, after all, were exactly what they were looking for.

Since creating a whole new securities market in the 1970s based on the junk bond concept they had pioneered, Drexel and its innovative bond trader/super salesman Michael Milken had used such bonds to assist hundreds of small companies like ZZZZ Best in raising the capital they needed for expansion.

Previously, loans for these unproven companies had been extremely difficult to obtain from traditionally conservative lending institutions like banks and insurance companies. But Michael Milken's concept of junk bond financing would change all that and, in the process, the face of Wall Street.

Milken, the classic Jewish outsider, first at the prestigious Wharton School at the University of Pennsylvania in the 1960s, and then at the elite, old-line investment banking firm of Drexel Harriman Ripley, had, like Barry Minkow, grown up in the San Fernando Valley, albeit in the middle-class, well-to-do enclave of Encino. And like Barry, Michael Milken seemed pathologically driven to succeed, to work eighteen- to twenty-hour days, and to make money for money's sake—as a way of keeping score and bending the world to his will.

It was when the WASPish Drexel, then on hard times, merged with the mostly Jewish Burnham and Company in the early 1970s that both companies and Michael Milken really came into their own.

Milken, who had been assigned to the sale of previously disdained low-grade junk bonds at Drexel, convinced both the bosses at his newly constituted firm and scores of big-time investors that a diversified portfolio, containing many different kinds of junk bonds, would minimize the risk and absorb the loss of any one of those different bonds failing. The reduced risk, combined with the high interest to be obtained, would, therefore, actually make them a more profitable investment than top-rated corporate bonds.

By the time Drexel officials sat down to talk with Barry, their company—due to its success in using junk bonds to finance expanding companies and big-time corporate raiders like Carl Icahn and Ivan Boesky—had become *the* junk bond market, accounting, by 1988, for almost half of the $17 billion worth of junk bonds sold. Throughout the eighties, financiers would be falling all over themselves to invest in Drexel's bonds, while money for those bonds was, as Boesky would say, "falling off the trees." And Drexel—not yet hit with the mammoth fines and most of the indictments for insider trading that would occur later—was finding itself in the enviable position of actually having to *seek out* companies with potential like ZZZZ Best in which to issue new junk bonds for their hungry investors.

It wasn't only ZZZZ Best's potential for growth, however, that attracted Drexel executives; it was Barry Minkow himself. After all, for a company like Drexel—intent on the short-term bottom line and with all that money to spend—there were only so many people with what Mark Morze was so fond of calling the "sizzle factor," only so many people who could make things happen and make big bucks for everybody. There were the T. Boone Pickenses at the top and the dynamic, young Barry Minkows at the bottom.

The executives at Drexel, along with the rest of Wall Street, had watched Rooney, Pace put this twenty-year-old kid in a dog and pony show and come up with every share of stock completely sold out. If he could make that happen at twenty, can you imagine what he could do at twenty-five or thirty-five?

It was as if Barry were Eddie Murphy and Drexel Burnham were a giant talent agency, say, ICM. Put Eddie in a movie, and he makes everybody rich. Buy Barry KeyServ, and who knows how far he could take it?

Barry had been wining and dining the three guys from Drexel for a couple of days before the *big meeting*, so Tom figured their guard would probably be down when they all finally got together, what with them being exposed to Mr. Charisma for practically twenty-four hours a day.

The meeting was to be held in Barry's recently renovated oak-paneled, plush-carpeted offices, which were now suitable for a conference with the representatives of Drexel Burnham Lambert, now suitable to meet with men who, as Tom Padgett would later note, were the epitome of big-league, New York, suspender-wearing success.

Prior to Tom, Roddy, and Brian "Logan's" arrival at the mid-morning meeting, Barry had presented a slide show detailing ZZZZ Best's progress, and Mark had shown the Drexel representatives some of his fantasy figures.

While driving to Barry's, Tom and the albino had gone over their rap "like two pitchers in the bullpen loosening up their arm before going into the big game." Tom was dressed in his Brioni black power suit with gray silk tie and was also wearing his Rolex with diamonds. Since he was at the meeting as a favor, he could show how successful he was. What do I look like, a failure or what? He certainly didn't feel like a failure, not driving his signature black Lincoln Town Car, a car with an important message: "Get out of my way; I'm big, black, and powerful."

Nor did he feel at all nervous. After all, if he didn't know what he was saying by *this* time, he might as well give it up. They'd done this on so many different occasions, Tom told Roddy, that there should be a Gallery of Saps on the wall of Barry's office, featuring the people from Union and First Interstate Banks, Bank Hapoalim, Ernst & Whinney, Hughes Hubbard & Reed, and all the investors—a financial Hall of Shame. Still, before going in, he decided to focus on a Zen saying he had just read: "When you stop seeking, it is then that you will find."

Barry, Mark, and the three men from Drexel had already finished up the slide show when Tom, the Ultimate White Man, and Brian "Logan" arrived.

The meeting went exceedingly well, starting out cordial and remaining so. While as usual having to shy away from certain lines of questioning, they were fully able to answer other questions because of the preparation they had done. For example, when asked if Tom would have any objection to them checking around with some of the local insurance companies to see if they knew of Interstate, Tom was able to reply confidently that, no, that would be fine, no problem, that they should go right ahead.

For, anticipating such a question (Mark's genius again!) and the possibility of a visit to Interstate from the men of Drexel, Tom and Roddy had bought four desks for Interstate's outer office, and then hired four men to sit behind them. Their primary function was to be Men in Suits, bodies to fill seats, should the guys from Drexel stop by. But secondarily, for their $500 per week, the Suits were expected to send insurance companies the literature about Interstate that the boys had had printed, and to call as many insurance companies as possible, soliciting new business—mainly auto claims. If the Suits drummed up any business, that was fine, but their main mission was simply to spread Interstate's name around so that if the Drexel underwriters contacted an insurance company, someone would say, "Interstate? Sure, I've heard of them."

Because of the preparations, the meeting, which lasted about an hour and a half, was one of the most successful they ever held. The only slight foul-up came near the end, when, with everyone talking in different directions, the albino began to nod out, and Tom had to give him the elbow.

In all, the boys spent about $20,000 getting Interstate Appraisal Services to look legitimate enough so that not just the men from Drexel but *any* investor could stop by, look around, and feel good. And here, once again, the UWM proved invaluable. He really knew how to give an office a power look. He'd read books on it.

For example, there was the time they'd gone shopping for a desk, and Tom decided to purchase what he considered a nice, although somewhat ordinary one, and the albino had had to tell him, "No, no, that's not for you. You need a *big* desk; you're the executive," and they'd found one then that suited Tom's image—for $2,000.

And when they'd opened their second office in Culver City, which, while not a beach community, was at least within a twenty-minute drive of the beach, it had been Roddy's idea to call it the "Marina office" (the original shoe box office in Van Nuys then becoming "headquarters"). And it had been the albino who'd designed the Marina office's decor: dark blue walls, lots of naval paintings, and just the right frames for Tom's college degrees and citations from his insurance courses like "Auto Damage" and "Writing General Policy." Fortunately, Roddy had decided and Tom had agreed that the certificates from his gun repair and small arms courses, as well as his mercenary school diploma, would be inappropriate for business.

Finally, with Sandra at the beach so much, they hired a second secretary who wasn't a friend of Tom's. Barry was really pissed off about Sandra, telling Tom, "Get somebody else, goddamn it, this is too important. If Sandra ever works twenty hours in a week, I'll blow you and give you time to draw a crowd."

And Barry *was* right; it was everybody's worst nightmare that Drexel would phone Interstate in the middle of the day and get an answering machine. Just when they were so close.

Meanwhile, Joel Hochberg was making his own preparations for a visit from Drexel. Joel had been put in charge of a mammoth telemarketing center that ZZZZ Best had opened in an attempt to meet some of the expansion requirements of the public offering prospectus. But it had been an excellent idea on Barry's part too—a way to centralize the telemarketing operations under one roof and cut down substantially on costs.

Located at the far reaches of the Valley in Chatsworth, the center was in a 20,000-square-foot building and had 150 phones. From it, Joel and his telemarketers could work twelve locations from San Diego to Santa Barbara all under one roof. They'd simply make calls from listings in an area phone book and then fax the orders to the various offices.

It was an innovative concept and one Barry quite rightly wanted the Drexel representatives to see.

The problem, however, was that it was in no way yet fully functional. And Barry wanted it *humming* when the Drexel people came by.

So, much as he'd done with Jack and Jan Polevoi when he'd demanded pom-poms, placards, and cheerleaders, Barry told Joel to get out there, round up all the kids he could get his hands on, and have them sitting in the center with a phone to their ear when the Drexel people arrived.

And Joel, who'd been promised he'd be in charge of telemarketing if and when KeyServ was acquired, as usual did what he had to. He drove by every bus stop, schoolyard, doughnut shop, and playground he could think of, offering the kids $10, $15, or $20 cash to sit in a chair and talk on the phone. If they had to play hooky, that was OK. This was work experience, wasn't it?

And when Barry walked the very impressed Drexel representatives through the center, the phones were ringing off the hook, and all the chairs were filled with teenagers looking as if they were talking to customers and writing down orders obtained from Barry's TV commercials or from contacts they themselves had just made. In fact, what most of them were doing was using the ZZZZ Best 800 number to call each other back and forth.

— 23 —

IT WOULDN'T BE LONG, Jeri Carr thought after putting down the phone, before she became "the biggest PR person known." And it will all be because she'd been smart enough to attach herself to *him*.

Carr still recalls as if it were yesterday that call she got from Barry Minkow telling her that Drexel was going to do the deal, was actually going to buy him KeyServ.

The news was so good, so big, so staggering, that for once Jeri Carr wasn't annoyed when Barry told her he wanted to have a press conference—a big one that included all the majors and normally would have taken weeks to prepare—on the following day. If *he* wanted it done, she would do it.

For by now Jeri Carr, like Joel Hochberg and many others, was a true believer in Barry Minkow. Like Joel, she'd heard Barry say he was going to do a lot of things, and like Joel, she watched as he'd done them. So when Barry began saying in earnest that he intended one day to be president of the United States, Carr, although not a political person, took out some subscriptions to political magazines—determined to learn the PR aspects of politics and to be the person who would publicize him. She wasn't about to allow anybody else to take the glory. She'd worked too hard, and Barry had always been so good about paying his retainer.

He'd been so cute that day he'd called, so excited. And although he was snapping out orders as usual, he'd also taken the time to tell Carr that he, too, felt they were a team—a couple of great motivators—and that, now that he was going to own KeyServ, he wanted her to come aboard and head his in-house PR team. He even offered to help in phoning up the media and telling them about the imminent press conference. It won't be a problem, he assured her, "I'll just say I'm somebody else."

The press conference featured Barry at his brashest and made almost all the local evening news programs. Articles also appeared in the *Los Angeles Herald-Examiner* and *Daily News*, as did short blurbs announcing the acquisition in the *Los Angeles Times* and *Wall Street Journal*. "I always said my goal was to be the General Motors of the carpet-cleaning industry," said Barry Minkow at the press conference. "Today it's a fact."

The deal was a sweet one, sweeter even than Barry and Mark had anticipated. In addition to the $25 million purchase price and $15 million for merging and operating expenses, Drexel had agreed to provide another $40 million line of credit for further expansion and investment. It seemed incredible, but the boys were shortly to have both a national company and $55 million to play around with.

Even more astounding, according to Mark Morze, was an offer made to him and Barry by a Drexel official right around the time of the KeyServ announcement. Once you have KeyServ, said the official, and you make $1 million a month in profits (as Barry and Mark had honestly estimated they could) for nine consecutive months, then we (Drexel) will raise $660 million in junk bonds and buy you ServiceMaster (a billion-dollar-plus franchised commercial and residential janitorial/cleaning service). We feel, the Drexel executive told them, that ServiceMaster is ripe for a hostile takeover.

But that was in the future; for now, the boys were about to get KeyServ and the $55 million. If *that* wasn't the cure, what was?

He was on his absolutely worst behavior, and Oprah was not pleased. Already about halfway through the taping of the "Oprah Winfrey Show," Barry, acting as if he'd just washed down about a dozen uppers with two pots of coffee, had already insulted, demeaned, and alienated his fellow guests and his hostess as well. It was a combination of his constant interruptions, his cocky, high-strung manner, and the mouthing of his seemingly endless supply of platitudes that had everyone, in but a short time, *up to here* with this kid. He used all the standards: "Think big, be big"; "Tough times pass, and tough people last"; "Life is a movie, and you are the actor—if you don't like the script, change it." By the time Oprah was ready to break for a third round of commercials, the other panelists were giving each other who-*is*-this-guy looks. Oprah herself, on her fade, felt compelled to throw back her head and ask Barry sarcastically if he thought it took "*aggressive* behavior to get ahead."

Jeri Carr and her girls had been trying to get Barry on "Donahue" for several years, without success. When "Oprah" came on, they tried her too, this time meeting with immediate interest. When Oprah's producers countered with a suggestion that Barry appear with four or five other panelists on a segment called "Young and Rich," they were naturally a bit disappointed, having wanted the entire program to showcase Barry. But it is a cardinal rule of PR that you take whatever exposure you can get, and Oprah with her national audience was very good exposure indeed.

Judging by Oprah's opening remarks at the taping in Chicago in early April, things had promised to go well, Oprah uncritically mouthing the standard Barry spiel: "At fifteen, this whiz kid was making more money than his high school principal . . . at twenty he was chairman of a $150 million public corporation with twenty-one offices and over 1,000 employees; welcome . . . Barry Minkow!"

But it all went downhill from there. It wasn't just the platitudes or the interruptions or his style. It was the *substance* of what he was saying, too, that people found so objectionable. "I'm really not into the material things," he told the audience. "[My stock in] ZZZZ Best right now is worth $90 million, [but] $90 million is nothing. . . . Five to ten *billion* is the kind of range I want to move up to."

What really turned the tide, however, was the arrogant way he dismissed a fellow "Young and Rich" panelist. Barry had just given some condescending advice to another guest, who owned a string of frozen yogurt shops: "We have a saying where I work—there is no excuse for seasonality. *I* could sell frozen yogurt in a blizzard." When the third panelist objected, Barry turned and told him, "Neil, your sales are seventeen million, mine are fifty; end of story."

While Barry was taping "Oprah" in Chicago, Tom Padgett was sublimely tossing back Corona Extras as he took in the view from the balcony of his new home at the water's edge in Newport Beach.

Tom's revelry was short-lived, however, for just a week or two after moving in, he got a call from Barry Minkow that literally filled him with a cold dread. Old news was returning to haunt them.

Back in January, Ernst & Whinney had begun a routine new audit of ZZZZ Best, and among the paperwork the auditors had reviewed, they found a one-page copy of a work order from Interstate for an $8.2 million restoration job in San Diego.

Because of its staggering size and the fact that the job was supposedly still in progress, the auditors, as they'd done with the Sacramento project, told Barry they wanted to visit both the site and a warehouse where they'd been told the job's materials were being stored.

As previously, it had fallen on Tom and the albino to secure a building and set everything up for a guided tour for Ernst & Whinney that would once again be conducted by the silver-tongued Mark Morze.

And as with Sacramento, things had gone surprisingly well. They quickly found an unfinished eight- or nine-story building on Fourth and Cedar in which carpeting and acoustical ceilings had already been placed on a couple of the floors. And they just as quickly located the building's manager, who, anxious to lease the entire vacant floor that Tom was claiming he was interested in, agreed to turn over the building's keys on the weekend that Tom's boss supposedly would be coming down to give his approval for the rental.

Then, almost as smoothly as with the building, they found a warehouse in nearby Miramar, used a ZZZZ Best corporate check for $23,000 to lease it for the minimum year required, and called Mark Morze—who, through Barry's connection at Carpet Corner, had a huge supply of the cheapest carpeting available trucked to the warehouse. Like the suits behind the desks in Tom's office, the carpeting was strictly for appearance—to look as if it was soon to be laid at the restoration site.

Next, they fixed up the warehouse to look as if it were doing business, buying filing cabinets and maps for the walls of the warehouse's small office and having the name of the albino's company—Assured Property Management—painted on the door. Finally, they contacted a friend of Tom's and hired him as security guard for the day of the visit. Just be there, keep your mouth shut, and wear a uniform, he was told.

Then, when Mark had flown down the Friday afternoon before

the inspection, they'd gone over to ZZZZ Best's San Diego carpet-cleaning location and picked up a van as a prop to be parked outside the warehouse and some ZZZZ Best T-shirts to be placed strategically around the office and warehouse.

Right before the inspection, they'd even scattered some popcorn around the office so Mark could tell Larry Gray that it looked like that pig Roddy was still spilling his popcorn all over the place.

Popcorn, van, T-shirts, a uniformed security guard, filing cabinets, maps, signs, a building, *and* a warehouse—they'd done it all for that February inspection, and Gray, as he had in Sacramento, had bought it all. It couldn't have been more perfect.

But here it was April, and because fuckin' Barry had announced that the San Diego job had been successfully completed, Ernst & Whinney was saying, "How nice. Now we want to *see* that completed job before we submit our audit." Well, fuck, who knew if that goddamned building in San Diego was even finished.

And now Barry was calling Mark and telling him he had to grab Roddy and get back down to San Diego, find out if that building was completed—lease some floors whether it is or not—and if it isn't, *get* it completed. "You must be nuts," Tom told Barry when he called. "We can't do all that." And Barry had told him that there was no "can't," that it had to be the *same* building because Gray had already seen it, that Gray was going to do the inspection, and he was taking *no* excuses. If Tom and Roddy couldn't take care of that building, it was *over*.

Shaken, Tom called the albino to tell him to get ready for the trip to San Diego and to get a dose of Roddy's special brand of reassurance that always did so much to stiffen the backbone of Tom Padgett. But all Roddy could say was, "Don't get too attached to that beach house."

While Tom was down in San Diego trying to deal with just one aspect of the scam, Barry was keeping up with his usual killing schedule, sleeping just a few hours a night while dealing with Ernst & Whinney, negotiating with Drexel Burnham Lambert, traveling about the country hyping ZZZZ Best stock in anticipation of the KeyServ merger, and holding closed-door meetings with Rosario, Charbit, Schiff, and other investors.

Simultaneously, he was also preparing a massive three-day conference to be held at the Century Plaza Hotel for about a thousand ZZZZ Best and KeyServ employees and their spouses—approximately 600 of whom he was flying into LA at company expense. "The guy," Mark Morze frequently thought, "must be triplets."

Called "The Sky Is the Limit," the conference was supposed to integrate KeyServ's personnel with ZZZZ Best's and make everybody feel comfortable. It was, in a sense, another astute management move on Barry's part, for such a conference, designed to boost morale and put employees' minds at ease at a time of transition, was surely a smart motivational tool. And it must have also increased Drexel Burnham Lambert's comfort level to know that ZZZZ Best was doing so well that it could afford to spend hundreds of thousands of dollars on such an affair.

Had the firm known, however, that Barry had gone to Maurice Rind to borrow $750,000 to pay for the conference, Drexel might have felt less comfortable about it.

Maurice, of course, was well able to afford the loan, having recently sold most of the ZZZZ Best stock he'd jointly bought with Richie Schulman and Robert Victor at the time ZZZZ Best went public. For stock that cost $50,000, they had realized a profit of over $6 million.

— 24 —

"OUR MISSION," Tom Padgett kept repeating through clenched teeth to the albino on the way down to San Diego, "is to get this building *leased*. We gotta get it. If we don't, we're history."

Perhaps it was that urgency that caused Tom Padgett to make his first big mistake. It occurred as they were sitting in the manager's office. Tom told the manager, the same one he'd spoken to in February, that they had decided to lease the space after all. And not just the one floor they had talked about previously, but three floors. Moreover, it didn't matter that they were not yet completed. We'll finish the construction, said Tom, at our own expense. We'll pay cash, we want the shortest lease you have, and we want to sign today. The manager, fit, blow-dried, in his late twenties—a straight Republican voter if Tom Padgett had ever seen one—stood to make a lot of money from such a deal. But being the "you-bet"-after-every-sentence, church-usher kind of guy he was, the building manager was also taken aback by Tom's proposal. *Cash?* A one-year lease? And finish the construction at their own expense? *Nobody* does that. This is San Diego; what are these guys into, drugs or wetbacks?

Over the next several days, in spite of Tom's pressing him, the manager seemed reluctant to lease the space, finally telling Tom and the albino that the building had recently changed hands and the new owners had decided not to rent *anything* until the deal had been finalized and they had legal ownership.

The ownership finally did change hands, but not until the last week in April, leaving little more than two weeks before the inspection tour was due to occur.

By then everybody was frantic, and the calls from Barry and Mark grew hot enough that Tom felt compelled to tell them that he was no fucking Superman, and was doing the best he could.

The new manager, perhaps warned by the previous one, proved no more helpful, however. A sharp, abrasive woman in her midthirties, she clearly did not like Tom and the albino (even though Roddy tried to date her) and wasn't at all tempted by the big commission she stood to make on the lease.

In fact, she actually went as far as to throw Tom and Roddy out of the building's conference room where they had gathered some contractors to start work on completing the unfinished floors. "There will not be one nail driven until there is a contract that has been signed," she said.

As they walked out of the building, the perennially optimistic albino grabbed Tom by the arm and said, "We're not gonna make it. We're not gonna get this building."

That same afternoon, following a fitful nap, Roddy suggested they go and talk with Brian Morze, who'd just been sent down to San Diego by Barry and Mark to see if he could help out.

Sitting in Brian's room, Roddy ran down what had been occurring, and his fears that it was all over. But "all over" meant unthinkable things, so they continued kicking around ideas until they came up with one they thought might work.

Brian would fly to Denver, where the corporation that owned the building was headquartered, and deal directly with the owners.

His story would be that ZZZZ Best wanted to lease the floors because the company planned on going after the lucrative San Diego market in a big way. ZZZZ Best wanted to be discreet and not make a public announcement, however, to avoid having the company's stock fluctuate. With the KeyServ merger so much in the public eye and the SEC watching, they needed to be extra careful not to leave themselves open to charges of stock manipulation— hence the need for secrecy.

It was quite a good story, they all agreed, and Brian quickly flew off to Denver and succeeded in breaking the logjam.

But the boys received no favor. They were required to put down a $500,000 security deposit and lease the floors for seven years.

With eleven days to go, they started construction. They had eleven days to do what might normally be three or four months' work. They'd previously gotten the building's plans done in only two days by "waving a blank check," and now they proceeded to wave some others at local contractors and some electrical workers and general contractor friends of the albino's from LA, telling them to work their crews twenty-four hours a day and then fill in the blanks.

On the day before Gray's scheduled visit, Tom and Roddy stopped by the building for a final inspection. It was like a miracle. All the new drywall, painting, plumbing, carpeting, and electrical work had been completed. It was all perfect.

The contractors had done all they'd promised, and in just eleven days. Of course, they'd also filled in those blank checks—for almost $1 million.

It took Larry Gray and another CPA who accompanied him about twenty minutes to inspect that million dollars' worth of work and not much longer to tour the warehouse, which this time contained little carpeting, most of it having ostensibly been used for the renovation.

Then Mark Morze and the two accountants hopped a plane to Dallas, where, according to a recent announcement, ZZZZ Best was beginning work on a restoration job costing $13.8 million! When Gray heard about *that*, he'd asked to visit there as well.

They went to a rented warehouse, where much of the carpeting that had previously been in the San Diego warehouse had been sent.

While there, two events occurred that were perfectly timed to coincide with the visit. The first was a delivery of cleaning and chemical compounds to the warehouse. Before leaving LA, Mark had given instructions for the precise moment of delivery. Then a staged phone call for Mark came through. He listened intently, grinned, hung up, and announced that ZZZZ Best had just received two additional restoration contracts totaling over $10 million.

Finally, Mark's third prearrangement paid off. Unlike San Diego, in Dallas there was a warehouse, but *no* building. In fact, the address the boys were quoting for the restoration site was a vacant lot adjacent to a freeway off ramp.

To avoid the scheduled visit to a building that didn't exist, Mark had deliberately booked the flight back to LA from Dallas so tightly that everything would have to go like clockwork for them to inspect both the warehouse and the restoration site before their flight took off. Then Mark made sure to stall at the airport, on the drive to the warehouse, and at the warehouse itself. By the time they were ready to go to the restoration site, it meant either missing the inspection or missing their flight and having to stay overnight. As Mark had anticipated, Gray said, "Screw it, I've seen enough," and back to LA they flew.

Meanwhile, back in San Diego, Tom Padgett accepted congratulations from Barry for a job well done. Feeling triumphant, he then went out with the albino and found a bar, where they spent the next five or six hours. "I can't wait to get back to Newport," Tom told Roddy. "I need a break in the action."

Flying back from Dallas the night of the inspection, Mark Morze too felt some of the tension draining away. As the first-class flight attendant stopped to make him a drink, he noticed that sitting across the aisle was the then Commissioner of Baseball, Peter Ueberroth.

To be polite and also because he genuinely admired the man who'd brought LA such a successful Olympics, Mark struck up a conversation, in the course of which Ueberroth happened to ask Mark what he did. "I'm in charge of restoration for ZZZZ Best Carpet Cleaning," Morze replied. Had Ueberroth ever heard of them? Certainly, said Ueberroth; in fact, he understood some people from his office were meeting soon with its owner, Barry Minkow, about his interest in purchasing the Seattle Mariners.

As Barry on more than one occasion had mentioned his desire to own a professional sports franchise, Mark wasn't at all surprised. Prior to the pending deal with Drexel Burnham Lambert, however, that desire had simply been what Chip always called a "Minkow pipe dream."

Now, such a buy was not only possible, but absolutely doable. Within a week or two of Morze's chance encounter with the baseball commissioner, Barry, along with Mark Moskowitz, Larry Gray, and a representative of Prudential-Bache (from whom Barry had just secured a $5 million line of credit), had actually met with a group of people from professional baseball to discuss buying the Mariners.

At the meeting, the question was raised of whether Barry planned to move the franchise if he bought it, and Minkow assured them he had no intention of doing so. He wished instead to sell shares of the team to the fans.

The matter of Barry's ability to meet the purchase price—rumored to be about $30 million—also came up. But the baseball people were assured by Barry's financial team that he had all the money needed. In less than a year, not only would he be able to sell his $100 million worth of stock, he would be head of KeyServ and CEO of ServiceMaster—a billion-dollar company. Thirty million dollars would be chump change.

Almost simultaneously with the San Diego and Dallas inspections, the KeyServ conference took place. Thanks to Barry and people like Jeri Carr and the Madrinan sisters who helped put it together, it proved a grand success. Barry held candlelight dinners for his present and future employees, told jokes, participated in panel discussions, introduced honored guests, gave inspirational speeches, received standing ovations, and publicly speculated on one day becoming President.

About a week later, ZZZZ Best issued a press release that, given its extraordinary claims, should have been viewed with some skepticism. But, perhaps because of all the success that preceded it, the release hardly caused a raised eyebrow.

"ZZZZ Best Co. Inc., . . . has entered into the largest single insurance restoration contract in its history, for carpeting and related work, for approximately $13.8 million," the release read. "ZZZZ Best also announced that, including this contract, it has entered into contracts for approximately *$25.7 million of new insurance restoration work during the past 30 days* [italics added], also a record for any 30-day period in its history."

Part IV
Coming Apart

— 1 —

AT ABOUT A QUARTER TO NINE on a Friday morning in May, Joel
Hochberg arrived as usual at ZZZZ Best's Reseda headquarters,
stepped through the door, and wondered what all the commotion
was about. Instead of working at their desks or chatting quietly
over morning coffee, most of the employees were milling about the
cramped quarters of Barry's secretary, Sherrie Maloney, asking
her what it all meant and if their jobs were in jeopardy.

When Joel asked what was happening, someone shoved the *LA
Times* in his face and said, "Here, read this." It was the lead article
on the front page of the business section, dated that day, May 22,
1987:

Behind Whiz Kid Is a Trail
of False Credit Card Billings.

Beneath the headline was a picture of Barry Minkow.

"Holy shit!" Hochberg thought. Gulping down a cup of coffee,
he read on: ". . . Through ZZZZ Best's lawyer, Mark Moskowitz,
Minkow acknowledged to the *Times* this week that ZZZZ Best rang
up $72,000 in false charges from November 1984 to March 1985 . . .
[but] said ZZZZ Best made good on all the charges . . . and blamed
12 unscrupulous carpet-cleaning subcontractors." The story, quoting a credit card fraud investigator, then added, "Because the
money from the charges was paid into a . . . corporate account . . . it
seems unlikely that an employee could have benefited."

One of his early scams, combined with his high public profile,
had finally caught up with Barry Minkow. The enemies he'd made
during the Floral Fantasies credit card fraud were now doing him
in. They, and some good reporting.

A few of them, including Robin Swanson—whose husband had
been beaten by Danny Krowpman, Jr.—had contacted a reporter
at the *Los Angeles Times* named Daniel Akst. Akst had previously
written a favorable story about Barry and, intrigued by the complaints and tips he was receiving, decided to do a follow-up. The
result of his investigations was the story now causing so much
consternation at ZZZZ Best. (Akst and other reporters around town
were also getting calls from "short sellers," who buy stock betting

its price will go *down*, and who were now self-servingly questioning the validity of the restoration jobs.)

Maloney took Joel aside and told him that Barry, away at a speaking engagement, had been calling every ten minutes for news ever since he'd heard about the article. Barry's main concern seemed to be whether the story was only in the *Times*'s Valley edition—in which case the damage might be minimized—or in its main full-circulation metropolitan paper too. He'd even had Sherrie send someone "over the hill" to LA to buy a city edition. The guy had just come back with the bad news. It was everywhere.

About that time, Barry called again, and when Sherrie told him how concerned the employees in the office were, he got on the speaker phone. At his absolutely most reassuring, he told everybody what was to become *the* story: the subcontractors had done it, it had all been taken care of, and the *Times*, because he was the Boy Wonder, was out to slander him.

Joel and the others were much relieved and began to calm down and settle in for the day.

Chip Arrington was also out of town when the *Times* story broke, visiting a KeyServ location in New Jersey. When Barry called *him*, he was far less reassuring. "Get home," he told Chip. "We've got serious problems."

About 4:30 that afternoon, Barry's lawyer, Arthur Barens, also received a call from Minkow. Barry was one of his favorite clients, as he paid Arthur a $1,500-a-month retainer for doing little more than deal with ZZZZ Best customers unhappy about spots remaining in their rugs.

Barry was always fun to talk to, but this time he sounded a bit odd. "I'm at the airport," Minkow said, "and I need to see you *now*." Barens told him to come right over. When his client arrived, Arthur was somewhat startled. The loose, freewheeling Barry Minkow with whom he had perennial running gags was disheveled and visibly upset, appearing to be almost in a state of emotional shock. "Have you seen the article in today's *Times*?" Barry asked.

That morning, Tom Padgett, still feeling good about his triumph in San Diego, worked out and at about ten drove from Newport to his office. As he sat down and propped his feet on his $2,000 desk, the new accountant he and Barry had just hired as a favor to Roddy—a thin, big-eared man whom Tom Padgett could not *stand*—came over, handed him the *Times* article, and said, "Take a look at this." As Tom read the story, the accountant, a CPA in his fifties named Norm Rothberg, hovered over Tom's shoulder like a goddamned gnat.

Finishing reading, Tom looked up at Rothberg, not much fazed—due as always to his superb ability to rationalize *anything*—and said "So what? No one's been hurt. No one's lost any money. What's the big deal?"

Rothberg looked at Tom as if he already knew what was going on. "This could really lead to problems," he said, walking away.

That same morning, a young, LA-based U.S. attorney named Jim Asperger sat down with the *Times* at his kitchen table and, while eating breakfast, also spotted the credit card story. "Well," he thought, *"this* looks interesting." When he got to his office, Asperger, the deputy chief of the district's Major Frauds Unit, called the SEC, spoke with an official there with whom he'd worked previously, and asked if anybody had seen the article. "Yeah," she said, "we've already been looking into it."

— 2 —

WHEN BARRY AND CHIP MET after quickly returning to LA, they were both tense. Unlike Padgett, Barry recognized the danger the *Times* story held. For the first time, he told Chip exactly what he'd done to pull off the credit card fraud, and how Drexel Burnham Lambert was now demanding some serious answers about what had happened. If they didn't come up with answers right away, they could lose everything, Barry said—the entire company in a matter of days.

After they discussed the problem for a while, Chip agreed their only option was to lie. Who, after all, was going to invest $80 million in a guy who just two years earlier was ripping off consumers in such a petty, venal way?

It was decided to tell both Drexel and an independent law firm hired by ZZZZ Best's board of directors to investigate the allegations, that Chip had been the true owner of Floral Fantasies, and that the overcharges had been caused by both the subcontractors and the shop's previous owner. Chip, in other words, had inherited the problem, and neither he nor Barry had anything to do with it.

With that decision, Chip was now in—part of the scam, although, like Dan Krowpman and others, in a very limited way. There was a $100,000 bonus—payment for his work in connection with the KeyServ merger—that was at stake. But no one who knew Chip Arrington ever thought *that* was his primary motivation. There was, far more importantly, five years of work for a company, a boss, and co-workers to whom he was devoted.

So within days of the publication of the credit card article, Chip met with investigators from Drexel Burnham Lambert and told them the lies that Barry and he had concocted. But, as Arrington was later to say, "They didn't exactly believe the story and . . . said that they wanted backup paperwork in order to prove it."

Meanwhile, a second potentially calamitous situation for the boys was also coming to a head—one that never would have occurred had Tom and Barry followed their instincts. But, no, because Norm Rothberg had that all-important CPA stamp that would lend credence to Interstate's paperwork, and because Roddy *asked* him, Tom, after consulting with Barry, had hired Rothberg as Interstate's accountant. He and Roddy had even gotten Barry to loan Rothberg $5,000 in December 1986, when Norman was about to get evicted from his apartment, asking only for some of that CPA validity on Interstate's documents in return. For that, in addition to the loan, they'd put Rothberg on the payroll at $400 a week and allowed him to move his computer into his own cubicle in the "Marina office" and to use the phone freely.

It was a disaster from the start. In Padgett's eyes, Norm Rothberg had a million things going against him. First, he was a rhymer, infuriatingly rhyming everything with *shm*: "taxes, shmaxes," he would say, "table, shmable." That alone was enough to drive you *crazy*. Then there was his smoking. OK, you want a cigarette, have a cigarette. But Rothberg would have one perennially dangling out of his mouth, allowing the smoke to swirl up into his eyes and the ashes to fall all over his clothing. And that was another thing: his clothes and grooming, thought Padgett, were an embarrassment to the office! There was no excuse for Rothberg's baggy, unkempt clothing and slicked-down, Brylcreem look. No matter that the guy was just coming out of a failed marriage with no place to live and hadn't made any money in years. Tom Padgett could well understand that, and what a woman could do to you, but a man should at least keep up his goddamned grooming.

And of course there was the fact that Norm was Jewish, one of that "5 percent that were *so* bad they caused Jews to be hated around the world."

He should have listened to Barry, Tom thought. The day after they'd hired Norm, Barry had called and said that he didn't like Rothberg, that he could be trouble, and that with access to Interstate's paperwork, he could well put it all together and discover what was going on.

And that was exactly what happened.

For in spite of having fallen on hard times, Norm Rothberg was nobody's fool. In addition to being a CPA, he was a law school graduate and a former IRS agent with seven years' experience. With his cubicle right next to Roddy's, Norm Rothberg overheard a great deal more than he was intended to—the boys goofing and laughing about the Sacramento inspection tour, for example, or how they'd put up ZZZZ Best signs and run Larry Gray through the building without him even questioning anything. He'd also overheard Tom and the albino reminiscing about how high they'd lived down at La Costa during the San Diego inspections.

After overhearing these and other conversations, and reviewing Interstate's checkbooks and paperwork, Rothberg realized there was a major scam going on, and that that information would be very valuable to Ernst & Whinney.

He also hoped, given his pitiful situation, that it could somehow prove valuable to him. But if he were just to report the information to Ernst & Whinney, and they acted on it, he might well be out of a job, an office, and a free phone. So in early April he decided to contact the accounting firm and see if he could cut a deal.

Calling an acquaintance at Ernst & Whinney named Howard Levy, Rothberg made arrangements to meet. Subsequently he outlined the information he had without mentioning ZZZZ Best or Interstate by name. But he did indicate that one of the companies involved was an Ernst & Whinney client. The meeting then adjourned, but when they met on two subsequent occasions, Norm was more demanding *and* more forthcoming. At the second meeting he asked Levy for $25,000 to $30,000 to be more specific. The money, he said, was to compensate him for what he would be losing from his client. And although Levy turned him down, during their third meeting in mid-May, Rothberg revealed that the company in question was ZZZZ Best, and that the Sacramento job didn't exist. He also mentioned, but was vague on another point—that about $500,000 was being run through a loop, making it seem like several million, and creating the appearance that ZZZZ Best's restoration work was real. As much as 80 percent of that work, he added, might be fake.

Within five days of the appearance of the *Times* story, ZZZZ Best stock had dropped from almost $17 a share to $6. It was clear that something had to be done immediately to stem the tide, prop up the stock, and keep Drexel in the deal.

So on May 28, Barry issued a press release announcing record preliminary results for the fiscal year ending April 30, 1987. New bookings were said to be at their highest level; the acquisition of KeyServ was proceeding on course; and an independent investigation of the credit card fraud had found, to date, no wrongdoing on the part of ZZZZ Best or its management. In addition, earnings were sensational: over $5 million as opposed to just under $1 million for the same period the year before.

Buoyed by the upbeat report, the stock rose in the next day or two to just over $10 per share.

Norm Rothberg's allegations couldn't have come at a worse time. ZZZZ Best's credibility with investors and Drexel Burnham Lambert had already been severely strained by the *Times* article. Additional charges would surely destroy whatever hope remained of completing the KeyServ merger and restoring investor confidence.

Although Rothberg had been meeting with Ernst & Whinney for over a month, he had not revealed ZZZZ Best's name and the specifics of the allegations until just days before the *Times* story broke. When Ernst & Whinney advised Barry of Norm's charges shortly thereafter, he seemed offended. "Rothberg?" he asked, "Who's Rothberg? Why are you listening to a crank call like this?" Without making any public announcement of the allegations, Ernst & Whinney then entered into an agreement with Minkow to have an internal investigation conducted by ZZZZ Best's board of directors and Kadison, Pfaelzer, the same independent law firm that was currently looking into the credit card charges.

Barry also alerted Padgett and Roddy to Rothberg's allegations and sent Brian Morze over to Interstate. "Their mission," as Tom Padgett later put it, was to persuade Rothberg to recant his allegations to Ernst & Whinney and the independent investigators. It was their only option. For the boys, desperate as they were, were not thuggish enough to think of, say, knocking off Rothberg. Such was not their style, save perhaps for Tom Padgett, who actually did rant and rave about picking up a gun and killing Norm. Reason overcame bluster, however, and he was dissuaded by Barry and the Morze brothers from even threatening Rothberg. Instead, Padgett and Roddy took a picture of Adolf Hitler that Tom kept in his desk drawer and hung it on the wall for Rothberg to see when he walked in.

But Brian did use a gun when he and the albino talked to Rothberg about recanting his charges. In a novel form of duress, Morze pulled a .45 semiautomatic out of Tom's desk, put it in his own mouth, and said in effect, if you don't do what we ask, I'm going to blow *my* brains out.

Brian then told Rothberg that he was aware of Norm's financial difficulties and that they were willing to raise his salary from $400 to $1,000 per week—guaranteed for three years—if he would cooperate and "mitigate what [he'd] told Ernst & Whinney." Rothberg agreed but demanded the money up front because "Once I talk, you won't need me."

Shortly thereafter, Norm met with Barry and Brian Morze at a Baker's Square restaurant. Rothberg repeated what he had earlier told Brian—that he wanted a $100,000 bonus before he told *anybody* he'd been mistaken. Barry agreed on the condition that Norm take the hundred grand in ZZZZ Best stock—an offer, given the company's precarious position, that Rothberg rightly found insulting.

Instead, it was agreed that Norm would receive a $25,000 cash bonus, *plus* the $1,000 per week for three years.

Chip was crestfallen after the meeting with Drexel Burnham Lambert. Paperwork! They wanted to see paperwork from Floral Fantasies, he told Barry. But Barry, to Chip's surprise, was unperturbed. "Don't worry about that," he told Chip. "Just call Mark Morze, because he can do anything."

Chip called Mark, who was as blasé as Barry. "Get me one of your blank checks from that Floral Fantasies period, as well as a bank statement from that time," Mark said, "and I'll make it look like you [not Barry] bought and paid for that flower shop."

Dropping off the check and bank statement at Mark's house, Chip returned later to find they'd been transformed. Most of the front of the new check had been left blank to be filled in by Chip. The date would reflect the period about two and a half years earlier when Chip supposedly had bought the flower shop. The amount would reflect the shop's purchase price—$20,000. The memo would read "purchase of Floral Fantasies," and the check would be made out to the shop's previous owner.

On the back of the check, Mark had already placed the previous owner's endorsement signature. And on both sides, he'd put bank stamps and numbers making it appear that the check had been negotiated.

Morze had also added a $20,000 withdrawal to Chip's bank statement as proof he had made the purchase.

Arrington brought the check and doctored bank statement to Barry, who passed them on to the Drexel investment bankers.

A few days later, Chip had a startlingly abrupt meeting with the Drexel officials. Calling him into a room, they told Arrington they didn't believe his story, and then asked him to write the numbers zero through ten, and then in reverse order ten through zero. With that, they pulled out a photocopy of a Floral Fantasies charge card deposit slip, looked at it, looked at what Chip had written, looked at each other, said, "OK," and left.

The following day, on June 1, Drexel Burnham Lambert, without public comment, quit the ZZZZ Best account. A Drexel spokesman, denying that his company and ZZZZ Best were close to an agreement, would later say as his firm withdrew that Drexel "hadn't even priced the deal."

But according to highly placed law enforcement officials as well as Mark Morze, the *Times* story had broken just three days before Drexel was to have signed the papers and turned over to Barry Minkow and ZZZZ Best a check for $40 million. Three days. Within a month, if the deal had gone through, they would have given Barry Minkow and ZZZZ Best $40 million more.

The weather was beautiful in Newport that first week in June, and Tom Padgett was enjoying every minute of it.

One day, Sandra and her mother came down for lunch, sunning on the beach and then going with Tom to Mimi's, a nice little French restaurant in nearby Costa Mesa.

It was a memorable day, made unfortunately even more so when, late in the afternoon, Tom got a call. It was from the albino, who said four words that shattered Tom Padgett's tranquility: "Ernst & Whinney resigned."

First Drexel, now Ernst & Whinney.

Tom Padgett immediately called Barry.

The conversation made him feel even worse. Minkow and Morze were at a loss for ideas, which was very unusual, Barry and Mark *always* being full of ideas. And Barry sounded tired, which was even more unusual. Barry *never* sounded tired.

Just a few days before, there had been cause for mild optimism. At a meeting with Mark and Roddy at Barry's house, Barry reported that he'd been able to work things out with Rothberg, and that they still had a good shot at KeyServ. Now it was all coming apart.

Drexel hadn't bought Chip's story *or* Mark's paperwork, and one question too many had finally been raised in the minds of Ernst & Whinney. First, there had been Rothberg's fraud allegations, then the *Times* story, then the distribution of the May 28 press release—the one with all those fantastic profit figures—without anyone even notifying *them*—ZZZZ Best's own accountants—that the company intended to issue such a release. Lastly, there was that check they'd just found in the course of their year-end audit, that $5,000 check Barry had given Norm Rothberg as a loan back in December 1986. Barry had told them no more than two weeks before, when they'd confronted him about the allegations, that he didn't even know who Rothberg was. Why, then, had Barry written him a check for $5,000? No, something wasn't right.

In spite of their reservations, Ernst & Whinney made no effort to notify anyone other than ZZZZ Best of their resignation. The accountants' attitude was that an investigation by an independent law firm was now in progress, and that until that investigation was complete, there was nothing to report. In any case, they were not obliged to notify anyone other than their client. Under SEC regulations, it was up to ZZZZ Best to notify the SEC that Ernst & Whinney had resigned. And they had fifteen days to do so. A lot could happen in fifteen days.

— 3 —

SHERI ELOWSKY WAS FLATTERED. The first-class ticket from New York to LA that Barry Minkow was paying for, along with the big basket of fruit and bouquet of flowers that he arranged to have waiting in her hotel room, had all made Elowsky—who was about ten years Barry's senior—delighted about the weekend "lark" she had decided to share with him.

It was June 26, and this was the second time that Elowsky was spending a weekend in LA as Barry Minkow's guest. She had met him several months earlier at a KeyServ road show in Manhattan. A loan officer and vice president for Prudential-Bache, she had recently approved a $5 million personal line of credit for Minkow. Ever since, Barry had been, well, attentive.

At first, it was just friendly phone calls, talking about personal things as well as business. Then Barry had asked her to fly out to LA over Memorial Day weekend while he was starting negotiations for the Seattle Mariners. She had protested that it wasn't necessary, that the people from their West Coast office who were part of his financial team could handle it. But Barry had insisted that he wanted *her* to be there, assuring Elowsky he'd pay for her first-class ticket and other expenses.

At ZZZZ Best headquarters, Barry had greeted her with a hug, which surprised Elowsky; it was, after all, a business headquarters. Of course, they *had* talked a lot on the phone and become friendly. Still, it kind of surprised her.

Memorial Day was the weekend after the *Times* story, and although Barry had already used much of his $5 million line of credit, the article had not alarmed Elowsky in the least. Barry's explanation seemed totally plausible to her. And as she sat there while he took calls from investors and the press, the credit card allegations actually *boosted* her confidence in him. She thought to herself, "Well, there was a problem, he found out what it was, and he solved it and stopped it." And in Elowsky's mind, that was usually the sign of a good manager—isolating and solving a problem.

The following day, they had lunch. The conversation centered on social rather than business matters, and much good-natured flirting took place.

After Elowsky returned to New York, Barry's calls became more frequent—three or four times a week—culminating with his invitation to come out to LA on this last weekend in June that Elowsky was now regarding as "such a nice little lark."

On a tour of ZZZZ Best headquarters, Barry pointed out a locked room where he said all credit card charges were now *double-checked*. He also showed her ZZZZ Best's latest statement of earnings and the telemarketing center.

The proper impression having been made during the day, Barry pulled off the road on the way to dinner that night and bought Sheri some flowers, afterward taking her back to her hotel room, where he finally came to the point. Writing three checks—the first two in reimbursement of Elowsky's expenses for her trips to LA, the third a check for $2 million, postdated to July 10—Barry told her, "Now I still owe $1,775,000 on my Pru-Bache line of credit, but I have a slight cash shortfall right now. If you could let me have another $225,000, I'll be able to pay you back the entire $2 million probably around July 3, when some insurance restoration payments come in."

Elowsky replied that she didn't know. What he was asking was very unorthodox, and she'd have to think about it. She then flew back to New York. The next day, however, she called and told Barry she had decided to lend him the money. "I love you," Barry said as he hung up the phone.

By late June, a man without Barry Minkow's incredible stamina, without his naive fearlessness, without his deceitful ingenuity, and without his total disregard for the feelings, lives, and concerns of anybody but himself, would have given up. But Barry Minkow was now as addicted to the game as he was to the result. There was no way that he would give up before trying every possible cure.

Earlier in the month, he had successfully dealt with his most pressing problems involving the investigations going on all around him.

Through Brian Morze, Barry saw to it that the bonus payments to Norm Rothberg were made—payments that were to ensure Norm's vague, noncommittal answers when he met with the lawyer/investigators from Kadison, Pfaelzer.

Then, following Ernst & Whinney's resignation, he'd secured

the services of another Big Eight accounting firm, Price Water-house, and ensured that Mark Moskowitz from Hughes Hubbard & Reed would continue to innocently defend him.

He had even managed to finesse the SEC-mandated announce-ment of Ernst & Whinney's resignation—fifteen days after that resignation had taken place. He simply stated that recent news reports linking the accounting firm's resignation with the false credit card billing story were "incorrect and/or misleading," and that Ernst & Whitney's resignation did not "relate to any disagree-ment over accounting principles or auditing procedures." Buying more time, Minkow also announced that ZZZZ Best's board of directors had "voluntarily authorized" a special committee to investigate the recent charges and that their findings would be reviewed by a "major, highly respected law firm."

But now with the month reaching its end, the boys once again needed money desperately, and were tapping anyone still willing to give it to them. Old sources like Richard Charbit and Ken Pavia came through with loans of about $600,000 and over $400,000, respectively.

And relatively new sources like Sheri Elowsky had also been approached. About the same time that he was wooing Elowsky in LA, Barry was also seeking a loan from Mike Malamut, a boyish-looking auto dealer, who had met Barry through the Polevois and accepted a position on ZZZZ Best's board of directors. Lured by the big profits reported by mutual friends and investors and attracted by Barry's winsome personality and Horatio Alger story, Malamut mortgaged his and his mother's homes as well as several pieces of property that he'd acquired over fifteen years of work, and loaned Barry $1 million.

Meanwhile, however, the *Los Angeles Times*, the *Wall Street Journal*, and the *Los Angeles Daily News* were all taking hard looks at ZZZZ Best. Now they were asking not just about the credit cards but the entire restoration scam, too. Short sellers on Wall Street were bombarding the papers and Tom Padgett with calls. Restoration jobs of the size ZZZZ Best had been reporting simply did not exist.

As Tom Padgett later said, with some understatement, "this was a very disturbing development."

— 4 —

THE WALLS IN THE HOTEL SUITE in Vegas were wafer-thin, and Kathy Carter overheard snippets of the conversation going on outside while she rested in one of the bedrooms: "ZZZZ Best," and, "The shit's gonna hit the fan."

It was June 30, and Carter, a sometime waitress and freelance artist in her midthirties, was in Las Vegas at the invitation of Jerry Polevoi, aka "Mini-Bucks" and "Gofer Two."

Initially, when Jerry had invited her, she'd been delighted, for "going to Vegas" to Kathy Carter meant "gambling and having a good time."

The Polevois, too, loved to gamble, but it quickly became obvious that they'd made *this* trip for other reasons. When they'd gone downstairs to the casino, Jack had started playing 21, but Jerry busied himself cashing a bunch of traveler's checks, asking Kathy and another woman whom Jack had brought to do the same. They would cash $5,000 or $6,000 worth of checks, bring the money to Jerry, and he'd give them more. All told, Kathy Carter cashed about $30,000 worth of checks.

Later that evening, around one or two, a friend of Jack's named Eugene Lasko arrived at the hotel suite. With him he'd brought thirty-five more cashier's checks, made out for $9,500 each in order to avoid the $10,000 trigger that requires disclosure to the IRS. Altogether, there was $332,500.

These checks, along with the ones Kathy and the others had been cashing, were part of more than $700,000 Barry Minkow had given to Jack Polevoi to launder. They included about half a million Barry had quietly withdrawn from ZZZZ Best's corporate funds and the $225,000 loan Sheri Elowsky had just made him.

That same night, Barry called Tom, who was settling in with some popcorn and a Steinlager, a New Zealand import, at his house in Newport. After some initial small talk, Barry said something that, given the situation, should in no way have startled Tom Padgett. But it did anyway.

"If something goes wrong," said Barry. "I want you to know that . . ."

"The fuck you talking about?" Padgett cut in angrily. "Nothing's going to go wrong; I don't want to hear that shit." (The worst thing that could happen, thought Tom, was for Barry, the master of positive thinking, to start talking like that.)

"I know, I know," Barry continued, "but *if* something goes wrong, I want you to know the only person I really care about is you. You were there with me when it all started, and we'll be together until the end."

Tom was touched. On at least four or five of the nine times Tom had seen the movie *Platoon,* he'd asked Barry to go along with him, but Minkow had always been too busy. Nor had Barry ever been able to find the time to at least *see* his house in Newport or the "Marina office." Barry's changed so much, Tom had recently complained to Roddy, he never seems to have time for his old friends. "Everybody changes a lot from fifteen to twenty-one," the albino had told him, "Think of yourself, the guys you grew up with." And Tom had to agree that that was what had happened with the Boy Wonder—multiplied a hundred times, that is.

But now Barry had taken the time to call and talk to him on a personal level, just like in the old days. Tom appreciated that. "Don't worry about anything," he told Barry. "It'll all work out; let's talk again tomorrow."

It seemed to Eugene Lasko that Jack Polevoi was on the phone with Barry the entire night, trying to convince Minkow that they couldn't cash all those checks immediately. The people at the casinos were growing suspicious, Polevoi said. They didn't like people depositing $95,000 or $100,000 in cashier's checks and then making $5 and $25 bets and trying to get cash back. At the very least, they'd have to wait until the following day so that the casinos' personnel could verify the cashier's checks.

Early the next morning, Barry called *again,* and even the devoted Jack was now frustrated. He told Minkow there was *no new news* for Christ's sake, that he'd call him later, and that what Minkow wanted him to do wasn't that easy.

But by depositing the checks in different casinos and pretending to gamble, the Polevois, their dates, and Eugene Lasko were able, over the next several days (and during a subsequent trip), to cash, launder, and return to Barry Minkow about $500,000.

That evening at about 5:30 or 6:00, Jack and Jerry asked Kathy Carter to go to the Vegas office of PaineWebber, the stock brokerage firm. They wanted her, the Polevois told Carter in a phrase that seemed to Kathy most odd, "to buy some shorts." Kathy didn't understand what that meant, but it seemed to have something to do with purchasing stock.

At PaineWebber, she met with a broker named Vic and gave him the false social security number and address that Jerry had provided, as well as about $35,000 in cash and traveler's checks. Then she waited until the broker received a call from Jerry who instructed him to sell ZZZZ Best stock short.

She sat quietly for a few moments after Vic hung up, then went into a main room to monitor ZZZZ Best's shares. In a relatively brief time, the stock declined three-quarters of a point. She knew that was good news because when Vic phoned Jerry back, they were both "ecstatic." It was then that Kathy Carter realized she'd been buying stock that Jack and Jerry had felt certain was going to go down.

While Kathy Carter was selling ZZZZ Best short in Vegas, Tom Padgett was in Eddie Carroll's in Beverly Hills getting his hair styled. That taken care of, he was off to the airport in his Lincoln Town Car to pick up a friend flying in from San Francisco. From there, they went to Hollywood and met a mutual pal for dinner. The meal was on Tom, who, as successful as he was, could certainly afford it. Dropping off his friends after dinner and heading south on the 405 freeway back to Newport Beach, Tom Padgett felt on top of the world.

And then his car phone rang. A rare occurrence.

It was the albino. "Tom," he said, "Barry's been trying to reach you. He *really* wants to talk."

"Now fucking what?" thought Padgett as he dialed Barry's home.

When Minkow got on the line, he was talking slowly and sounded tired. "It's over," he repeated several times as if in a daze, neglecting even to say hello. "It's over. The stories are gonna break in the press any day now, and there's not a thing I can do to stop it. It's over."

"Barry," interrupted Tom, "stop this shit. My parents are coming out to Newport next week. It can't be over. Not now!"

"Look, the press is . . ."

"Fuck the press!" Tom screamed. "There's got to be *something* we can do. We can say it was the fault of foreign insurers."

"No," replied Barry, sounding really weary now. "Akst and [Patrick] Lee [of the *Daily News*] are on to us. Akst has talked to Tengberg. Tengberg told him everything. They've been to Sacramento; they've found no permits were ever issued. I'm telling you, it's *over*."

Tom's cellular phone kept fading out, so he hung up, pulled off at an exit, found a pay phone, and immediately called Barry back.

"Get out of that house," Barry told him, "tonight. Checks are gonna bounce everywhere tomorrow. I'll get you the best lawyers money can buy, I'll take care of you, just get out of there!"

By this time, Tom Padgett had stopped listening. "We can come back, we can come back," he kept on saying, still halfway believing that somehow Barry or Mark, who'd always come through in the past, would be able to do so again.

But all Barry said was, "I'm resigning tomorrow for health reasons—my ulcer. Give me a phone number where you'll be in the morning, and get out of that house! Tomorrow I'm getting my number changed. I'll call you in the morning." Then Barry hung up.

"Guess what?" said Jeri Carr's husband to her less than 36 hours after Barry and Tom's frantic conversation, "You no longer have a client." Lying in bed, barely awake, Carr accepted the morning cup of coffee and the copies of the *Times* and *Daily News* her husband handed her.

In the papers, Carr immediately saw what he'd been talking about: Barry had resigned! The *Daily News* was *also* reporting that Barry and his company were "under investigation by the Los Angeles Police Department and [that] the police had been in contact with the State Department of Justice, the Securities and Exchange Commission and the U.S. Attorney's Office."

The *Times* story contained some additional dismaying news: ZZZZ Best stock had fallen more than $1 a share as a result of the announcement, closing at $3.50 in extremely heavy trading.

The *Daily News* also mentioned an intriguing little sidelight. The very afternoon of the resignation announcement, according to the story, Barry had gone to a Woodland Hills sports store and purchased "$750 worth of weight-training equipment. A clerk at the store," the story continued, "said Minkow appeared healthy and in good spirits at the time."

Carr remained in bed, staring at the papers for at least ten minutes. She'd talked to Barry just a couple of days earlier, and he'd told her everything was fine. They even discussed again the possibility of Carr bringing her company in-house as ZZZZ Best's publicist. And now *this*.

Her mood of disbelief was finally broken by Ana and Elenora calling to ask if she'd seen the papers. Like her, they seemed in shock.

When Carr got to her office, it was pandemonium. All of the media, who hadn't wanted to take her calls before, were bombarding her for some answers: *Time*, *Life*, "60 Minutes," *Newsweek*, *USA Today*—name the major, they called that day or sent someone over.

— 5 —

THURSDAY, JULY 2—RESIGNATION DAY

Jeri Carr's office was not the only place where Barry's resignation was causing pandemonium. Immediately following the announcement, worried investors and TV crews had descended on ZZZZ Best's Reseda offices.

Among them was Paul Schiff. The movie producer had over $1 million personally invested in ZZZZ Best, and was serving as the middleman for several million more that Swiss banks had loaned the company.

Barry had told Schiff about the credit card problem right before the *Times* article appeared, and, as a result, Schiff hadn't paid it much attention. After reading the story, however, Schiff became mildly uneasy. If Floral Fantasies had been bought by Chip and his wife, why was the story pointing so emphatically at *Barry*? But eventually Schiff had dismissed his misgivings. The amount was so insignificant compared to what Barry had made, Schiff reasoned, that even if Barry *had* been involved, it was just a young man's mistake.

Unable to get in touch with Barry after hearing of the resignation, Schiff immediately went to Minkow's office, where he met other investors like Ken Pavia and Kay Rosario, who were already waiting outside. Bruce Andersen, ZZZZ Best's controller, and an accountant from Price Waterhouse were also there. Talking with them, Schiff realized that *nobody* seemed to know the extent of the fraud and exactly why Barry had resigned. Perhaps the company was just overextended, or maybe 50 percent of the jobs were bad and the rest could be salvaged. They'd know more this evening, Andersen told them, when the board of directors was scheduled to meet. Schiff then asked the Price Waterhouse accountant if he was aware of ZZZZ Best having any accounting problems, and the man replied that, no, everything seemed sound.

THURSDAY AFTERNOON, JULY 2

Back in New York, Sheri Elowsky was feeling a little panicky. She had tried reaching Barry five or six times, but for some reason he was always unavailable.

Although it was the day that Barry had publicly announced his resignation, whoever was taking the calls never mentioned that little detail to Elowsky, who, because it had not yet been reported in the New York media, was still unaware of the fact.

She was calling instead to instruct Barry on how to wire the $2 million he owed, and also to ask what was going on with ZZZZ Best's stock—why it seemed to be continually dropping. By her third or fourth call, however, Elowsky's concern had shifted almost exclusively to ZZZZ Best's stock. Not only was it dropping, it was "falling through the floor." And it was Barry's shares of ZZZZ Best that were securing his loan from Prudential-Bache. When she finally tried Barry's home, she got a queasy feeling along with the disconnect message.

THURSDAY EVENING—RESIGNATION NIGHT

At the board meeting the first night of the resignation, Andersen and Chip were instructed to secure the company's assets, change the locks on the office, and notify the banks to freeze ZZZZ Best's accounts.

Andersen then told the board that in the last fiscal year alone, ZZZZ Best had paid Marbil Management (Mark's bogus company) approximately $18 million, ostensibly for labor and materials, and was due to receive over $8 million from (Padgett's) Interstate Appraisal that coming Monday.

Then he delivered the bad news: He and Chip had spoken with Mark Morze immediately upon hearing of Barry's resignation. When they asked him if it was true that the restoration jobs were fraudulent, Mark had given them "some basis to [believe] the rumors that much of the restoration business did not exist." Morze had said, "A little bird is telling me [that] the whole thing is probably made up."

FRIDAY, JULY 3

By Thursday—Resignation Day—Norm Rothberg had already received over $17,000 of his bonus, and was scheduled for another payment as well as a salary check. But when he called Brian Morze to make arrangements to get together, Brian, who previously had always been most solicitous, seemed rushed and asked Norm to call back the next day. When he did, Brian wasted no words. "Look at the papers," he told Norman Rothberg. "Your money tree has melted."

Jeri Carr tried calling Barry and found his phone had been disconnected. *Imagine.* Disconnecting his phone without even telling her. And now the media were asking *her* the hard questions and accusing *her* of not doing her homework. After an hour of being hassled, Carr turned on her answering machine and stopped taking calls.

Sheri Elowsky cancelled her plans to go away for the fourth of July weekend and nervously began calling ZZZZ Best headquarters, finally reaching Chip Arrington. When Chip told her Barry had resigned, Elowsky felt as if someone had knocked her to the floor. "What about my $2 million?" she asked. "Where is Barry?"

Chip had no answer to either of these questions. But he told her the board of directors had met the night before and was reconvening that evening. Someone would call back then.

Meanwhile, Ada Cohen in Las Vegas received the bad news by phone from Bobby Rosario. Kay was *very* upset, Bobby told her, and was saying over and over, "How can he do it to me? I'm going to kill myself."

Ada, in turn, "became hyperventilated and had to terminate the conversation."

Friday morning Tom Padgett woke up at a friend's place, went out and got all the papers, returned, and waited for Barry to call.

By late afternoon, when the local news shows started coming on TV, he was still waiting. They were all reporting rumors that Barry had taken millions of dollars in cash that he had secreted away, and fled the country. *Fled the fuckin' country!* Jesus Christ!

That night, the albino stopped by, and they talked about what to do—get new IDs, lawyers, contact the feds, what?

Tom kept saying Barry should call any minute now, and the albino kept telling Tom that Barry was *not* going to call.

When Roddy left, Tom stayed in the living room, lay down on the floor, curled up like an embryo, and remained in a semicatatonic state until the following morning. By then he finally realized that Barry had left him high and dry.

FRIDAY EVENING

Several matters had to be taken care of at the board meeting that Friday night before the call to Sheri Elowsky could be placed. First, a board member and investor named Neal Dem reported that Mark Morze had contacted him and was willing to meet with them. Dem had also brought a bankruptcy attorney, who was in a waiting room outside should he be needed.

Next, Chip reported the company's cash flow situation. ZZZZ Best had been pulling in about $200,000 per week in income from the carpet cleaning, but paying *out* $350,000 in expenses. (The carpet-cleaning division had been losing that kind of money for eight or nine months.)

Following that, the board approved plans to sue Barry, Mark, and Tom for fraud.

Then Bruce Andersen placed the call to Sheri Elowsky in New York. After telling Elowsky there was a board meeting in progress and putting her on the speaker phone, Andersen and the others listened as Elowsky told them about the $2 million postdated check, and asked if they would acknowledge it and permit Prudential-Bache to put it through. Andersen replied that they had no knowledge of the check, didn't have $2 million in their account in any case, and had no intention of honoring it.

It was late when Jim Asperger returned home after being briefly out of town. Turning on his answering machine, the assistant U.S. attorney heard a message from a friendly lawyer in the state attorney general's office: Look at the article in today's *LA*

Times on ZZZZ Best, it said. Reading it, Asperger thought he'd better act quickly.

SATURDAY, THE FOURTH OF JULY

Schiff, Charbit, Rosario, Pavia, the press, the board, they were all asking Chip—the CEO—where Barry was. Had the guy split to Europe or what? And where was all the missing money? As if *Chip* knew.

So on July 4, in an effort to get some answers, Arrington drove to Barry's house and was met by an enormous heavyset man who appeared to be some kind of a guard. "Where's Mr. Minkow?" asked Chip.

"He's gone to the beach," replied the guard.

SUNDAY, JULY 5

The next day, the board met again. Half the payroll checks issued on Friday had bounced, they were told, and the company had no money left in its payroll account. Although the company had over $6 million in assets, it was *heavily* mortgaged. The meeting adjourned with the board agreeing unanimously to file for bankruptcy under Chapter 11.

In a meeting the following day, Mark Morze was suspended from the company. Dan Krowpman was asked to resign from his position on the board of directors, "due to information regarding payments by ZZZZ Best to Cornwell . . . Tools." Chip was suspended as the company CEO because of his acceptance of "certain unauthorized payments by Mr. Minkow from corporate funds." ($70,000 of the $100,000 bonus Chip had been promised.)

Surprised by how much was being uncovered so quickly, Jim Asperger called John Orr and Buck Sadler of the FBI, the postal inspectors, and the SEC personnel with whom he'd been working on the case. He wanted, he told them, to begin preparing search warrants. He didn't realize at the time that the Los Angeles Police Department was doing the same thing.

MONDAY, JULY 6

By Monday, the story of Barry's resignation had finally made the New York papers. In fact, when Sheri Elowsky at last steeled herself and marched into her boss's office to tell him they'd just lost

$2 million, he was reading all about it in the *Wall Street Journal*. He continued reading as she explained how they were now "in the hole for $2 million."

Later in the day, Elowsky wrote her resignation, handed it to her boss, and told him he could accept it, tear it up, or hold it for future use.

He immediately accepted it.

A day or so later, the check for $836 that Barry had given Elowsky to cover her trip to LA bounced.

TUESDAY, JULY 7

On Tuesday, ZZZZ Best's stock closed at ninety-three cents a share.

By the end of the week, the story was really breaking everywhere, and Carr and her staff went out and got the *Times*, got the *Herald*, got the *Daily News*, got *USA Today*, got *Barron's* and the *Wall Street Journal*, and got a couple of buckets of fried chicken, too. Then they went into the office, kept the answering machine on, sat down on the floor, and started reading to each other.

— 6 —

THE STORY HAD EVERYTHING: a psychopathic young con man, beloved by a press that had first used him to fulfill its Ronald Reagan–era Horatio Alger fantasies and was now selling copy with its fallen-angel angle; a neo-Nazi; the Jewish Defense League; mob hangers-on out of the Over-the-Hill Gang; a girl-crazy, action-loving, silver-tongued former UCLA football player; the ex-wife of a pop star; little old lady investors; Charlie's Angels; antidrug campaigns and very public acts of charity; a PR firm that was proving that anything or anybody was promotable, not just a U.S. President; "Lifestyles of the Rich and Famous" ostentatiousness; Big Eight accountants and an old-line prestigious law firm; short sellers in Vegas and elsewhere and the real possibility of stock manipulation; stock underwriters who had gone bankrupt and were themselves having trouble with the law; the mighty Drexel Burnham Lambert; the attorney who defended Joe Hunt and the killer of Vicki Morgan, now gearing up to defend the scorned Boy Wonder; and a series of scams that would have been deleted from a screenplay like "The Sting" on the grounds that they were too farfetched for any audience to believe.

And as if *all that* weren't enough, six days after Barry's resignation Daryl Gates, the chief of the Los Angeles Police Department, held a much publicized press conference in which he announced, to the utter astonishment of everybody—including the principals accused, the FBI, the U.S. attorney, and the SEC—that ZZZZ Best and Barry were strongly suspected of being part of a nationwide drug ring that was laundering huge amounts of cocaine money for organized-crime families.

Gates, whose department is one of the toughest, most powerful, and least accountable to civilian authority in America, is also well known locally for his often intemperate remarks.

During the conference, the chief went on to say that the department's Organized Crime Intelligence Division (OCID) had uncovered information linking Minkow and ZZZZ Best with organized-crime figures and legitimate and front businesses associated with organized crime that were used in the money laundering. Among the organized-crime figures said to be involved were Maurice Rind, Richard Schulman, and Robert Victor.

A year and a half later, the chief's charges remained unsubstantiated and were regarded by almost everybody connected with the case (excluding the LAPD, which maintains that its investigation continues) as a figment of somebody's overeager imagination and someone else's desire for the big bust and resultant publicity.

Whose imagination is difficult to know, the LAPD remaining close-mouthed about the sources of its allegations. Important among those sources, however, was certainly Dirk Summers, an archnemesis of Maurice Rind. Summers was then doing a three-year, eight-month sentence at the California State Prison at Chino on a bad-check conviction.

Summers and Rind had been at each other's throats ever since they had coproduced a show starring Jonathan Winters at the Sands in Las Vegas. The show closed after just six days. But during and after the show's production, Rind and Summers managed to hurl so many charges and countercharges at each other that the facts are now hopelessly obscured.

Several things, however, *are* clear. One is that Summers, an extraordinarily charming, urbane, well-spoken man in his late fifties, is an easy man to find credible, unless, that is, one is at all familiar with his con man background and always vivid recollections of the past. Among other things, for example, the blue-eyed, silver-haired Summers has claimed the FBI set fire to his house to keep him quiet after he'd solved the D. B. Cooper skyjacking case; claimed that he was married to the actress June Allyson, an allegation denied by Allyson, who said Summers had run up thousands of dollars on her credit card in Europe; and been charged with forging Liberace's signature in connection with a celebrity golf tournament he was trying to put on in Las Vegas in the entertainer's name but without his knowledge or permission.

Then in 1984, Summers became a key government witness against Maurice Rind and four others charged with manipulating the price of First City Properties stock through brokers and bank accounts in Texas. It was then that Rind signed a consent agreement with the SEC promising not to engage in such practices but not admitting any wrongdoing.

Later, Summers told the FBI that Rind was "washing money for the syndicate."

And now apparently Summers had told the same thing to the LAPD, but with greater success.

Rind, Summers told the OCID, had said to him when they were in the Bahamas together in 1984 that there "wasn't a key [kilo of cocaine] that went into Florida that he didn't get a piece of." And he also told them about Rind's problems with the SEC.

As for ZZZZ Best, says Summers, well, "he may have hypothesized" that drug-money-laundering was taking place, but he never directly alleged that.

In any case, searches carried out by the LAPD at sixteen locations and on nine different persons as part of the money-laundering investigation turned up only a minute amount of coke, which was obviously for private enjoyment, in the personal effects of Rind's wife.

But in fairness to the LAPD—which did embarrassingly shoot from the hip, and which did unquestioningly try to tailor its case to prove its preconceptions—who would have thought that a twenty-one-year-old like Barry Minkow could have pulled off all he had without a mob mastermind in the background playing him like a marionette in some plot out of a two-hour special of "Miami Vice"?

While Tom Padgett lay curled up like an embryo on his friend's floor, Barry Minkow seemed to his attorney, Arthur Barens, to be "undaunted," displaying—given the circumstances—a remarkable "strength, boundless energy, and resilient manner."

With the more than $500,000 the Polevois had laundered for him in Las Vegas, plus the more than $100,000 he'd received from the sale of his Testarosa, Barry had recovered from his initial panic and was now taking steps to make the best out of a very bad situation indeed.

With the bulk of the money—just under $400,000—Barry hired Barens and a legal team to defend himself. That team, in addition to Barens, consisted of the highly respected attorney Don Re, and the equally well-regarded private investigative firm of Palladino & Sutherland, both of whom had worked with Howard Weitzman on John DeLorean's successful defense.

Then Barry invested somewhere between $45,000 and $70,000 as a silent partner in an Encino restaurant called More than Waffles and an additional $15,000 to $30,000 in two other small, ultimately unsuccessful businesses called No-Pest Pest Control and Novelty Carpet Cleaning. On paper, No-Pest was owned by Barry's main man, Tony Scamardo, but in reality, Barry was 80 percent owner.

Most of the rest of his possessions, including tens of thousands of dollars worth of paintings and furniture that, like the Testarosa, he sold before his soon-to-come bankruptcy hearing, went to pay off the money still owed to Maurice Rind on the KeyServ convention loan.

In mid-August, when Barry filed for bankruptcy under oath, he neglected to mention, as required by law, his ownership and involvement in his three new businesses, nor did he list, as was also required, the assets like his Ferrari that he'd sold within the preceding three months.

It was around this time that Barry asked Tony Scamardo and another hanger-on named Jimmy Mulhern to dispose of a couple of boxes of papers and documents for him.

Don't look at them, don't go through them, don't throw them in a public trash can. *Burn* them, said Barry.

Which they did.

These moves, as well as the phenomenal run of success that had until recently been his, seem to have filled Barry Minkow with the certainty that he would beat what now lay before him, just as he had beat everything else in his young life.

Shortly after Barry's resignation, when Mike Malamut went to see him in an unsuccessful attempt to retrieve some or all of the $1 million loan that he'd made to him just weeks before, Barry informed him that he (Barry) was "going to come out of this smelling like a rose. No one's going to believe a twenty-one-year-old could have done this. The other guys are going to take the heat."

It was Barry's plan to use the I-didn't-know-what-was-going-on "jujubes" defense. But perhaps feeling he needed a backup, and perhaps inspired by Chief Gates's imaginative mob drug-money-laundering theory, Barry decided in August to make it look as if someone—maybe the mob—was out to shut him up. So along with Tony Scamardo, he took his father's handgun, drove to No-Pest's office, parked Tony's Chevy truck, and shot two holes in it.

Then they drove to Malibu, threw the gun in the ocean, and reported the incident to the LAPD, filing a report saying they were driving down the Santa Susana Pass when a white Lincoln Continental (Jack Catain's old car) pulled up alongside of them and fired two or three shots.

Shortly thereafter, Arthur Barens told the LA Times of his concern for Barry's safety.

"Things are getting a little blown out of proportion when a client's life is being jeopardized," said Barens.

While Barry Minkow remained in his big house in Woodland Hills, planning his next moves in relative calm, Tom Padgett was nervously lying low in the less-than-exclusive Half Moon Hotel, a few blocks from the now abandoned "Marina office."

Tom was busy chugging down twelve-packs of Coors rather than Steinlagers in recognition of his newly scaled-down lifestyle, when he noticed a tall, attractive brunette, about thirty-five, constantly passing his room to use the pay phone in the parking lot, the goddamned Half Moon being so cheap that it didn't even have phones in the rooms.

She was in room 8, Tom in 7, and with her door open and the TV blaring, what could Tom do but sit down on her bed and watch the eleven o'clock news, the news on which *his* name and picture were being featured? Yeah, that was him, he told his hostess, who it turned out was a madam and therefore an outlaw herself. She seemed drawn to Tom, who had, after all, been getting over on "the man" for years. The relationship was quickly consummated before the news ended and "Nightline" had begun.

A short time later, Tom was flat broke, having foolishly given his remaining savings of about $17,000 to the albino, who supposedly knew a guy who could help them out, but who had instead split with the money. Tom was delighted, therefore, when later the madam proposed he motel-hop with her as she made her calls and set up dates for her girls. Why not, he thought, broke and future jailbird that he was. Besides, they got along pretty well.

Shortly thereafter, Tom and Roddy contacted Buck Sadler of the FBI. It was late Friday afternoon when Sadler called his fellow agent, John Orr, telling him to cancel any plans he had for that night. Then they drove to a deserted field near the campus of UCLA and sat in their cramped government sedan and listened while Tom Padgett and the albino spilled their guts to them for hours.

Mark Morze, meanwhile, had immediately retained a high-powered attorney named Anthony Glassman, said to be one of the finest white-collar lawyers in town. A former U.S. attorney himself, Glassman put Mark in touch with the federal prosecutors, and Mark Morze, who would always do the smart thing, soon began singing like an opera star.

— 7 —

UNLIKE THE LOS ANGELES POLICE DEPARTMENT, the U.S. Attorney's Office took its time, both in its investigation and in handing down indictments. It was not, in fact, until more than seven months after Barry's resignation—in mid-January 1988—that indictments were finally brought.

Absent from those named were Rind, Schulman, Victor, and others mentioned by Chief Gates as having ties to the mob as well as to ZZZZ Best.

But Barry and eleven others were charged, including, of course, the boys: Padgett, Mark Morze, his brother Brian, and Roddy. Also accused of "participating in and aiding and abetting various fraudulent activities" were Dan Krowpman, Chip Arrington, Norm Rothberg, and Ed Krivda (who had falsely represented selling large quantities of carpet to ZZZZ Best for the restoration jobs).

In addition, Jack and Jerry Polevoi were charged with aiding

Barry in the theft of the $500,000 they had laundered for him in Vegas, while Eugene Lasko was accused of conspiracy in that theft, as well as money laundering.

Specifically, Barry was charged with bank, stock, and mail fraud, money laundering (in Vegas), racketeering (an ongoing criminal conspiracy), and tax evasion. He was being charged with 54 counts and was facing 350 years in prison and a $13.5 million fine.

Mark was facing most of the same charges and looking at 182 years and an $8.5 million fine; Padgett, 177 years and $8 million; the albino (who was already in prison from his latest coke bust), 115 years and $5 million; Brian Morze, 80 years and $4 million, and Chip Arrington, 50 years and $2.5 million.

"This case is the most massive and elaborate securities fraud perpetrated on the West Coast in over a decade," said Robert Bonner, the U.S. attorney for Los Angeles. "The resulting losses to investors in ZZZZ Best stock and to banks are estimated to be in excess of $50 million" (a figure later revised downward to about $26 million).

Bonner also added that Barry was one of the youngest persons ever to be prosecuted in a major white-collar crime.

Setting the tone for Barry's "jujubes defense," Arthur Barens insisted not only on his client's innocence but that Minkow hadn't even participated in the restoration business. "He was an eighteen-year-old boy from the Valley who got lucky and [then] got exploited. He had a clever idea, and he was willing to work hard. Unfortunately, he was misled by the more savvy and sophisticated people around him."

About three days before the indictments and arrests, Chip Arrington got a call from Barry. He must have spent forty-five minutes telling Chip how he'd turned to the Lord and was now back on his hands and knees cleaning carpets.

"I know I'm gonna get arrested," said Barry, "but I'm gonna beat this. And while I'm out on bail, I want you to work with me cleaning carpets like in the old days—I'll pay you 50 percent!" The Lord's name must have been mentioned twenty-five times by Barry as he first tried to talk Chip into going back to work, then read him a list of those who were shortly to be arrested. Chip's name, Barry assured him, was not among them. And the *sick* thing, Chip Arrington said later, was that he believed him.

Soon afterward, as Chip was sitting down to watch "LA Law,"

nine cops—LAPD, FBI, SEC, IRS—with bulletproof vests and their overkill mentality surrounded Arrington's house, knocked on the door, and announced he was under arrest. Lulu and their little girl woke up crying.

When he got to the holding cell in downtown LA, Chip was surprised to discover Morze, Padgett, and the others, who had been picked up in simultaneous police raids that night. Chip, facing fifty years, was in a state of shock. He sat down next to Tom and Mark Morze, rocked back and forth, and kept repeating over and over, "What am I doing here? What am I doing here?" To Chip's amazement, Mark and Tom seemed almost cheerful. Mark was telling the story about lying on his back and snapping the Polaroid in Arroyo Grande, and both of them were speculating good humoredly about Barry's defense. It looked as if it would be the jujubes/know-nothing version. But then again, the Ollie North–Bill Casey defense might just work, too—Jack Catain, of course, being Bill Casey. Barry had gotten a large loan from Catain, this scenario went, he couldn't pay it back, was threatened with harm to his family, and got Tom and Mark to work for him and continue the scam because Catain made him do so.

But it wasn't *exactly* laughs, even for Mark and Tom, waiting in that holding cell at three in the morning for arraignment the next day, with people who didn't quite look like graduates of the Ivy League. In addition, Mark's wrists still ached from the force with which the LAPD officer had placed the handcuffs on him. And his brother, Brian, who suffers from a medical condition that requires medication at regular intervals, was pleading to have that medicine sent to him, but his pleas were falling on deaf ears.

The following morning, they were led from the LAPD's holding cell in Parker Center to the Federal Court House less than a block away for their arraignment.

Barry was already waiting in a cell there when the rest of the ZZZZ Best defendants, shackled together, snake-lined in.

Tom was actually glad to see Barry, whom he'd not been in contact with since that summer, even though Minkow had broken his promise and left Padgett with nothing to pay an attorney. (Tom would eventually have to get a public defender.) Strangely, he wasn't at all angry at Barry, and the natural affection he always felt for Minkow seemed to return immediately. Within moments, they had shaken hands and were goofing back and forth as if they'd just talked yesterday.

It had not been an easy seven months for Tom Padgett. He had gone back to Newport with his madam-girlfriend but was forced to depart hurriedly after a repo man tried to kick down his garage door one night and take his car.

Ultimately, he was reduced to living in a tiny singles apartment in Beverly Hills, listening all day to the phone ringing while his new girlfriend asked, "What are you looking for, a blond? a redhead? black? white?" *Fuck that.* He finally left her and moved in with his aging aunt and uncle, working odd jobs until his arrest, which, given his situation, was kind of a relief.

When Barry turned from shaking hands and goofing with Tom, and found himself standing toe to toe with Mark Morze, Barry's smile slowly faded, his mood changed, and his face dropped. He looked petrified, thought Mark. For Barry had been telling everybody in town that "Morze did everything, *every* fucking thing," and that he, said Barry, "knew nothing about what Morze was doing with the company . . . had absolutely no knowledge of *anything.*"

"He thought I was gonna beat the shit out of him," Mark said later. But Mark Morze was not about to do anything stupid, and he just sat down.

In little more than a week after Barry's resignation, Mark had shown up at the U.S. attorney's office with his high-priced, high-powered lawyer and two boxes of materials, literally asking the government what he could do to help.

Eventually Mark would spend over thirty-nine hours talking to various government investigators, including two full days in his lawyer's office being deposed by the SEC.

Right after the resignation, he'd also called dozens of people who'd been scammed and let them know the bad news. Not long afterward, he had landed a job as a financial consultant for $1,000 a week, and he started coaching inner-city kids and doing volunteer work for MADD. Waist-deep in shit, Mark Morze intended to do whatever was necessary to pull himself out as painlessly as possible.

Joel Hochberg was sitting with Chip's wife, Lulu, in the front row of the spectators' section of the packed courtroom when Barry and the others were brought in. Close by sat Barry's girlfriend, Joyce, holding on her lap a Bible and three Alcoholics Anonymous books. Every once in a while, she'd look at Barry and throw him a smile, and he'd either wink or smile back at her.

Once he'd even looked over and winked at *Joel*, a move that literally set Hochberg's false teeth rattling. Having recently been rather unpleasantly questioned by the LAPD about $15 million worth of restoration contracts to which Barry had forged his name, Joel, there to support Chip, didn't want *anybody* thinking he might be exchanging signals with Barry, and he quickly turned his head away.

Barry was wearing a gray-and-red sweatshirt and black sweatpants and, although in good spirits and joking during the breaks, he seemed tired. Later he would tell Joyce that the other prisoners had kept shaking him awake the entire night asking if he wasn't "the ZZZZ Best guy."

Before the start of the proceedings, Arthur Barens had eased over to Jim Asperger, now prosecuting the case, and good-naturedly asked the U.S. attorney to "let my people go." Barens was hoping to arrange reasonable bail, but Asperger's reply was "Tell your client to bring back the [unaccounted for] money, and we'll discuss it."

"You don't understand," Barens said, turning on his heel. "There *is* no missing money."

But Asperger was able to convince the court that there was, and that Barry was a definite flight risk. His bail, therefore, was set at $2 million, an amount he couldn't make. Tom's was $200,000, which he couldn't make either. The other ten defendants, however, did make their bail, and only Barry and Padgett were later bused out to the federal prison at Terminal Island, where Barry told Tom to enjoy the ocean view.

— 8 —

BY AUGUST 1988, more than a year after his resignation and seven months after his indictment, the trial of Barry Minkow was about to begin. By then, all but he and Norm Rothberg had pleaded guilty. The rest of the defendants either were awaiting sentencing or had already been sentenced.

But Barry Minkow was hanging tough, no easy thing to do with the full weight of the federal government coming down on you in a high-profile case, with a paper trail pointing at you like a road sign, with ten of your eleven codefendants providing the feds with all they wanted to know, and with all of them telling the prosecutor essentially the same thing: they were the planets who revolved around the sun that was Barry Minkow.

Adding to Barry's problems was the prosecution team the government had assembled. At first glance, Jim Asperger and his coprosecutor, Gordon Greenberg, with their relative youth and understated nice-guy manners, did not appear particularly formidable. But they were perhaps better prepared to prosecute an intricate paper crime involving a long-running, multifaceted investigation than many a more grizzled career prosecutor.

The son of an upper-middle-class tax attorney, Jim Asperger, an intense, athletic man with square-jawed, straight-arrow good looks, had grown up in Fresno and attended the University of California at Davis before graduating with honors from law school at UCLA. He had then clerked for liberal California Supreme Court Justice Stanley Mosk, and the conservative U.S. Supreme Court Justice William Rehnquist, now the Chief Justice. After three years with the large national law firm of Latham and Watkins, he joined the U.S. Attorney's Office, specializing in complex fraud cases, which he calls "cops and robbers on a grand scale."

Gordon Greenberg's experience was more hard-edged. He grew up alternately well-to-do and poor in a financially troubled household on the north side of Chicago, before going to the University of Illinois at Champaign and to law school at the Illinois Institute of Technology. As a young assistant DA in Chicago, he worked with a gang unit that would arrive with the police at the scene of gang murders "while the bodies were still warm." On a desk in his office, he still keeps a copy of a full page of the *Chicago Tribune* showing a small picture of the dozens of gang members who had up to that date been convicted of murder. Outlined in red are the six that Greenberg prosecuted.

Tall and thin, with a neatly trimmed black beard, Greenberg's quiet, Henry-Fonda-as-young–Mr. Lincoln demeanor and self-effacing humor almost perfectly concealed the competitiveness and strong ego that is the very essence of the trial lawyer he is to his bones. Since joining the U.S. Attorney's Office in 1983, Greenberg, in his midthirties, had become an expert in the prosecution of money-laundering cases.

On fast-track careers with a case attracting national media attention, the easy thing to have done would have been to indict

Rind, Schulman, and Victor as well as the others—say, for stock manipulation—and take on the Mob as well as the Boy Wonder in headline-grabbing stories. But Asperger and Greenberg were in no way certain that Rind and the others were culpable and, with a sense of justice rare in such a media-conscious law-and-order era, declined to indict them.

Their motivations, however, were not entirely altruistic. Smart prosecutors rarely indict unless they think they can convict, a major reason why, in addition to tough new federal laws and the use of electronic surveillance, a U.S. attorney's office like LA's can boast a 98 percent conviction rate overall and almost 90 percent on cases that actually go to trial.

Moreover, the two prosecutors didn't want to muddy the waters and confuse a jury with subsidiary plots to a case that was already amazingly complex.

Largely for that reason, when new, similar charges were added against Barry right before his trial was to begin, the prosecutors dropped the racketeering count, which was based on the draconian Racketeer Influenced and Corrupt Organizations (RICO) Act prohibiting and severely penalizing an "ongoing criminal conspiracy." Nevertheless, with the new indictments, Barry was now facing 403 years in jail instead of 350.

On the issue of Barry's bail, they also continued to play hardball, successfully arguing before a magistrate and a judge against reduction of Minkow's bail, a wearing-down tactic frequently used by prosecutors to get a defendant to plead to the charges and thus avoid the risk and cost of a trial. On the other hand, Barry *had* gone around bragging to people about having money stashed in Europe and at least some money was still unaccounted for. But remaining in jail made mounting a defense that much more difficult.

Moreover, because of some clothing the guards at Terminal Island had found hidden in an air vent in the common area near Barry's cell, he had been placed in the "hole," a five-by-seven-foot cell where he was forced to spend twenty-three hours a day. (Later, when prison authorities offered to let him out, he chose to stay for his "own protection.") It was there that Barry Minkow, "with a great transistor radio" and his "religious readings," was to spend the months of his trial. His bail had been reduced from $2 million to $1.5 million, but he still couldn't make it.

By the start of the trial, Asperger and Greenberg had worked out their strategy: slowly and deliberately build their case, call no

one as a witness who wasn't squeaky clean or very close to it, and
paint Barry as the charismatic, lying, sociopathic leader of dozens
of cold, calculated scams.

Barry Minkow was not happy with Arthur Barens. For one,
Barry Minkow was in jail, and everybody else was out on bail. And
two, he was now sitting in the hole, twenty-three hours a day in a
room the size of a closet. And before letting him out of the closet for
that one hour to take a shower or go to eat, they always made sure to
slap the cuffs on him, as if he were some kind of crazy animal. The
hole is a form of deliberate mental torture, tough on anyone; to
Barry, hyperkinetic as he was, it was particularly painful.

The hole had not, of course, caused Barry the kind of trouble it
had caused Tom Padgett. Barry was too disciplined for that. He
was too well adjusted in an odd sort of way not to adjust to even
that madness-creating situation. With Tom Padgett, it had been a
different story.

After a "60 Minutes" segment they'd both appeared in aired
while they were in prison—the one in which Barry blamed it all on
Mark and Tom, and managed at the same time to coyly flirt with
Diane Sawyer—the prison officials, getting their con men mixed
up with their violent criminals, had placed Tom and Barry in the
hole "for their own safety."

And *that* had truly driven Tom Padgett to the brink of insan-
ity. Single, a veteran of two tours in the army, and possessed of a
nineteen-year-old's delight in male camaraderie, Padgett was probably better suited to do time than any of the other defendants. But
not in the hole. Please, God, not in the hole. After a month of it, he
could stand it no longer, and he had his parents mortgage the house
they'd worked a lifetime for, in order to get him out on bail.

But Barry never could make his $1.5 million bail, which Ar-
thur Barens, who didn't typically do federal case work, had told
him would be *much* lower. Never mind that it was Barry who had
shot his mouth off to his $1 million investor Mike Malamut and to
the Polevois about having money stashed away in Italy, and was, as
a result, having his ass busted about being a flight risk. Barry
Minkow never was very good at accepting responsibility for his
problems.

And where was Arthur when they'd discovered that clothing in
an air vent and threw him in the hole again, saying he might try to
escape? Escape from Terminal Island! Were they nuts or what?

Now he was locked away again, and where was Arthur? Away on some goddamned ski trip or off to New York just when Barry was caught short.

Even before all this happened, however, Minkow had been growing displeased with the way his defense was proceeding. Speaking with the other inmates, he was surprised to find that few of them had ever even heard of Arthur Barens.

When Barens returned to LA, he was not pleased to hear that Barry had begun interviewing for a new attorney. Their parting of the ways came quickly, with Barens retaining the $300,000 to $400,00 fee Barry had already paid him. With the loss of Barens, Barry also lost the services of the esteemed Don Re and the investigative team of Palladino & Sutherland.

With no lawyer and no money, it appeared that Barry had no cards left to play. But that was not the case. Because he was *Barry Minkow*, central figure of an upcoming trial that was sure to be splashed over the newspapers and airwaves, he *did* still have leverage. Whoever defended Minkow was sure to have his or her name in newspapers and airwaves along with Barry's, an excellent form of free publicity for a trial lawyer's practice. A smart attorney with some flair could even become nationally famous à la Howard Weitzman or F. Lee Bailey. And there were always book and movie rights. If Barry was found guilty, he could not profit from an account of his crimes, but he could tell his story *exclusively* to the attorney, who in turn could then have a book or movie script ghostwritten.

Among the attorneys Barry had heard good things about while at Terminal Island was forty-six-year-old David Kenner, well known in LA legal circles for his defense of suspected drug dealers and organized-crime and white-collar suspects. Short, small-boned, with a great mane of blow-dried black hair falling over his collar, and given to flashy suits, French cuffs, and lacquered nails, David Kenner was as different in style from Jim Asperger and Gordon Greenberg as one could imagine. But he was also shrewd and combative and as a single private practitioner had built up a practice that at any one time had between fifteen and fifty clients. For a case as intricate and time-consuming as Minkow's was sure to be, it was not unusual for him to command a fee of $500,000. Having handled many such cases since graduating from law school at the University of Southern California almost twenty years earlier, he could now well afford to take Minkow's case, in the hope of future payment. The shot at national prominence if he won was worth it.

Before agreeing to take the case, however, Kenner told Barry that if he were planning on sticking to the I-didn't-know-what-was-going-on defense, Kenner "wasn't his man." You *had* to know, he told Barry. You were the president; it couldn't have happened without you knowing.

"After twenty years," Kenner later said he told Barry, "you develop a sense of what's salable and what's not. . . . I'm not going to stand up in front of twelve people and ask them to believe you had no knowledge of what was going on—particularly when all the other defendants [excluding Rothberg] have already pleaded."

"What else," he asked, "was going on?" When Barry again began with the I-didn't-know story, Kenner steered him to Daryl Gates's press conference.

"No, no," said Barry, "Gates was completely wrong. There was no [drug] money laundering."

But Kenner was insistent. "There's got to be some merit to the fact that certain [organized-crime] people were around you." And, says Kenner, Barry's new defense simply "flowed from there."

David Kenner was absolutely right. Given the voluminous paper trail, the dozens upon dozens of witnesses the government could call to testify about Barry's activities, as well as the pleas of his codefendants, the I-didn't-know defense wasn't just unbelievable, it was ludicrous. And Asperger and Greenberg were offering no deals worthy of consideration.

For whatever reason, perhaps the recent headline-grabbing indictments of Boesky, Levine, and others on Wall Street, or perhaps because of a general perception that the situation on the Street and in the savings and loan industry had gotten out of hand, sentences for white-collar criminals were becoming more severe—the harshest in memory, in fact. Crimes that five or ten years earlier might have drawn a fine, probation, or a couple of months in a halfway house, were now routinely resulting in serious time—two, five, seven years—in the federal pen. Twenty-year sentences for financial crimes were becoming more and more common.

It was not a good year for Minkow to face the man.

Other than copping a plea to the twenty or so years the prosecution was offering—something Barry, who had never had a big loss before, wouldn't even consider—the only real option was the one David Kenner and he finally settled on: the duress defense.

Simply put, such a defense admits the defendant committed the crime, but maintains that he or she was *forced* to do it.

While this was their only option, it wasn't a particularly good one. F. Lee Bailey, for example, had tried duress in his defense of Patty Hearst. She had *clearly* been kidnapped and threatened, but had lost anyway.

In Barry's case—irrespective of the fact that it simply wasn't true—the duress defense would be extremely difficult to present.

Under the law, for Barry to be found innocent by reason of being coerced into committing his crimes, Kenner would have to show that for the five-year period that Barry was stealing and scamming, he was under constant, *immediate* threat of death or serious bodily injury; that he had a well-grounded fear that if he did not do as he was told, death or serious injury would result; and that he had no opportunity to escape or to report the matter to law enforcement officials.

To further complicate Kenner's task, he would have to show that over that five-year period, Barry had been coerced and made to do all that he did by a cast of totally unrelated characters, first by Dan Krowpman, next by Jack Catain and his bent-nosed gumbas from LA and New Jersey, and finally by Maurice Rind, his associates, and "family." For five years, in other words, Barry Minkow was a frightened innocent, who, fearing for his life and that of his girlfriend and family, allowed himself to be passed around like a pack of Kools.

Moreover, in such a defense, most judges—and Barry was to have a *very* tough judge—require that a defendant prove more than just a "state of mind" (i.e., a fear that dire consequences would occur if he or she didn't obey orders). He would also have to show *evidence* of specific threats, at specific times and places, and show how they related to the crime committed. Being afraid because you thought a guy might be associated with the mob and you'd just read *The Godfather* wasn't enough to prove duress.

It was a dubious defense at best, but it was all they had, and it was worth a shot. After all, Barry had been a teenager—a kid—when many of the crimes had taken place, and there were guys with mob connections involved—guys with vowels at the end of their names and multipage rap sheets.

The duress defense, with all its problems, also offered another faint ray of hope. Paradoxically, while Kenner had to meet various criteria to prove duress, Greenberg and Asperger would also have to prove that Barry had *not* been placed under duress, and if he had, that at least he had had the opportunity to escape. Moreover, Kenner correctly assumed that the prosecution would be loath to call Padgett and Morze (who were incredulous when they heard of Barry's new defense), Krowpman, and the others, all of whom had admitted to committing many crimes and therefore would be generally unsympathetic witnesses.

So the defense settled on its strategy: Barry was passed around like a joint at a party. Barry as Mr. Big? No way; try Mr. Used. You've heard of the battered-wife syndrome, haven't you? Well, Barry was a battered child, the battered child of organized crime. And a battered child, frightened and beaten, doesn't leave. "Money has been traced to seven different Mafia-related families." Barry was "the puppet" of several New York crime families. He daily feared for the life of his girlfriend and family. The government knew of the involvement of organized crime but for some reason was covering it up. The government didn't want to do the hard work and uncover the *real* story. Organized crime was using ZZZZ Best to gain a foothold on the West Coast (this last courtesy of Chief Gates).

In short, as David Kenner was to put it during a pretrial hearing, "Barry Minkow simply had no alternative once the die was cast. . . . [He] was simply not able to remove himself from the threats and intimidation."

Such was the position of Barry Minkow as he awaited the opening of his trial.

— 9 —

WITH THE EXCEPTION OF A fanatical law-and-order man or a publicity-hungry jurist looking to inflate his ego, Dickran Tevrizian was the worst kind of judge Barry or the other ZZZZ Best defendants could have drawn.

The son of hardworking Armenian immigrants, Tevrizian, now forty-seven, had been a judge since he was thirty-one. Appointed to Los Angeles's Municipal Court bench in 1972 by then Governor Ronald Reagan, Tevrizian was the youngest person ever appointed to California's judiciary. Later, he became a Superior Court judge and briefly retired to private practice before being named to a federal judgeship by President Reagan.

Named 1987 Trial Judge of the Year by the California Trial Lawyers Association—the first federal judge ever so honored—the balding, portly Tevrizian was also considered to be among the nicest and least arrogant of LA's federal judges by the courthouse press corps.

A strict constitutionalist who was not loath to let lawyers know he didn't much approve of new liberal defense theories, Tevrizian seemed the epitome of the tough-minded judge the majority of the American electorate, through Ronald Reagan and George Bush, has been saying it wanted.

That may have been fine in the voting booth, but one would *not* want to stand before Tevrizian as a defendant. For the judge, as cordial a man as you'd want to meet at a party, seemed on the bench to exist solely in the world of the cop—the kind of cop who routinely refers to people as "the good guys" or "the bad guys," and sees no gray areas in between.

He seemed unable to empathize with anybody who had fallen out of the law's narrow perimeters and who stood in front of him for judgment. *He*, the immigrant's son, had made it and been accepted, and he appeared now to have little feel and no understanding of weakness or the fallibility of those who had not. It was ironic to hear him quote his father quoting Woody Guthrie at the beginning of Barry's trial: "Some men will rob you with a six-gun, some with a fountain pen." His tough, even harsh, sentencing seemed as far from what Guthrie stood for as a well-meaning man like Tevrizian could get.

Once, for example, Tevrizian listened to the impassioned pleading of a public defender *and* a probation officer not to send to jail a mother of two who had violated her probation by taking a couple of hits from a PCP cigarette at a local park. Responding to their pleas, Tevrizian came up with what he clearly felt was the most lenient sentence possible: sixty days in jail and five years' probation. Commenting on his "leniency," Tevrizian said he hoped he'd done the right thing because *he* "was going to have to live" with his mistakes "for the rest of [his] life."

So while Barry was sure to get a fair and orderly trial, he was not likely to get any breaks. Nor were any of the other eleven defendants who would appear before the court. "Nobody walks [away from this without doing time]," the judge had told the prosecution and defense attorneys in open court. "Nobody walks."

— 10 —

THE CASE OF *United States v. Barry J. Minkow* opened on Friday morning, August 26, 1988, in the U.S. District Court for the Central District of Los Angeles.

The cavernous courtroom, with its dark wood, red leather, and marble motif, is packed, and the whispers of the eighty or so people there to hear the opening arguments in the trial of Barry Minkow seem to bounce off its high ceilings. The bald, fat man who will mysteriously say only that he is "from the studios" is there, as he will be intermittently throughout the trial. So too are the old court groupies, four or five somewhat unkempt, casually dressed men who look like the last surviving members of the Abraham Lincoln Brigade. Oblivious to the echo of their voices in the courtroom, they will, in yentalike fashion, gossip throughout the length of the trial, serving as a kind of Greek chorus, while seldom missing a day.

Off to the right of center—near the prosecution side—Barry's mother, father, sisters, other family members, and Joyce are seated on the hard wooden benches reserved for spectators and the press. Not far away, a local TV newsman points at Joyce, who is wearing high-waisted black slacks and a gray silk blouse, and comments to another reporter on the wedding ring she is wearing. Overhearing, she nervously twists it off and holds it in her palm.

Off to the left, behind the long, highly polished prosecution table beside which Greenberg, Asperger, and FBI agent John Orr are standing, is seated Asperger's young, soft-spoken wife, Julie, herself an assistant U.S. attorney, and his silver-haired father. "I heard it this morning," says Julie Asperger of the opening statement her husband will shortly deliver. "It's really fine."

At the long table to the right of the mammoth desk of the judge that divides the defense from the prosecution, Barry rocks back and forth on one of the red vinyl–covered swivel chairs provided counsel and defendants. He is dressed in the same black-and-white plaid shirt, baggy black pants, and drooping socks he will wear for weeks on end during the trial. Bright-eyed and alert, he chews nervously on a Styrofoam cup and whispers last-minute thoughts to David Kenner, sitting beside him. During the length of the trial, he will

*alternate between an animated, keenly interested, note-taking in-
volvement, a slumped resignation, and unconvincing attempts at
teenage innocence.*

*Also with them at the defense table are Paul Palladino (of
Palladino & Sutherland, recently rehired by Kenner) and Norm
Rothberg and his lawyer, Richard Burda. During the pretrial
hearings, the judge had ruled that all of the ZZZZ Best defendants
would have to stand trial together, and Barry and Rothberg are the
only two who haven't already pleaded guilty. Rothberg is being tried
as a coconspirator, and for accepting a $25,000 bribe to conceal his
knowledge of the fraud. Throughout most of the trial, Rothberg and
Burda will seem part of the furniture, as the trial focuses almost
exclusively on Barry.*

*Just before the judge makes his appearance, four or five young
beat reporters, who regularly cover the federal court, enter en
masse, mildly disturbed that no seats are available.*

*Shortly thereafter, as everyone rises, Tevrizian and the jury
come in. Noticing the reporters standing in the back, the judge
thoughtfully motions for them to sit in a small section of seats that
have been roped off.*

There were few surprises in the opening statements of Jim
Asperger and David Kenner.

For fifty minutes, Asperger, rarely referring to notes, portrayed Barry Minkow as a conniving supersalesman and a con
artist, without conscience, who had been defrauding people since
he was sixteen. "[Minkow] lied to make his business grow and to
make money. The lies started early, and as the business grew, so
did the lies," said Asperger. "He was a very quick study and an
incredible salesman. He had that uncanny ability, the gift of gab.
. . . [He] latched onto others more expert than himself. Some were
legitimate bankers and consultants, and some were crooks. Defendant Minkow willingly embraced all of them . . . and he paid them
very well." Much of Asperger's presentation, which was animated
but coolly professional, was spent in this vein, the rest on detailing
the intricacies of the various scams.

David Kenner's opening was more compelling for those who
had not been attending his assertive, impassioned, but sometimes
vague press conferences, not only because of Kenner's flamboyance
but also for the sheer audacity of what he had to say. It is the nature
of such proceedings to present diametrically opposing views of

incidents and alleged crimes, but the difference between Asperger's and Kenner's versions of events seemed to carry *Rashomon* to its most extreme.

True, Kenner *did* agree with Asperger that the crimes alleged had occurred, calling them a "fraud of gigantic proportions." But there the similarities ended. "What started out as the American dream—a young entrepreneur starting a business in a garage—came squarely into conflict with the American nightmare: the infiltration of organized crime into a legitimate business," said Kenner. In but a short time, Barry became a frightened puppet of the mob, forced by loan sharks, stock market crooks, bookmakers, and even pornographers into fronting a multimillion-dollar fraud: "He's told, you are a front man, a PR man. Your job is to convince the press this company will succeed because it is run by this young, brilliant, entrepreneurial whiz kid," said Kenner. Various enforcers, like "Michael" and "Mel," were always around to ensure that Barry did what he was told. Often Barry would protest, getting "for his reluctance," on one occasion, "a beating the likes of which Barry never saw before." On other occasions, Barry, who claimed to be petrified of water, had had his head submerged in water by "Mel," a 300-pound brute; had been "grabbed . . . by the back of the hair" by Michael, "an enforcer for Schulman"; "punched . . . in the stomach and [had his face] repeatedly . . . smashed into the kitchen table until Barry rolled off the table."

As to the admitted fraud, Kenner made his most telling point to a jury whose members, as required, knew little of the case: "Did Barry Minkow [from the years he was sixteen to twenty-one] fool all these law firms, all the trained investigators, all the accountants, and the SEC? Did he fool law enforcement and all the organized-crime figures, or was he used and abused by the Mafia for their own ends?"

Kenner's opening also included, however, an easily refutable point that Gordon Greenberg gleefully zeroed in on during his cross-examination of Barry: "He was not the designer of a fraud. He was the unwitting victim of the ZZZZ Best experience," said Kenner, adding quite extraordinarily that all Barry had even gotten for his pains was one Japanese sports car that he'd bought for $6,000.

The trial had promised to be a circus: twelve defendants tried simultaneously with a battery of lawyers present, clashing with each other and the prosecution, while the media was being fed delicious quotes in the halls by attorneys eager to try the case in the press. Howard Weitzman had used such a tactic with great success during the DeLorean trial, the prosecutor Lea D'Agostino, with disastrous results in the John Landis prosecution involving three deaths during the filming of the movie *Twilight Zone*. Admonishments from judges to the contrary, what appears in the media has a way of getting back to a jury.

But the circus never materialized. Ten of the defendants had already pleaded guilty and thus were not present at the trial; Rind, Schulman, and Victor—the "alleged mob associates"—hadn't been indicted; Kenner's strategy of admitting to Barry's participation in the restoration frauds ensured that the titillating details of those scams would not for the most part be dwelt on; and Asperger and Greenberg's strategy of using only squeaky-clean witnesses precluded them from calling Tom Padgett, Mark Morze, or Dan Krowpman—witnesses with whom Kenner might have made some sparks fly.

Kenner, for his part, didn't want to call Padgett and Morze as witnesses either, for they were in a position to know that the duress defense was a sham.

As for Dan Krowpman, each side wanted the other side to call him. This was due largely to trial protocol. Whichever side *calls* a witness to testify—be it the prosecution or defense counsel—is limited in the areas in which questions can be asked as well as the *way* they can be asked. On cross-examination, however, a lawyer has far more latitude. For example, if Kenner were to subpoena Krowpman, he could not ask any leading questions or delve into many areas of Krowpman's past. And he wanted to do exactly that in order to try to establish that Danny was engaged in loan sharking and to repeat the allegations Barry was now making of being beaten by Krowpman. The prosecution, on the other hand, while not believing Krowpman had beaten Minkow, knew it would be Danny's word against Barry's, so they too refused to call Krowpman and other controversial witnesses like Rind and Victor. They simply didn't want Kenner to have a chance to delve into Maurice's and Victor's pasts.

Also contributing to the trial's initial lack of excitement was the fact that Judge Tevrizian had made it abundantly clear early on that decorum *would* prevail during the trial.

In fact, as Gordon Greenberg and Jim Asperger presented a seemingly endless parade of credit card victims, loan officers, slides, and documents, the only real fireworks in the first tedious

weeks of the trial came from the clashes between the judge and
David Kenner.

Tevrizian, who was clearly familiar with the case, appeared to
have already made up his mind that Barry was guilty, and seemed
more than a little annoyed that a trial with a defense he clearly
considered a lie and a farce was even going forward. (Later he
would refer to Barry's defense as "El Toro poo-poo" and say, "I have
to ask myself: 'Is he trying to clean my carpet or what?'")

Moreover, Kenner, whose flashy Vegas style clashed with that
of the straight-arrow middle-American Tevrizian, had gotten off on
the wrong foot with the judge even before the trial had begun. "The
judge," Kenner had said at a crowded press conference, "has a
predisposition [against Barry] that borders on being biased and
prejudicial."

Shortly thereafter, at a pretrial hearing, when Kenner in-
quired of the judge if he had read some motions he (Kenner) had
recently filed, Tevrizian replied that, yes, he'd "read everything,"
adding pointedly, "even a summary of your press conference."
Later, during the trial, when Kenner introduced another motion,
Tevrizian looked up from his papers to say, "Every week we have
something new Mr. Kenner thinks of. I call this legal foreplay."

Not many rulings were to go David Kenner's way in the months
to come.

— 11 —

*IT IS NOT EASY in the early weeks of the prosecution's case to
fathom exactly what is going on in the mind of Barry Minkow.
Sometimes animated, sometimes passive, all that is clearly obvious
is that he's lost weight and a good deal of muscle as a result of being
off steroids and in the hole.*

*His sense of humor, however, has not been lost. "Nice tie," he
says one afternoon to his father, who has faithfully appeared at
each court session, and whose blue-, green-, and white-striped
neckwear is of the widest variety imaginable.*

*During the recesses, Bob Minkow hangs over the railing, en-
thralled with the conversations of Barry's and Rothberg's attorneys.*

*But in the hall outside the courtroom, one finds, judging at least by
the questions he asks, that there is a great deal going on he simply
doesn't understand.*

"Thanks for coming, Dad," Barry says on another occasion.

*"Oh, I didn't come to see you," says Bob Minkow, laughing a
little too loud. "I came to see David [Kenner] here."*

"Did you get the letter I sent you?"

"Yes," says his father, "but you forgot to write about . . ."

*Barry snaps, "I wasn't writing a book. I was just writing to say
I love you." This last, however, seems not directed at his father but
at a more general eavesdropping audience. "My dad's a great guy,"
he adds sotto voce.*

*Barry and Bob Minkow spend as much time as possible trying
to warm up the stony-faced U.S. marshals sitting in back of Barry
and guarding him. They vary in age and appearance from a tough-
looking young woman in autumn tweeds and cowboy boots to a
prune-faced older man in a powder blue suit who constantly ad-
monishes anybody attempting to talk with Barry, including his
father.*

*One afternoon, as the court is preparing for noon break, Barry
complains about the food to his father and a reporter. "They give
you a choice here for lunch," says Barry. "Bologna and cheese or
cheese and bologna. And an apple or an apple," he jokes as the
prune-faced marshal puts the cuffs on him. Laughing, Bob Minkow
leans over to pat Barry affectionately on the arm, thinks better of it,
and asks the marshal, "Can I touch him?"*

"Yeah," says the marshal, leading Barry out, "in twenty years."

Jim Asperger and Gordon Greenberg had been building their
case slowly with their victim and banker witnesses, so it wasn't
clear exactly what they were leading up to when they called Chip
Arrington to the stand.

Thus far, in addition to establishing Barry's abilities as a con
man and his lack of conscience, the trial had been a sparring match
between the prosecutors and Kenner, who, while asking specific
questions of specific witnesses, were also asking pro forma ones of
seemingly everyone. David Kenner would ask if they knew Maurice
Rind, Richard Schulman, Robert Victor, Joseph Mangiapane, and
so forth, going on to name a seemingly endless list of Jack Catain's
gumbas from Jersey. Exasperated by Kenner's tactics, Jim Asperger countered by asking witnesses about Jack the Ripper: "How
about Jack the Ripper? Did you know Jack the Ripper?"

But Asperger and Greenberg had their series of stock questions, too. Had the witness ever seen Barry threatened? Had he or she seen Barry with any cuts, bruises, or black eyes? Were there any bodyguards around?

The set-piece questions of both parties were, after all, the heart of the matter; Barry's guilt had already been established.

The answers, however, were almost never favorable to Minkow's case. Nobody *had* seen a bruise, cut, or any other sign of bodily harm on Barry. Nobody knew of the Jersey gumbas, and the few who had seen Barry interacting with Krowpman, Rind, and Catain said they all appeared very friendly.

That essentially was how the case went until the Friday before Labor Day weekend and the testimony of Chip Arrington.

Although he was facing 403 years, was just twenty-two, and was alleged to have undergone five years of ruthless intimidation by thugs, Barry had not generated much pity in the courtroom. He was, if not cocky, at least self-confident, and while his lawyer was trying to portray him as a coerced teenager, Barry didn't have much heart for acting like one.

The first moments of genuine emotion and compassion came, therefore, when the prosecution examined Chip Arrington.

Chip was scared, literally trembling as he waited to be called to the witness stand—and with good reason. As a result of a few days of weakness, a few hours of venality, a favor to a friend, he was in a position where the prosecution had him by the balls and was squeezing to the tune of fifty years and a $2.5 million fine.

Nothing is ever overtly stated in a situation like this, but Chip was a friendly witness for the prosecution, the only defendant the prosecutors would call, and they intended to use his testimony to introduce some key evidence. Do well by us, was the tacit agreements, and we'll do the best we can by you.

David Kenner understood all this and knew that Chip might well be the only "dirty" prosecution witness he'd get to cross-examine. He did not intend to be easy on him.

Chip Arrington—a simple, honest, not unintelligent man—was facing a nightmare, caught up with con men and shrewd professional cops and lawyers whose job it is to go for the jugular. Waiting in the hall outside the courtroom, he must have smoked half a dozen cigarettes before John Orr of the FBI came out and told him they were ready to swear him in.

Struggling to stay in control, and looking every bit the handsome, clean-cut, Southern California all-American boy he essentially was, Chip finally awakened a jury that had been somnolent throughout the opening weeks of the trial. It wasn't so much what he said—which was that Barry and Barry alone was in control of ZZZZ Best, that Dan Krowpman was a great guy whom he'd let baby-sit his (Chip's) little girl, and that he never saw any evidence of Barry being beaten, threatened, or controlled by Krowpman, Rind, Catain, or anybody else. It was the *way* Chip was saying it. He was dying on the witness stand, not just scared, but humiliated. He was playing in the big leagues, and he didn't even know the score, couldn't even *play* the game.

Greenberg and Asperger had chosen shrewdly. When Kenner got up on cross-examination, he tried to make Chip out to be a liar who knew far more than he was willing to say. Instead, he succeeded only in showing how naïve, trusting, and gullible Chip had been. It was not a good morning for the defense.

But the afternoon was to prove far worse. The afternoon, in fact, was devastating.

With Chip still on the stand, the prosecution introduced the videotape of the 1985 post–public-offering Christmas party at the Bonaventure Hotel, the one with Barry wearing the white tux, playing Bert Parks, giving out awards and listening to the "Barrrrrrry!" chants of his hundreds of adoring employees. The one in which he was obviously, charismatically, powerfully in charge.

Shown to the jury and a hushed courtroom on four or five TV monitors, the tape—given the context—was a heartbreaking, disastrous body blow from which the defense would find it hard to recover. The tape was disastrous because, after seeing it, it was going to be more than just a little difficult to convince the jury that *this* guy, this grinning tux-wearing, mike-swinging guy, was under duress.

And it was heartbreaking to watch Chip Arrington cry as he viewed what once was and realized what he was now doing to someone for whom he once had so much affection. It was heartbreaking as well to watch Barry Minkow at his pinnacle and then to look at him watching himself, hands over his eyes, softly sobbing.

Exactly one week later, it happened again. It was an audiotape this time, and it was so bad that Judge Tevrizian, out of the hearing of the jury, told David Kenner that the tape of a wiretapped conversation between Barry and Dan Krowpman that the prosecution was intending to introduce was evidence of "the most damaging kind . . . devastating to your client."

Kenner already *knew*—if not the specifics, at least in a general way. That's why he had spent the entire morning—while the jury was sequestered—arguing against its admittance.

Made in October 1987, after ZZZZ Best's collapse but before the indictments, the lengthy audiotape, like the video that preceded it, *was* devastating. For it unequivocally contradicted the defense contention that Barry was simply a frightened teenager doing what he had been forced to by a thuggish Dan Krowpman and others. For the conversation with Krowpman showed much more directly than even the awards video that the situation was exactly the reverse: a frightened Krowpman was asking *Barry* what to do, and Barry was coolly telling him. Since Kenner in his opening remarks had already portrayed Krowpman as the Svengali-like master of the "whipped puppy dog" Barry for the first year and a half of ZZZZ Best's existence, the role reversal was particularly telling.

And that was just for starters. There were also contemptuous assessments by Barry of Rind, Schulman, and Catain, and once again the blaming of everything on Mark Morze—*not* the mobsters he was now saying made him do everything.

It was no wonder then that David Kenner was especially forceful on this Friday morning in arguing against the admission of the tape. As a lengthy argument ensued over its playing, Kenner demanded more time to prepare to defend his client against a tape he was now claiming had never been given to him. The prosecution attorneys countered that they were certain Kenner had received it.

If Tevrizian was to rule that the tape would be allowed in evidence that day, said David Kenner heatedly, then he would ask for a mistrial on the grounds that Barry was being represented by "either a fool or a liar."

Two days earlier, Tevrizian had rudely chastised Kenner for his "professional immaturity," calling it "akin to bed-wetting." "You have a habit of trying to bait judges . . . and you're not going to bait me . . . or you and I are going to have some difficulty at the conclusion of this trial."

Now he simply told Kenner he had no intention of dismissing him or granting a motion for a mistrial, adding, "In your opening statement, you stood up and said that there was a massive fraud . . . and your client committed those acts under duress. . . . The contents of this tape basically undermine that defense. I'm going to permit its playing."

Dan Krowpman, like Chip Arrington, was in an understandable panic over the enormity of what he was now facing. And, like Chip, he was in way over his head. He had, as a result, agreed to cooperate with the LAPD, which had been conducting its own investigation simultaneously with the FBI. (Eventually the LAPD would turn over its case to the FBI and U.S. Attorney's Office.)

With a tough, veteran LAPD detective named Mike Brambles listening in, Krowpman agreed to call Barry, engaging him in the wiretapped conversation that was now to prove so revealing.

Prompted by Brambles, Krowpman, sounding scared and confused, called Barry from a local police station, asking him about a wide variety of characters and events.

And Barry, sounding strong and confident, replied with what he may have guessed were the right answers back then (in October) but were clearly the entirely wrong ones now.

Richie Schulman (in whose condo Barry would later testify he was repeatedly terrorized)? "A big nothing, that's what he is . . . a big nothing. A big bag of wind."

Jack Catain (who Kenner and Barry were claiming had close links not just with the DeNunzio brothers but with Marty Taccetta, reputedly of the Lucchese crime family of New Jersey, and other "mob" figures who supposedly were investing the profits from the restoration jobs in a porno operation)? "Jack Catain wasn't even organized crime. It's all bullshit. . . . You [Krowpman] know more organized-crime figures than I do—[like] that bookie."

Robert Victor (who Kenner and Barry would say was an associate of the Colombo family and one of the major "organized-crime figures" coercing Barry)? "He's not a crook, Danny. He's not—Bob Victor is as innocent as can be, if you can believe that. I know you can't believe it, but he has nothing to do with nothing. He's an innocent guy."

Ronnie Lorenzo (another of the alleged mob guys who forced Barry into committing his crimes)? "He's a nice guy, and he doesn't deserve anything he's getting."

As for Mark Morze, Barry again went on at length to repeat that it was Mark who had perpetrated the whole restoration fraud without Barry's knowledge. "Are you crazy?" said Barry when Dan Krowpman asked if he knew the restoration jobs were phony. "I had no knowledge in a million years that these were phony jobs. None. . . . When I went to San Diego . . . I just went through the warehouse and said [to Mark Morze], 'OK, everything's here, good-bye. I trust you. Good-bye.' . . . It's Greek to me . . . the stuff that

Morze was pulling without my knowledge, and the money that he embezzled."

Tom Padgett? "I introduced Morze to Tom. And what they did behind my back without my knowing . . . let me tell you . . . he [Tom] had offices, he was expanding to Newport Beach, he bought this beautiful . . . house, I thought the guy was rolling in dough."

Dan Krowpman—who, as part of his "cooperation" with the LAPD and at Brambles's urging, was trying to elicit every piece of damning information against Minkow that he could—also got some advice from Barry: "Danny, you take the Fifth Amendment," said Barry eight different times over the course of the conversation. "You don't say a fucking word."

The tape would be played again later, near the end of the trial, when its effect was maximized, as the jury listened a second time to a strong, confident Barry Minkow and a cowering Dan Krowpman, as they listened a second time to Barry's dismissive characterizations of the men he had been testifying for weeks under oath had made him live in terror, as they listened a second time to evidence completely contradictory to the defense's case.

Barry, to be sure, would later have an answer for the tape under aggressive cross-examination by Gordon Greenberg. He'd been instructed by Krowpman and various of the gumbas to say what he did in order to get them and everybody else (excepting presumably Morze) off the hook. He had known, said Barry, that the call would be coming and that it would look bad for him, but by then he was so beaten down that he just went along with it. To ensure that he did, there was, of course, an alleged mob thug standing over his shoulder (as Krowpman had Brambles over *his*), telling him what to say.

Later, however, after Barry had testified to this version of events, the prosecution brought Barry's main man and "dear friend" Tony Scamardo to the stand. Scamardo, like Chip and Krowpman, did what he had to do—what with the FBI and IRS breathing down his neck. No mobbed-out musclehead had been there during that conversation, Scamardo told the court. He knew, because *he'd* been there and remembered distinctly that Barry had motioned repeatedly to him for help in getting Krowpman off the phone. Tony's memory had also been recently refreshed by the FBI, which played the tape for him. On it, he could distinctly hear his own voice talking to Barry in the background.

On Friday, when the tape was played for the jury, it proved to be a powerful piece of evidence that seemed to leave everybody in the courtroom slightly numb. Walking out, a veteran wire service reporter who had generally been skeptical of the prosecution's case looked at another reporter and said, "That's it for this kid."

Barry Minkow was eating his second Styrofoam cup of the day as the prosecution, after introducing thousands of exhibits and calling forty-seven witnesses, rested its case.

"Don't do that," said Norm Rothberg's lawyer, Dick Burda, during a break, as he reached over and took the cup away from Barry. "It makes too much noise."

"Let him eat it," said the macho little marshal sitting behind him. "I hear they're toxic."

Barry, however, had good reason to be nervous on this day. He was facing the biggest decision of his life.

After ten exhausting weeks, with the prosecution's case completed and the defense attorneys gearing up to present theirs—which promised to be equally lengthy—there was now strong talk that the trial might go no further; a deal was in the works. The deal was one David Kenner found "tempting": Barry would plead guilty to ten counts, the government would ask for twenty years, and the judge, who allegedly had informally concurred in the agreement, would sentence Barry to twelve years.

Everybody seemed to want the deal: Tevrizian, whose calendar was backed up and who appeared more than ever convinced of Barry's guilt; the prosecution, which because of Barry's age and the general belief among the public in the omnipotence of the mob, was worried that two or three jurors might buy the duress story and a hung jury would result; and the defense, which, as one local reporter put it, knew it "had a case for shit." Everybody seemed to want the deal except for Barry Minkow, who was to agonize over his decision for an entire weekend.

A sentence of twelve years meant Barry would be eligible for parole in four, although, practically speaking, he stood almost no chance of getting out that soon. Probably he would wind up serving seven or eight years.

Because of complex sentencing and probation guidelines, however, if Barry *were* convicted and got, say, twenty-five to thirty years, the likelihood was he would still be out after about ten years. So the difference in time Barry would actually serve by pleading guilty was perhaps three or four years. But three years was three years. And Judge Tevrizian had also let it be known that he definitely would not be disposed toward leniency if a jury found Barry guilty.

Kenner, for his part, gave no advice one way or the other, letting his client make the decision. "I never tell Barry what to do," said Kenner. "He has a way of blaming everybody else for his problems."

Court never met on Mondays, so Barry had a long weekend to consider what to do. The first hint of his decision came on Tuesday morning, when Judge Tevrizian, as usual, asked the attorneys if they had anything to bring up before the jury was brought in. When the question was put to Rothberg's lawyer, Dick Burda— whose consistent good humor throughout the trial had made him popular with everyone—he rose and said to some knowing laughter that he did: "I lost $2 over the weekend, Your Honor," said Burda. "I bet the wrong way on what I thought was a sure thing."

Barry Minkow had decided to go for broke. "He's a con man," said a legal observer close to the trial, "and he thinks he can get all twelve jurors."

— 12 —

BARRY WAS TENSE, tenser than he'd ever appeared throughout the entire trial, as he rose to take the stand. Reaching over the railing, David Kenner's wife patted his hand as the prune-faced marshal snapped, "Don't touch."

He started off well, hanging his head and speaking in a near whisper, pausing sometimes for dramatic effect, answering, yes, he *had* done it, *all* of it, as David Kenner read the charges against him, and a hushed, crowded courtroom listened intently. "It's true I made those claims, and they were all lies," he said of the fraudulent statements he'd made about the restoration jobs.

"Did you manipulate ZZZZ Best securities?" Kenner asked him.

"ZZZZ Best and many more," Barry replied almost shyly. He offered a little boy's hand-in-the-cookie-jar "yes" or "that's true" to every question David Kenner was to ask him in the next hour.

Barry was admitting to almost all the crimes he'd been accused of.

To many in the court, this was the most effective moment of Barry Minkow's defense, as he actually sounded like the scared teenager Kenner had pictured, a young man who had lived in fear for five years.

In the days to follow, David Kenner would lead Barry time and again through the litany of his crimes, and in each telling, Barry would explain why he had committed them: the threats and beating he had suffered at the hands of Dan Krowpman and his sidekick, the frightening 300-pound "Big Mel"; the beatings he endured from the Jersey gumbas at the behest of Jack Catain; the threats of death from Robert Victor; the instructions from Maurice Rind on how to perpetuate the stock fraud; and the thugs Maurice had placed all around him to ensure that he did what he was told. In all, said Barry, fifteen guys, most allegedly related to the mob, had beaten or threatened him, bouncing his body off walls and his head off kitchen tables, submerging his face in sinks full of water, shoving guns in his face, and even trying to rape him.

By the time Kenner had finished questioning Barry, the prosecution still had the upper hand, but the old court groupies, the fat man "from the studios," and especially the press corps were asking each other if it might, *just might*, be possible that Barry was telling the truth. For Barry Minkow had had an answer—an explanation—for everything he had done. And although much of it sounded farfetched it was just plausible enough to raise that little nagging doubt that might trouble a jury later. That was its beauty.

Asperger and Greenberg had decided it would be the soft-spoken Gordon Greenberg who would handle the cross-examination of Barry.

By this time, Greenberg was not bothering to hide his outrage at what he regarded as several weeks of total lies and outright fabrications by Barry. And, it seemed, he could not wait to have at him.

When he stood up to at last question Barry, it seemed that outrage had gotten the best of Gordon Greenberg and that he had succumbed to that fatal flaw of any professional: being guided by raw emotion.

Greenberg started off by attacking Barry's character *hard*—struggling, it appeared, to rein in his contempt.

Barry at first responded coolly, but after an hour or so of such grilling, Greenberg got what he wanted. Barry came back at him just as hard—combative and filled with righteous indignation and anger. He had risen to Greenberg's calculated bait, and was now coming across as strong and assertive—someone not accustomed to allowing *anybody* to push him around. Someone, in short, as far as one could imagine from the terrorized teenager who supposedly allowed himself to be dominated by small-time hoods.

And once Greenberg had gotten Barry into that pattern of behavior, which, after all, came naturally to him, Barry Minkow seemed powerless to step back out. For the rest of his time on the stand, that was the Barry Minkow the jury was to see, not the scared little boy.

Even under David Kenner's gentle questioning, Barry was rarely sympathetic, wanting too much to be in charge to play sympathetic for any length of time. Now, reacting with anger to Greenberg's attacks and sarcasm, Barry wasn't likable either. He was a bit too cocky, a bit too much of the show-off in spite of the extraordinarily frightening position he was in. And this, too, was harmful to Barry Minkow. As Ollie North has shown before Congress, you can overcome adverse facts if people just like you. But Barry Minkow didn't seem to know how to be likable in this situation.

Given his big, egocentric personality, the only way he might have come across as likable would have been as a kind of Murph-the-Surf lovable con man, a little David who had slain the Wall Street Goliath.

And one sensed while he was on the stand that, in spite of the ordeal he was undergoing, there was a part of him that wanted very much to do that. Not to feel cleansed but to claim recognition for his cleverness. But the part of him addicted to the game was to remain in control.

Day after day, as Greenberg zeroed in on Barry, setting him up to be caught in the lies he'd told the previous day, Barry, with remarkable fluidity, would manage to slither out. Somehow he would always come up with the explanation that, although highly unlikely, *could be* true.

Paradoxically, however, the more agile he became in inventing excuses, the worse it got for him in the eyes of spectators and the jury.

For if you didn't believe Barry's story—and after the second playing of the Krowpman tape, it was a very hard story to believe—

then Barry was answering the only truly troubling question remaining: How could a kid so young have been able to lie so brazenly and convincingly and to fool so many people for so long? Well, here was your proof, right before your very eyes.

Three-quarters of the way through Barry's cross-examination, he and David Kenner realized this, but by then it was too late. Coming off the stand one day, Barry turned to Kenner and said, "Sorry, David, sorry if I disappointed you." And to a reporter during a break as he walked to a water fountain outside the court room, David Kenner said, "I'm surprised. I thought Barry would be a better liar."

But in the end, the defense's problems proved greater than just an unconvincing performance by Barry Minkow.

For the story simply didn't fit the facts. Barry had been under duress for five years, the defense was claiming, yet in all those fives years, not one person—not Barry's mother, father, girlfriend, not Tony Scamardo, not Chip Arrington, not Tom Padgett, not Mark Morze, not Joel Hochberg—not one of the people who lived and worked with Barry Minkow ever saw it.

And while Catain, Rind, Schulman, and even Krowpman at least had the reputation of being capable of thuggish behavior, Judge Tevrizian had ruled that their reputation and previous convictions were inadmissible as evidence, and that Kenner could call as witnesses to corroborate threats against Barry only those who had actually seen or heard such threats.

Undoubtedly, someone *had* threatened Barry, or even perhaps jacked him up against a wall on occasion. But the remarkable thing—given whom he'd been dealing with—was that Barry Minkow had apparently never been seriously beaten. For, as with the threats, nobody ever saw a bruise, a cut, a black eye, a contusion, or any other injury on Barry. Not the people closest to him, and not his doctor. One had to wonder, for example, how Barry's face could have been "repeatedly smashed into a kitchen table" and yet show not a mark.

Given the mob reputations of the men he was blaming, if they had been more violent or if Barry had been a meeker individual with a tighter rein on his ego, he and Kenner just *might* have gotten that hung jury they were looking for. And with that hung jury, there might have been some real bargaining power for a deal the

Boy Wonder could have lived with. But for all those ifs to come together would have required a run of luck too incredible even for the Barry Minkow story.

The jury's verdict interrupted a last-minute round of plea negotiations that Barry had insisted on in spite of Kenner's objections. Although conceding that even the chance of a hung jury was slim, Kenner was not ready to give up. Besides, even if Barry was convicted, there was still a shot at an appeal.

But Barry, reportedly on the advice of a "spiritual counselor," insisted that Kenner reopen negotiations; he was ready now to accept a deal for an eighteen-year sentence. Before it could be finalized, however, the jury returned, court was reconvened, and Barry sat quietly as over the next twenty minutes the verdicts were read. After nearly four months on trial, after fifty days of testimony, after considering 25,000 exhibits and more than 100,000 pages of evidence, the jury found Barry J. Minkow guilty on all fifty-seven counts.

Interviewed later by the *Los Angeles Daily News*, the jurors let it be known they had not found their decision difficult. Although expressing some sympathy for Barry because of his age, they were not kind in assessing him. "The only duress I think Barry had was his own self," juror Curtis Baker, a thirty-one-year-old bus driver, told the *News*. "But he didn't come out smelling like a rose at all."

"It's amazing how people can take other people's lives and throw them away," said another juror, Lela Bolden.

A third, a nurse named Lori Bohannan, said that, while some jurors had been convinced that people associated with organized crime had been involved with ZZZZ Best, they didn't believe the duress defense: "For one thing," said Bohannan, "he said he got constant beatings, but the people who saw him every day said they didn't see any signs of it."

"Escape was a big key," said jury foreman Melvin Tiedemann. "He had too many chances [to escape], and he wasn't dumb. We thought he was in charge, generally, all the way to the end. He did it out of greed, naturally. And ego in large part."

The *Daily News* also managed to contact Barry's sister Gail Foy, who said Barry was in the process of writing apology letters to his victims.

"He broke down crying," said Foy, "when he called my father and told him about the conviction. But he doesn't want an appeal. He wants to work with the government and help them in any way he can."

Epilogue

EVER SINCE THE STORY BROKE and his name was splashed all over the papers, Mark Morze had been too embarrassed to see famed UCLA football coach Terry Donahue, whom he used to know on a first-name basis, or many of his old Bruin friends and acquaintances.

But in spite of that, Mark had managed, for the most part, to remain upbeat. While fully cooperating with the federal authorities, he also got a job, making a grand a week counseling companies on leveraged buyouts. He was buoyed, too, by the knowledge that the prosecutors were keeping a large journal, eventually numbering hundreds of pages, enumerating how helpful he had been.

That journal, he was sure, would put him in even more solidly with the federal probation officer writing his presentencing report, a man with whom he already had an excellent rapport.

No matter what, he knew his sentence was sure to be less than half that of Padgett's. Tom had pleaded guilty to four courts, Mark to only three. Mark had raised the money to obtain a top-flight lawyer; Tom was destitute and had only a public defender. And Tom had gotten the absolutely worst presentencing report. He was telling the presentencing officer too many gleeful war stories about the scams, and not showing enough remorse. "Fuck those old ladies; they should have checked it out," was not the proper attitude to show before a man recommending your sentence to a judge.

True, Mark had had that little misunderstanding with Asperger and the IRS agent about how much money he'd actually made from the scam. Mark had told them a number that had turned out to be a little on the low side, and the deal he and his high-priced lawyer had originally negotiated had to be revised upward. His maximum sentence could now be fifteen years instead of the seven originally agreed to. But he'd explained the mix-up, and his lawyer had assured him the feds understood and wouldn't hold it against him. Mark figured he'd now get six years and do two—two and a half max.

And he knew one thing: whatever time he *did* get, he intended to use fruitfully. He would definitely be going to a minimum-security federal prison, not exactly the "Club Feds" that outside suckers like to make them out to be, but still the easiest time one can do in prison within the United States. While there, he would study arbitrage and international finance, maybe write a couple of works of fiction—Ken Follett or Robert Ludlum kind of stuff.

Mark was also feeling upbeat about the future. He'd seen, in his year at ZZZZ Best, the art of the possible and learned the art of the deal. He now knew how to speak *bank*. And that made him in demand. He'd already had dozens of job offers for when he got out, from people who knew what he'd done at ZZZZ Best and looked at it as a real plus!

Half the people, in fact, who should have wanted his hide now seemed to want to climb into bed with him. But Mark intended to work for himself. High venture capital. He figured that with what he had learned, he'd be able to raise $20 to $50 million the first year he was out, at a 2 to 10 percent finder's fee.

Oh, he'd be squeaky clean next time, wouldn't even touch the paperwork, just raise the money and let the lawyers and accountants take care of the rest. Mark Morze wouldn't, he knew, be wearing a scarlet letter all his life.

But Dickran Tevrizian had a view of Morze's accomplishments at ZZZZ Best that differed from the attitude of all those venture capitalists so eager to hire Mark. And one day in early January 1989, he let it be known.

"The integrity of the American financial system is at stake," said Judge Tevrizian, "and I don't think you can just do some wrist-slapping." With that, he sentenced Mark Morze to eight years in federal prison and five years probation, and ordered him to make restitution in an amount to be later specified.

The morning of Tom Padgett's sentencing, he decided he wasn't going to wear his black Italian power suit. He wanted to send a message, but it wasn't "give me twenty years." So he decided on his light brown summer suit. He was strangely calm that morning, in remarkable contrast to his behavior just days before, when, sitting in a West Hollywood restaurant after a couple of beers, he'd almost lost it—loudly and most sarcastically singing "God Bless America," while pounding his fist on the table in frustration at the injustice of it all.

Mark Morze had been right. Tom's presentencing report had been bad—really bad—recommending "a substantial period of incarceration" and probation, and stating that "restitution was applicable." And the IRS was also saying he still owed $130,000 in back taxes!

All *that* for being a bit actor in the Barry Minkow story. He'd signed on for a small role, and all of a sudden he'd been promoted to costar!

The back taxes and restitution bothered Tom as much as the prospect of doing time. One hundred and thirty thousand dollars. He'd never get out from under that, even after he was finally released. And with the presentencing report he'd received, that could well be ten to fifteen years from now.

The very morning of the sentencing, in fact, Gordon Greenberg had confidently predicted that Tom would get "ten or eleven years" of the possible twenty and at the sentencing he was now facing after pleading guilty to four counts of fraud, Jim Asperger had strongly argued for several years more than that *and* restitution. But Judge Tevrizian, perhaps taking into account how little Padgett had actually made from the scam compared to Barry and Mark, the fact that he was now broke, and perhaps as well his relative unimportance compared to Minkow and Morze, surprised everyone by giving Tom Padgett a lesser sentence than the prosecution had asked for: eight years and probation—the same time as Mark Morze would get six months later—and with no restitution requirement.

Now in a minimum-security federal prison in California, Tom Padgett must surely have been one of the few white-collar criminals in recent memory who, after being sentenced to eight years in jail, walked out of the courthouse relieved and smiling.

Dan Krowpman, on the other hand, seemed dazed when in late February 1989 he was sentenced to three years in federal prison, five years' probation, and a $5,000 fine for falsely certifying the sale of millions of dollars' worth of equipment to ZZZZ Best.

"I never meant to hurt anyone," Dan Krowpman told Tevrizian prior to his sentencing. "If I'd known what was going on, I'd never have been involved."

"You don't get $600,000 over a short period of time just standing around," replied the judge dryly.

At about the same time, Ed Krivda, who had signed sales slips showing vastly exaggerated sales of carpets to ZZZZ Best and then lied to the SEC when asked about it, was sentenced to sixty days in a halfway house and 300 hours of community service.

Several weeks earlier, Chip Arrington came back from the Michigan farm country where he'd been living close to his wife's family while out on bail.

When ZZZZ Best collapsed, his father, who was a stockholder, lost about $50,000, other relatives about $17,000. Chip had been hoping for a sentence of probation and a fine, but Greenberg, who seemed genuinely fond of him, had told Chip that, given Tevrizian's "nobody walks" dictum, that was probably not in the cards.

At the sentencing, Greenberg said he found himself "in a unique position in arguing for leniency for Chip," and asked that Arrington be given a fine and time in a community treatment center or halfway house. Chip was "a peripheral player," Greenberg told Tevrizian, "a decent human being."

Again, repeating, "Nobody walks," the judge, apparently moved by Greenberg's plea, gave Chip six months in a halfway house, five years' probation, and a $4,000 fine.

Mark Roddy, the Ultimate White Man, already doing time on his drug bust and facing twenty years and a $1 million fine for his ZZZZ Best crimes, got five more years in prison from Judge Tevrizian.

Mark Morze's brother, Brian, who had helped the boys in San Diego and in dealing with Norm Rothberg, was sentenced to three years, with Tevrizian recommending that he be allowed to serve his time at the federal minimum-security prison at Lompoc, California, so that Brian would be able to receive the daily treatment he needs in connection with a combat wound he'd received in Vietnam.

Norm Rothberg, the Interstate accountant who had demanded a bribe from the boys to conceal the fraud, was found guilty by the same jury that convicted Barry, and was sentenced by Judge Tevrizian to one year and one day in prison. In pleading for leniency, Dick Burda, Norm's lawyer, pointed out that it was Rothberg who had initially raised the suspicions of outside lawyers and accountants. "He was the whistle-blower in this case," said Burda.

"Yeah, well, the whistle got plugged up," said Judge Tevrizian.

Jack and Jerry Polevoi, Big Bucks and Little Bucks, who had laundered the $500,000 for Barry in Las Vegas, were sentenced to eighteen months.

Eugene Lasko, who was with the Polevois during their money-laundering spree in Las Vegas, received thirty days in a community treatment center, thanks largely to Asperger's intercession on his behalf.

"Barry's like a disease," Bob Minkow had once rather inartfully said, referring to his son's infectious enthusiasm. It was a characterization with which Chip Arrington, Eugene Lasko, Ed Krivda, Brian Morze, and Dan Krowpman could only agree.

When Maurice Rind was subpoenaed by David Kenner to testify at Barry's trial, he took the Fifth Amendment ninety-two times.

This was *proof*, David Kenner triumphantly declared in the courthouse hallway afterward, that Maurice had something to hide. And he may well have.

But he, Robert Victor, and several others whom David Kenner also called, and who also took the Fifth, may also just have been following their lawyers' advice.

For Rind, Victor, Schulman, and others remain objects of at least three ongoing investigations. The U.S. Attorney's Office is continuing to look at allegations of insider trading, stock manipulation, and other crimes by the three men. So are the SEC and the LAPD.

It is not possible to measure the cost of the ZZZZ Best fraud in human terms. The damage permanently affected the lives of thousands of small-income investors—people like Kay Rosario's elderly friends—Bernard Pincus and his wife, who lost their life savings of $71,000—or Ada Cohen, the owner of a small motel with two employees, who trusted in Barry and lost $100,000. And Mike Malamut, who mortgaged almost everything he owned, including his mother's house, to lend Barry Minkow $1 million less than two weeks before ZZZZ Best went bust.

It *is* possible, however, to trace in a general way, some of the money—perhaps as much as $70 million—pumped into and paid out by ZZZZ Best over a two-year period.

Currently, the best guess is that the net loss to banks and

investors (taking into account winners and losers in the stock trading up and down) was about $40 million:

- Fifteen million dollars was lost by the purchasers of ZZZZ Best shares during the original stock offering.
- Seven million dollars was lost by Union Bank.
- Prudential-Bache's loss was $3 million.
- First Interstate Bank's was nearly $2 million.
- Kay Rosario and her group of investors also lost about $2 million.
- Individual investors like Mike Malamut, Ken Pavia, and Paul Schiff were each out about $1 million.
- The Swiss banks for which Schiff was serving as a middleman also lost about $4 million.
- The equipment-leasing companies lost about $400,000.
- Millions of dollars more were lost by small-time investors left holding worthless ZZZZ Best stock.

There were also companies that ZZZZ Best owed money to at the time of bankruptcy:

- Pearlman Wohl Olshever Marchese, the Los Angeles advertising firm that did the ZZZZ Best commercials featuring Barry, wound up losing $900,000.
- American Express lost $146,000.
- AT&T lost about $125,000.
- Pacific Bell lost about $100,000.
- Ernst & Whinney lost $120,000.
- Hughes Hubbard & Reed lost about $117,000.
- The *Los Angeles Times* lost over $50,000, a newspaper in Tucson over $30,000.
- Price Waterhouse lost $30,000.

At least six class-action suits by investors are currently pending in U.S. district courts. Although Barry, Mark, Tom, most of the ZZZZ Best defendants, and most of the company's board of directors have been named in the suits, little can be expected to be recovered from them. The suits' real targets are Greenspan & Co., and particularly Ernst & Whinney and Hughes Hubbard & Reed, whose pockets and those of their insurance companies are *very* deep indeed. (Having gone bankrupt in late 1987, Rooney, Pace can be expected to contribute very little to any settlement.)

As with the actual dollar amount of the loss, just where all the money went remains highly speculative, what with so much cash having been passed around.

According to his own testimony—and what can be traced—Barry alone spent over $3 million. That's excluding the currency he spent, and Barry did a lot of business in currency, in addition to living off it.

Mark Morze is estimated by the U.S. attorneys in a final tally to have made and spent (along with his brother Brian) between $2.5 and $3 million.

Between $600,000 and $1 million was paid to Dan Krowpman for his part in the phony equipment-leasing scheme.

Tom Padgett, for his efforts, got to live in his house in Newport Beach for about a month and probably received, all told, about $200,000.

About $1.5 million was spent by the boys on frantically finishing and then leasing the building in San Diego right before Ernst & Whinney's inspection tour. Another $1 million was used for putting on the KeyServ convention—flying in over 1,000 employees and putting them up at the Century Plaza Hotel.

Barry's various award ceremonies, money that was paid for television advertising, and fees to Ernst & Whinney, Hughes Hubbard & Reed, and Rooney, Pace account for several million more.

Minkow's investments in failed stock deals—including $1 million in Maurice Rind's company, Art World—cost about another $1.5 million.

And several million dollars were also lost in running the carpet-cleaning side of the business and setting up subsidiary services, such as the telemarketing center, the generator company, and the cleaning-chemical company.

Finally, millions more went to pay juice, or interest, to investors and lenders who got in and out early before the pyramid collapsed.

In the end, however, according to Greenberg and Asperger, due either to no bookkeeping in some cases or the clever disguising of funds and their ultimate use in others, millions of dollars are simply unaccounted for.

It was right around Christmas of 1988, and Barry Minkow, who'd always wanted to do the "Johnny Carson Show," finally made it. Not physically, of course, but he was *mentioned*. For after being found guilty, Barry was spending his Christmas in the Metropolitan Correctional Institution in downtown LA, leading regular Bible study classes—explaining the Word to about ten or eleven other inmates.

It was ironic, Barry being mentioned on "Carson" now, for Johnny's people had tried to get him on the show about the time of the stock offering. But the underwriters had told Minkow absolutely no, it might get them all in trouble with the SEC at a very delicate time in the offering process. So Barry had had to pass up the opportunity of a lifetime, the opportunity to banter with Johnny.

But now Carson was doing his annual parody of the Season's Greetings cards that the famous might send:

There was one from then-President Reagan . . .

And one from then-President-Elect Bush . . .

And one from Geraldo . . .

And one from Elvis . . .

And one from Barry Minkow . . .

On its front was a picture of Barry smiling. "I'll Be Home for Christmas . . . ," it read. When Carson opened up the card, the greeting, imposed over a second picture of Barry, this one behind jail bars, continued, ". . . in the year 2391." Johnny had given Barry the maximum sentence—the entire 403 years.

Judge Dickran Tevrizian would be less harsh, sentencing Barry on March 13, 1989, to twenty-five years in federal prison and $26 million in restitution.

Chronology of Events

Late 1982

At sixteen, Barry Minkow founds ZZZZ Best Carpet and Furniture Cleaning Company Inc. in the garage of the Minkow family home in suburban Los Angeles.

Early 1983

Minkow moves ZZZZ Best into small offices in Reseda, California.

June 1984

Minkow graduates from Grover Cleveland High School, where he is voted Class Clown and Most Likely to Succeed.

June 1985

Already deeply in debt, Minkow meets Jack Catain and through him gets big investment loans.

September 1985

Robert Victor introduces Barry to Maurice Rind and Richie Schulman. Victor and Schulman invest heavily in ZZZZ Best.

December 1985

Jack Catain files civil suit against Barry Minkow. Catain later drops the suit after Minkow agrees to pay him $670,000 plus interest.

January 1986

With the assistance of Maurice Rind, ZZZZ Best becomes a public company.

December 1986

ZZZZ Best raises $15 million in a public offering of its stock.

April 1987

ZZZZ Best stock peaks at about $18 a share. Minkow is said to be worth about $100 million.

May 1987

The *Los Angeles Times* reveals that Minkow was involved in a credit card fraud. Within a week, the stock is trading at $6.

June 1987

Ernst & Whinney resigns as ZZZZ Best's independent auditor.

July 1987

Minkow resigns from ZZZZ Best, citing health reasons. ZZZZ Best stock closes at pennies a share.

January 1988   Minkow and eleven associates are indicted in
                  federal court.

August 1988   Barry Minkow's trial begins.

December 1988   Barry Minkow is convicted on all fifty-seven
                  counts.

March 1989   Barry Minkow is sentenced to twenty-five years
                  in federal prison and $26 million in restitution.